A CRITICAL EVALUATION OF ALBERT HENRY NEWMAN, 1852-1933, CHURCH HISTORIAN

William Glenn Jonas, Jr.

Mellen Research University Press
San Francisco

Library of Congress Cataloging-in-Publication Data

Jonas, William Glenn, 1959-
    A critical evaluation of Albert Henry Newman, 1852-1933, church
historian / William Glenn Jonas.
      p. cm.
    Includes bibliographical references.
    ISBN 0-7734-9798-6
    1. Newman, Albert Henry, 1852-1933. 2. Church history-
-Historiography--History--19th century. 3. Church history-
-Historiography--History--20th century. I. Title.
BR139.N48J66   1992
270' .092--dc20   92-19310
                                                          CIP

Copyright   ©1992 William Glenn Jonas.

Editorial Inquiries:

Mellen Research University Press
534 Pacific Avenue
San Francisco
CA 94133

Order Fulfillment:

The Edwin Mellen Press
P.O. Box 450
Lewiston, NY 14092
USA

Printed in the United States of America

DEDICATION

This book is dedicated to my wife Pam,
who inspires me and makes me a better person.

TABLE OF CONTENTS

CHAPTER I
The Life of Albert Henry Newman

CHAPTER II
Albert Henry Newman as a General Historian

CHAPTER III
Albert Henry Newman and Anabaptist Historiography

CHAPTER IV
Albert Henry Newman and Baptist Historiography

CHAPTER V

FOREWORD

The study of religion in the United states has flourished in the past thirty years: scholars have produced textbooks, source collections, atlases, bibliographies, biographies, and monographs in abundance. Students of the discipline have been keenly interested in self-reflection, charting their changing presuppositions, approaches and interpretations. Recently a growing number of studies have been devoted to historiographical monographs which examine the life and writing of individual church historians and historians of religion. Glenn Jonas has made an important contribution to these studies by providing a careful analysis of the scholarly career of Albert Henry Newman.

Newman was a superb linguist who devoted his skills principally to understanding the place of Baptists in the history of the church. He taught exclusively at Baptist institutions: Rochester Theological Seminary, Toronto Baptist College, McMaster University, Baylor University, Southwestern Seminary, and Mercer University. He was shy, and his classroom manner was uninspiring; but students respected his academic achievement, and colleagues appreciated his irenic spirit. Newman's teaching career spanned the period 1877-1929, but his productive publishing career was concentrated in the last decade of the nineteenth century (1891-1902). All of his major books were published at this time – during his days at McMaster University. Jonas has worked diligently to locate all relevant archival materials and has reconstructed Newman's scholarly career. He has discovered interesting connections between Newman and fellow church historians Philip Schaff, Harold Bender, and W.H. Whitsitt.

Jonas finds three strands of church history writing which shaped the work of Newman. In his typology, church historians who took the theological approach looked for the growth of the Kingdom of God in history. The scientific approach urged that historical claims be limited to documentary evidence, that standard historical methodology be followed without appeal to providential explanations, and that the church be studied as a human rather than divine institution. The sectarian approach emphasized denominational distinctives and sought to defend them. Jonas evaluates the strands of each of these approaches in Newman's writings. He affirms that Newman drew from, but modified all three.

Newman published books relating to three different subjects: general church history, Anabaptist history, and Baptist history. Newman's most enduring work is his two-volume *Manual of Church History*, a general survey which was widely used as a seminary textbook. The highest royalties for the book were paid in 1953, over a half century after the original date of publication. A major theme in all of Newman's work was the idealization of the apostolic age and measurement of the rest of church history by this norm. He was critical of Catholicism; he thought medieval sectarian groups more nearly approximated first century Christianity and so devoted special attention to them. Newman studied the Anabaptists as forerunners to the Baptists. Although he rejected the idea of lineal descent of Baptists from earlier dissenting traditions, Newman did believe in a "spiritual kinship" of many of these groups to the apostolic age. Of these groups he taught that Anabaptists were second only to Baptists in approximating apostolic Christianity. Harold Bender wrote of his appreciation for Newman's work, but Bender's own scholarship (and that of the "Goshen School") along with Newman's apologetic agenda soon rendered his perspectives on Anabaptist studies obsolete. Newman's scholarship was recognized by the academic community, and he was commissioned to write the the history of Baptists for the monumental series sponsored by the American Society of Church History. Jonas also traces Newman's preoccupation with the question of Baptist origins, and his involvement in the Whitsitt controversy, a debate

date of Baptist beginnings and the date when Baptists began to immerse. It was Newman's desire to understand and communicate the preeminent place of Baptists in church history. His bias is evident and it undermined his credibility in the twentieth century which demanded a more objective approach. Nonetheless Newman advanced the discipline of church history, and his contributions deserve to be remembered. Jonas' study serves as a very helpful guide to the life and scholarship of Albert Henry Newman.

The graduate program in religion at Baylor was established in 1966; it offers M.A. and Ph.D. level work in New Testament, Old Testament, Systematic Theology, Historical Theology, Ethics, Church History, and History of Religions. The program is broad-based and requires each Ph.D. student to do some work in Biblical, theological, and historical studies; additionally, the student must pursue a required minor outside the Department of Religion. Eighty students are currently engaged in some phase of graduate work. The present study is the second revised Baylor dissertation in church history published by Mellen. We are pleased that the publication is being made available to the academic community and hope that it may be a useful addition to scholarship.

Dr. William Pitts

PREFACE

This study analyzes and critiques Albert Henry Newman's life and work as a church historian. It shows his place in church historiography and explores his contribution to understanding Anabaptist and Baptist history; it also shows that his work was largely outdated by the beginning of the twentieth century because of his failure to incorporate new developments in the field of church history into his own historiography.

I first became interested in Newman in 1987 through a graduate seminar at Baylor University in American Religious History. The study of historiography interests me. Very little had been written about Newman, nothing which treated his historiography comprehensively. Consequently, a thorough treatment of Newman's life and work became the goal of this study.

Newman attended Mercer University and Rochester Theological Seminary, with an additional year of study at the Southern Baptist Theological Seminary. Though originally trained as an Old Testament scholar, Rochester Theological Seminary hired him in 1877 to replace R. J. W. Buckland, whose death left a vacancy in the area of church history. Thus, Newman began a career as a church historian lasting over fifty years. Other teaching appointments included Toronto Baptist College (later to become McMaster University), Baylor University, Southwestern Baptist Theological Seminary, Mercer University, and several visiting professorships.

During the last half of the nineteenth century, the study of church history became a professional discipline. Three different types of historical methodology were prevalent. Scientific church historians attempted to remove metaphysical speculation from their work by basing their conclusions on the sources alone. Theological church historians based their conclusions on primary source study but also retained the notion that history was the study of the movement of God through time. Sectarian church historians were concerned with identifying an organic connection between their confessional stance and the first-century church.

Although his historical method did not fit squarely into any of the three categories, Newman had some identity with the theological methodology and his use of the Spiritual Kinship theory of Baptist origins gave him a measure of similarity with the sectarian historians. His inability to identify with scientific church historiography, which was the dominant method by the beginning of the twentieth century, caused Newman's work to become obsolete as the twentieth century progressed.

Newman believed that the Baptists were the true inheritors of apostolic Christianity. This favorable bias toward the Baptists, coupled with his use of the Spiritual Kinship theory, served to foster an interest in the Anabaptists. Newman studied the dissenting groups in church history in order to determine how closely they resembled Apostolic Christianity and Baptists. Although he refused to posit an organic connection, he did believe that there was a "kinship" between these sects and Baptists. The Anabaptists represented for Newman the most complete renewal of Apostolic Christianity before the rise of the seventeenth-century Baptists. Although one of the first historians to assign to the Anabaptists their proper place in church history, free from pejorative assumptions, Newman's Anabaptist studies were surpassed as the twentieth century progressed, due largely to rapid advances made by Mennonite historians such as Harold S. Bender. Also, Newman's purpose as an Anabaptist historian was not to serve as a discoverer but to interpret the Anabaptists to his Baptist constituency in order to encourage their interest in Baptist history.

As a Baptist historian, Newman's work is also largely antiquated because he maintained adherence to the Spiritual Kinship theory of Baptist origins. His work exhibits a refusal to accept the English Separatist Descent theory, the predominant interpretation of Baptist origins by the beginning of the twentieth century.

While Newman's work is not used today by very many church historians, it should be noted that by nineteenth-century standards he ranks among the best in his field. He was a brilliant linguist and used this ability to become an expert on the dissenting sects throughout the history of the church. He was also among the pioneers in the field of Anabaptist studies. He should be classified as one of the premier Baptist historians.

This project has stimulated me to further areas of inquiry in the area of historiography. Much work needs to be done in the specific area of Baptist historiography. The debate about Baptist origins has not been settled and continues to interest me. Also, there are some other Baptist historians, both living and dead, whose work needs to be analyzed critically. Perhaps a study which examines a number of Baptist historians would be received well. The goal of the study would be to investigate the work of Baptist historians from the seventeenth century until present and then classify them according to the similarities and patterns that could be discovered from an analysis of their works.

Another area in Baptist historiography which needs further investigation is the history of Baptists in the United States. Newman's *A History of Baptist Churches in the United States* (1898), which was a part of the American Church History Series, was an excellent survey of American Baptist history in its era. The book, now out of print, needs to be revised and updated. This would be a worthy project especially in light of the many changes which have occurred in the twentieth century among American Baptists. Issues such as the rise of Fundamentalism and its effect on American Baptists, the Social Gospel Movement among American Baptists, and twentieth century divisions all need to be incorporated together with Newman's earlier work.

ACKNOWLEDGMENTS

Without the help of many people, the completion of this project could not have occurred. I am especially grateful to the members of my dissertation committee, Dr. William L. Pitts, Dr. Glenn O. Hilburn, and Dr. Gary W. Hull. They exhibited much patience with me as they guided me through the research and writing process. I wish to express my sincere thanks to them for their help.

Five professors at my *alma mater*, Mars Hill College, Dr. H. Page Lee, Dr. W. Thomas Sawyer, Dr. A. Ellison Jenkins, Dr. C. Earl Leininger, and Dr. Robert A. Melvin, share the sole responsibility for starting me on the academic pilgrimage which has reached its culmination thirteen years later. I loved Mars Hill as a student, and I continue to love it. The influence of these men will remain with me for the rest of my career.

Dr. William R. Estep, Distinguished Professor of Church History, emeritus, at Southwestern Baptist Theological Seminary gave to me the "passion" to study church history and contributed to my interest in Albert Henry Newman. Thank you Dr. Estep for all the encouragement you have given me. Also thanks to Dr. Jonathan A. Lindsey, my friend and "father confessor," who gave me much encouragement, created in me a desire to reach my fullest potential as a scholar.

The staff of Baylor University's Moody Library, especially the Reference Department, deserves special thanks. Barbara Cantrell worked diligently to secure materials through the inter-library loan process. Thanks

x

also to Mr. Kent Keeth and Mrs. Ellen Brown of the Texas Collection for your help. Miss Judith Colwell, librarian at the Canadian Baptist Archives helped secure vital materials from Newman's years at McMaster University. Mr. James Lynch, Director of the American Baptist Historical Society, also contributed assistance in securing sources, as did Mr. J. Kevin Miller of the Mennonite Historical Archives. A final word of thanks should go to the Southern Baptist Historical Commission for allowing me to copy the entire Albert Henry Newman Collection. This made my research efforts much more convenient.

Finally, a word of thanks goes to my family. My in–laws, Ben and Anna De Sopo gave me much support and love and I owe them a debt of gratitude. Thank you for making me one of the family. To my parents, Bill and Virginia Jonas, what can I say? You have loved me and encouraged me all my life. Without your support, I never would have reached this goal in my life. To my lovely wife Pam: you bring joy, excitement, and happiness into my life. I look forward to many years of mutual love and support as we strive to reach our goals together. It is because of your love, support, and patience that I dedicate this book to you.

CHAPTER I

THE LIFE OF ALBERT HENRY NEWMAN

Introduction

The last half of the nineteenth century in America was a period dominated by turmoil and change. The industrial revolution captivated America and caused the unprecedented growth of large cities. This led to the decline of the agrarian society, so admired by Jefferson at the beginning of the century, and the rise of a society dominated by names such as Rockefeller, Carnegie, and Vanderbilt.[1]

Waves of immigration added to what was already a heterogeneous nation. With new people came new ideas to challenge the existing norms. This, coupled with technological advances in communication, transportation, and industry created an environment filled with both anxiety and optimism.

Sectionalism began to dominate politics in the nineteenth century eventually leading to the Civil War. The Reconstruction era brought more bitterness to the already devastated South. Following Reconstruction the political climate in America for the remainder of the century was characterized by scandal and corruption.

---

1. Henry Steele Commager, *The American Mind: An Interpretation of American Thought and Character Since the 1880s* (New Haven: Yale University Press, 1950) Though this publication is somewhat old, it still serves as an excellent analysis of the changes in America during the last decades of the nineteenth century. Also see Henry Steel Commager, *The Era of Reform: 1830-1860* (Malabar, Florida: Robert E. Krieger Publishing Company, 1960) for an analysis of the period before 1880.

2

The publication of Charles Darwin's *Origin of the Species* (1859) and later his *Descent of Man* (1871), catapulted the scientific world into turmoil by proposing new ideas concerning the beginning of the world. The theory of evolution stimulated the growth of new disciplines such as sociology and psychology. The term "social darwinism" became popular as William Graham Sumner applied Darwin's ideas to society.[2]

The study of history encountered growth during this period. Historians such as Charles Adams and Herbert Baxter Adams went to Germany for their advanced degrees and brought the new German methods of historiography back to America.[3]

The theological world also saw change. Revivalism became big business as Charles G. Finney faded into the background and Dwight L. Moody came to the forefront.[4] New methods of Biblical criticism elicited responses from many who wanted to hold to traditional methods of study. Fundamentalism arose during the last quarter of the nineteenth century as an attempt to battle intellectual changes that seemed to challenge traditional understandings of society, the world, and God.[5] Modernism surfaced almost simultaneously with Fundamentalism resulting in intense denominational battles during the next century.[6] In the midst of this environment, shaped by new ideas Albert Henry Newman emerged as a leading church historian. Throughout his career as a scholar and teacher, Newman served as a mediating interpreter of church history attempting to address the issues of his day.

---

2.   Richard Hofstadter, *Social Darwinism in American Thought* (Philadelphia: University of Pennsylvania Press, 1944; reprint, Boston: Beacon Press, 1955), 3-67 (page references are to reprint edition).

3.   Henry Warner Bowden, *Church History in the Age of Science* (Chapel Hill: The University of North Carolina Press, 1971).

4.   William G. McLoughlin, *Modern Revivalism: Charles Grandison Finney to Billy Graham* (New York: The Ronald Press Company, 1959), 166-281.

5.   George M. Marsden, *Fundamentalism and American Culture* (Oxford: Oxford University Press, 1980).

6.   William R. Hutchison, *The Modernist Impulse in American Protestantism* (Oxford: Oxford University Press, 1976).

Edward H. Carr in *What is History?* said, "when we take up a work of history, our first concern should be not with the facts which it contains but with the historian who wrote it."[7] Therefore, the best starting point for a study of Newman's work is to examine his life and development as a scholar. This chapter will examine four areas of Newman's life: his childhood and education, academic career, personality, and retirement years.

Early Life

Childhood

In the small Edgefield district of South Carolina Albert Henry Newman was born 25 August 1852.[8] He was the third of five children born to John Blackstone and Harriet Whitaker Newman. His father was a farmer and saddle maker by trade. Though he had no formal education, Newman's father was an ardent reader. Newman's mother received a fairly good education because her father was a schoolteacher.[9]

Harriet Newman died as a result of an unusual accident when her son was a child. On the occasion of the oldest daughter's marriage, Newman's mother was unable to attend the wedding due to illness. She stayed with a neighbor until the family returned home. When she returned, the family dog

---

7. Edward Hallett Carr, *What is History?* (London: McMillan and Company Ltd., 1961), 16-17.

8. The only published biographical account of Newman is Frederick Eby, *Newman the Church Historian: A Study in Christian Personality* (Nashville: Broadman Press, 1946). Eby was Newman's son-in-law. In addition, there are two unpublished biographical manuscripts and one autobiographical essay in the Albert Henry Newman Papers, Dargan-Carver Library, Southern Baptist Historical Commission, Nashville, Tennessee. (Hereafter, this collection will be cited as Albert Henry Newman Papers). One of the manuscripts is 85 pages in length and was delivered by Eby at Mercer University 14 January 1927, in conjunction with the golden anniversary celebration of Newman's teaching career. The other manuscript, much briefer, is written by Eby, but corrections are written in Newman's handwriting. Eby's biography of Newman includes most of the material contained in the unpublished essays. Finally, there is an autobiographical speech delivered by Newman on 5 April 1929 at a dinner given by the Senate and Board of McMaster University honoring his retirement and fifty-three years of teaching. A copy of this speech is located in the Canadian Baptist Archives, McMaster Divinity College, Hamilton, Ontario.

9. Eby, *Newman the Church Historian*, 3.

in his excitement to greet her, scratched her leg. The scratch became infectious, eventually causing her death.[10]

Newman seems to have engaged in the normal type of activities which occupied young boys in the middle of the nineteenth century. Because he grew up in a rural area, he had opportunity to develop enjoyment of outdoor activities, especially fishing. This hobby remained with him throughout his life.[11]

There is one unique fact about Newman's childhood which may have distinguished him from other children of his age. He began reading at the age of three. This practice developed into "an unquenchable thirst for knowledge and an avid interest in books."[12] This quest for knowledge remained with Newman throughout his years of formal education.

Education

Childhood Education

Since Newman's father received no formal education he felt it imperative that his children be educated. Because there were no public schools in the area where the Newman family lived, Newman received his education from private schools, mostly conducted by the local pastor. Mr. H. I. Bird became Newman's first teacher and was responsible for giving him his start in the study of Latin, but most importantly, "he awakened in him an unflinching determination to secure a college education."[13]

Just after the conclusion of the Civil War, when Newman was fourteen, the family moved to Thompson, Georgia. There he came under the influence of Reverend Epenatus Alexis Steed, the local pastor. Steed was a well-educated man who graduated second in his class from Mercer University in 1851. For a number of years he was professor of Greek and Latin at

---

10. Hope Chavous to Frederick Eby, LS, 23 September 1940, Albert Henry Newman Papers, 5-6.

11. Eby, *Newman the Church Historian*, 4.

12. *Ibid.*, 5.

13. *Ibid.*, 5.

Mississippi College.[14] For nearly three years Steed tutored Newman in Latin, Greek, arithmetic, and orthography. Newman was an exceptional student. Under Steed's direction he completed the material equivalent to the freshman and sophomore years at Mercer University. In September, 1869, he entered Mercer as a junior. In a letter recommending Newman to Mercer, Steed said, "I send you a boy who is smarter than he looks. Take an interest in him and put him forward. He has more brains than many."[15]

Steed's influence on the young Newman was not confined to the academic realm. It was through the work of this pastor that Newman was converted and baptized in the local Baptist church. Also through the pastor's inspiration Newman developed a desire to study and teach theology, which became his vocational choice.[16]

Mercer University

Through his work with Steed and Bird Newman began to develop the intellectual acumen which he carried throughout his life, especially his ability with languages. At Mercer, Newman's academic abilities blossomed fully. Though the University was small at the time, it nevertheless offered a faculty and curriculum which was challenging. Newman chose the "Classical Course" as opposed to the "Scientific Course." The languages he studied were Latin, Greek, and French. In addition to the language requirements, the classical curriculum required courses in international and constitutional law, mathematics, logic, an introduction to the sciences, and philosophy.[17]

Newman worked more closely with Professor John Joyner Brantly, professor of *Belle Lettres* and modern languages, than any of his other professors. Brantly stimulated Newman's interest in German and convinced

14. *Ibid.*, 6.

15. *Ibid.*, 7-8. Writing to his parents Newman quotes a different version of Steed's recommendation: "I send you a boy who will pull at a stump if you tell him. Take an interest in him and put him forward. He has more brains than many." Newman to Family, 28 August 1869, as cited by *Ibid.*, 13. Eby says that both versions of the quote came from Newman.

16. *Ibid.*, 8. Newman's conversion occurred on 21 September 1868 according to the Minutes of the Thomson Baptist Church dated 27 September 1868. See Jerry Breazeale, "Albert Henry Newman, Historian and Theologican" (Th.D. diss., New Orleans Baptist Theological Seminary, 1960), 2.

17. *Ibid.*, 9.

him of his need to master the language as a necessary research tool. Because German was not taught in the curriculum, Brantly agreed to tutor Newman privately.[18]

Some insight as to the character of Newman as a student can be found in a letter from Dr. Kerr Boyce Tupper, one of Newman's classmates at Mercer, to Eby. Concerning Newman, Tupper said:

> He impressed the whole student body by his earnest studiousness, and fine recitations in the classroom....I cannot recall that Newman ever missed answering correctly every question asked when in the classroom, especially in Greek, in Latin, and in History....He never played baseball in the afternoon, but studied while the rest of us were striking the ball and running the bases![19]

Newman's experience at Mercer was not limited to academics. One of the most popular campus activities during his student years involved the two literary organizations at Mercer: the Ciceronian Society, to which Newman belonged, and the Phi Delta Society.[20] These literary societies provided a sort of extracurricular training for the students in debate, public speaking, and parliamentary procedure. The societies were highly competitive with each other for the new students and were an important part of student life at Mercer during Newman's college days.[21]

On 15 May 1869, the Chi Phi fraternity, a secret fraternal organization, was founded on the Mercer campus.[22] It is difficult to determine the exact reason for the organization of the fraternity. It may have been part of a trend that was taking place on other college campuses at the time.[23] It also

---

18. *Ibid.*, 10.

19. Letter from Dr Kerr Boyce Tupper to Frederick Eby as cited in *Ibid.*, 11-12.

20. Eby, *Newman the Church Historian*, 22.

21. *Ibid.*, 21-22.

22. Bartow Davis Ragsdale, *Story of Georgia Baptists*, vol. 1, *Mercer University: Penfield Period and Related Interests* (Atlanta: Foote and Davies Co., 1932), 304. A chapter of the Chi Phi fraternity had been organized at the University of Georgia in Athens, Georgia in 1867. It was disbanded by faculty action in 1874, but reinstated in 1878. See Spright Dowell, *A History of Mercer University 1833-1953* (Macon, GA: Mercer University Press, 1958), 149.

23. Ragsdale, 304.

may have arisen to provide its members with different social interests and activities.[24] The existence of the fraternity became known in February, 1870 when certain students appeared at chapel wearing purple ribbons, an action which signified mourning for the death of a fraternity brother who had lived in Athens, Georgia.[25]

Though the exact date he joined is hard to determine, Newman is identified as a member of the new organization by the minutes of the Ciceronian Society on 8 April 1870.[26] His reason for joining is also subject to speculation. Perhaps an important factor contributing to Newman's decision to join the fraternity involved the fact that membership was deemed an honor and only the top academic students were chosen.[27]

With the arrival of the Chi Phi fraternity, the literary societies began immediately to resist. The new fraternity claimed to be literary and intellectual and many felt it presented a threat to the Ciceronian and Phi Delta societies. The literary societies argued that the members of the Chi Phi fraternity had transferred their allegiance to another society.[28]

Another point of conflict generated by the new organization centered around its characteristic of exclusiveness. Fraternities as a rule were highly selective as to who was invited to join. This promoted an aura of resentment

---

24. Dowell, 149.

25. Ragsdale, 307. Ragsdale cites the account of the Chi Phi's public appearance from Nathaniel Willet, a Mercer student who witnessed the episode.

26. Excerpts from the minutes of the Ciceronian Society 8 April 1870, as cited by Ragsdale, 301.

27. Newman revealed in an undated letter to his family that he rejected the first invitation to join the fraternity: "I had been elected a member of the Chi Phi fraternity on account of my scholarship but I being on my guard refused to go with them. They continued to urge upon me to join. They said that it was considered a great honor to belong to that society and that only the best scholars were elected. Knowing that there was some trick in it [referring to initiation] I told them that I was obliged to them for the honor they conferred on me in electing me, but that I preferred not to join at present." Quoted in Eby, *Newman the Church Historian*, 15.

28. Dowell, 150.

and jealousy among the non-members.[29]   Many felt that the Chi Phi fraternity caused a caste system to develop at the university.[30]

The entire university found itself embroiled in controversy over the Chi Phi fraternity. Both literary societies passed resolutions that any member of their respective society who joined the new fraternity would be expelled from the society.[31] The fact that some members of the fraternity were the sons of professors, trustees, and prominent family members did not lessen the hostility toward the new organization.[32]

The Ciceronian Society expelled Newman on 15 April 1870 for being a member of the Chi Phi fraternity.   However, by the following fall, the controversy had lessened.   The campus became more tolerant of the fraternity. Also that year the Sigma Alpha Epsilon fraternity appeared.[33] Newman was reinstated into the Ciceronian society on 1 October 1870.[34] There is no evidence that the controversy over the fraternity or his involvement in it had any affect on Newman's career. In the sources that are available, Newman never mentioned his membership in this fraternity or the controversy on the campus during 1869-70.

The organization of the fraternity did have an effect on Mercer University. "So far as Mercer was concerned, the advent of Chi Phi in 1869-70 marked the beginning of changes that were to be of permanent and progressive influence."[35]

Newman graduated from Mercer in 1871 at the head of a class of fifteen. About twenty years after the class graduated, Professor John Joyner

---

29. Ragsdale, 306. Also see William J. McGlothlin, *Baptist Beginnings in Education: A History of Furman University* (Nashville: The Sunday School Board, 1926), 166.

30. Dowell, 150.

31. Excerpts from the minutes of the Ciceronian Society, 26 February-8 October, 1870 and excerpts from the minutes of the Phi Delta Society, 25 February-11 June 1870, as cited by Ragsdale, 300-03.

32. *Ibid.*, 300.

33. Dowell, 150. Other fraternities appeared shortly after 1870. In 1872 Phi Delta Theta organized a chapter on the Mercer campus followed by Kappa Alpha (1873); and Kappa Sigma (1874). Interestingly, Chi Phi disbanded voluntarily in 1880. See Dowell, 149.

34. *Ibid.*, 301.

35. *Ibid.*, 150-51.

Brantly said that Newman was "The most scholarly of all the graduates gone out from Mercer."[36]

Rochester Theological Seminary

During the year following his graduation from Mercer, Newman taught at two different village schools; one at Jeffersonville, Georgia and the other at Seale, Alabama.[37] He decided to attend seminary during this period.

Originally, Newman's intentions were to attend the Southern Baptist Theological Seminary, then located at Greenville, South Carolina. But through a subscription to a Baptist denominational paper from Cincinnati, Ohio called the *Journal and Messenger*, he acquainted himself with the Baptist seminaries in the north. The northern schools were older and more established and Newman believed they offered certain advantages that the Southern Baptist Theological Seminary could not match.[38] His decision to attend the Rochester Theological Seminary may have stemmed from his admiration of two Baptist scholars who were connected with the school: Dr. Thomas Jefferson Conant and Dr. Horatio Balch Hackett.[39] Consequently, in the fall of 1872, he enrolled at the Rochester Theological Seminary in Rochester, New York.

---

36. Eby, *Newman the Church Historian*, 25.

37. *Ibid.*, 26.

38. Albert Henry Newman to Frederick Eby, LS, 13 December 1926, Albert Henry Newman Papers, 1. Also see *Ibid.*, 26.

39. *Ibid.* It is unclear how Newman became acquainted with these men or why they impressed him so. They may have written articles for the *Journal and Messenger* or the periodical could have discussed their careers in some way. Conant was Professor of Hebrew and Biblical Exegesis at Rochester from 1851-57. *The New Schaff-Herzog Encyclopedia of Religious Knowledge*, 1952 ed., s.v. "Conant, Thomas Jefferson." When Newman decided to attend Rochester, he thought that Conant was still on faculty at the seminary. (See Newman to Eby, 13 December 1926).

Hackett was Professor of New Testament at Rochester from 1870-75. *The New Schaff-Herzog Encyclopedia of Religious Knowledge*, 1952 ed., s.v. "Hackett, Horatio Balch." Concerning these two men Newman said: "Their names meant more to me at that time than those of Broadus and Toy [professors at the Southern Baptist Theological Seminary]." Newman to Eby, 13 December 1926. Also see Newman's comments on these men in "British and American Theology in the Nineteenth Century," 37, unpublished manuscript in the Albert Henry Newman Papers. Here he describes Hackett as exemplifying the German standard of objectivity while avoiding the conclusions of the German scholars, while creating an appreciation of the German language and literature among his students.

During his time at the seminary Newman experienced something which had far-reaching effects on the rest of his life. On 15 July 1873, during his second year in seminary, Newman married Mary Augusta Ware, whom he had met while teaching school at Seale, Alabama.[40]

Though he maintained a good relationship with many of his professors, Eby reported that Horatio Balch Hackett, Professor of New Testament, had the most profound effect on Newman. Evidently there was a certain amount of respect for Hackett as evidenced by the fact that Newman named his first-born son after the professor.[41] At the beginning of his seminary experience Newman was interested in New Testament exegesis and systematic theology. However, by the time he was ready to graduate, he decided to embark upon a teaching career with specialization in Hebrew and Old Testament exegesis.[42]

This change of direction during Newman's seminary experience raises a question. If he was so impressed with Hackett, the Professor of New Testament, why did he decide to concentrate in Old Testament studies? Eby said that Newman's reason for choosing an Old Testament major involved the progress that had been made in that discipline during the middle of the nineteenth century, for example, Julius Wellhausen's Documentary Hypothesis concerning the Pentateuch.[43] However, the discipline of New Testament studies also saw monumental advances during this period.[44] Eby provided no solution to this contradiction and Newman gives no explanation for the change.

Another contradiction to Eby's statement concerning Hackett's influence is found in a letter Newman wrote to his wife several weeks before his graduation. Concerning Hackett he said:

40. Eby, *Newman the Church Historian*, 103-105.

41. *Ibid.*, 107.

42. *Ibid.*, 27-28.

43. *Ibid.*, 27.

44. See Werner George Kummel, *The New Testament: The History of the Investigation of Its Problems*, trans. by S. McLean Gilmour and Howard C. Kee (Nashville: Abingdon Press, 1972), and Stephen Neill, *The Interpretation of the New Testament: 1861-1961* (London: Oxford University Press, 1964).

> Dr. Hackett is rather tiresome since his memory is getting poor and he says the same things over and over again just as if he had never said them before. He is, I feel, perfectly useless to me since I can use German books about as well as he can and he gets almost all that he has from German books, and since his mind seems to be failing so I would just as soon trust my judgement as his.[45]

This comment is only a portion of a section within the letter in which Newman expressed negative feelings about other faculty members as well as the seminary itself. Referring to his Hebrew professor he said, "If he just had a little bit of life and energy about him and didn't talk so slowly and so much through his nose I suppose we would think more of him."[46] And concerning the seminary itself he said, "[t]here is nothing going on in the Seminary that interests me much."[47]

Do these statements reveal that Newman did not look favorably upon Hackett or his seminary experience? Most likely not. There is no other statement in any of his writings that would lead one to the conclusion that Newman did not value his Rochester seminary years. The statements in the letter may best be explained in light of the fact that Newman was eager to graduate. He said in the letter, "I am getting so tired of Rochester."[48] Also, it is clear from reading the letter that he was anxious to be reunited with his wife. Perhaps the desire to see his wife coupled with his desire to graduate provide an explanation for Newman's harsh words.

---

45. A. H. Newman to Mrs. Newman, LS, 16 April 1875, Albert Henry Newman file, Texas Collection, Baylor University, Waco, Texas, 1-3. Hereafter this collection of Newman's papers will be cited as Albert Henry Newman File, Baylor University.

46. *Ibid.*

47. *Ibid.* The letter was written to his wife who was evidently living elsewhere. No reason was given for why she was away, nor was there any indication of where she was except to say that she was "down south." Most likely she was living with her family. The tone of the letter however does not suggest that there was any marital problems between them. Except for times of travel to various places to deliver lectures and speeches, Newman's letters show that there was only one other time that he was separated from his wife. This occurred during the spring semester of 1881 while he was a professor at the Rochester Theological Seminary. (See below)

48. *Ibid.*

The Southern Baptist Theological Seminary

After he graduated from Rochester Theological Seminary in May, 1875, Newman felt he needed further instruction in the field of Old Testament studies. He desired particular training in the Semitic languages of Arabic, Syriac, and Chaldee. His wife's parents generously offered him the financial means to study in Germany. On the way from Alabama (his wife's home) to New York where he was to set sail for Europe, he stopped in Greenville, South Carolina. This was the location of the Southern Baptist Theological Seminary.[49] There he met Dr. Crawford H. Toy and Dr. John A. Broadus. Evidently in the course of conversation Toy was impressed with Newman's ability. He offered to give Newman private instruction in the Semitic languages if he would agree to remain in Greenville.[50]

Newman abandoned the trip to Germany and spent the year in Greenville. He studied Hebrew with the senior class of the seminary. In addition, Toy tutored him privately in Arabic, Syriac, and Chaldee. But in addition to this, Newman continued his study of New Testament and Patristic Greek with Broadus and studied Rabbinic Hebrew with Abraham Jaeger, a Jewish convert to Christianity, who was studying and teaching at the seminary. All this occurred during the academic year 1875-76.[51]

---

49. The seminary moved to Louisville, Kentucky in 1877. Norman Wade Cox and Judson Boyce Allen, eds. *Encyclopedia of Southern Baptists* (Nashville: Broadman Press, 1958), s.v. "Southern Baptist Theological Seminary," by Leo T. Crimson. Also see William A. Mueller, *A History of Southern Baptist Theological Seminary* (Nashville: Broadman Press, 1959).

50. Eby, *Newman the Church Historian*, 29. Crawford H. Toy taught at the Southern Baptist Theological Seminary, 1869-79. He received his educational training in Germany for two years and was influenced by the new types of Biblical criticism prevalent at the time. For instance, he accepted Darwin's theory of Evolution. He also accepted Wellhausen's Pentateuchal criticism. These views were judged out of character for Southern Baptists at the time. He was dismissed from his position in 1879 for his views regarding the Old Testament. In 1880 Toy joined the faculty of Harvard University as Hancock Professor of Hebrew and other Oriental languages. Eby says nothing about whether Newman followed Toy's views on these issues. See Mueller, 135-42. Also see: David Gordon Lyon, "Crawford H. Toy," *Harvard Theological Review* 13 (January 1920): 2-22; *Encyclopedia of Southern Baptists*, s.v. "Toy, Crawford Howell," by Gaines S. Dobbins.

51. Eby, *Newman the Church Historian*, 29.

Academic Life

Rochester Theological Seminary

Upon his completion of study at the Southern Baptist Theological Seminary in the fall of 1876, Newman moved to Charlotte, North Carolina where he taught school and served as pastor of a local congregation. Apparently this lifestyle did not agree with Newman. Several months later he received an offer from the Rochester Theological Seminary to teach the church history courses for the spring of 1877, a position which had been vacated by the death of Dr. Rabbi Joseph Wales Buckland, the seminary's church history professor.[52]

Because Newman's theological training was in biblical studies, the thought of teaching church history had not entered his mind until this point in his life. Nevertheless, Newman accepted the offer. As a result of this unplanned event, Newman began his long career as a church historian.[53]

Just before Newman returned to Rochester, the seminary acquired the personal library of Johann August Wilhelm Neander (1789-1850), professor of church history at the University of Berlin, from 1813 until his death. Newman's linguistic abilities, particularly his German knowledge, gave him the tools needed to study the materials. This in turn prompted the seminary to offer him a permanent position on the faculty. In 1880, he received promotion to Pettingill Professor of Church History.[54]

Newman enjoyed his work at Rochester. He believed that God had brought him to the seminary for a purpose and he desired to fulfill that purpose. "I believe I was brought to Rochester...by divine Providence. I

52. *Ibid.*, 31. Buckland's parents, though not Jewish, changed his name from "Smith" to "Rabbi" while he was a small child. They had a firm conviction that God had given them a child who would someday become a minister. The name "was to remind the boy as he grew – it was to remind the parents in their training of him – that he was to be a teacher for God." See Augustus Hopkins Strong, *Philosophy and Religion* (New York: A. C. Armstrong and Son, 1888), 338.

53. Eby, *Newman the Church Historian*, 32. Evidently he was comfortable with the field of church history and grew to enjoy it quickly. Just after he accepted the Rochester offer, the Baptist Theological Seminary at Morgan Park, Chicago, Illinois, which later became the University of Chicago, offered him the chair of Hebrew and Cognate languages. He declined the offer to remain at Rochester.

54. *Ibid.*

14

believe that God has work for me to do here."[55] He thought the work he performed at Rochester was more important than working at a job that would pay a large salary. "If I had an independent fortune I should choose to do just precisely the work I am doing."[56] Expressing pride in his work and the importance he saw in it, he said, "the whole Baptist denomination throughout the world would suffer by my withdrawal from my work."[57]

The success Newman enjoyed at Rochester was short lived. In the spring of 1881 he became involved in a controversy at the seminary which ultimately led to his dismissal. The controversy surrounded William Cleaver Wilkinson, professor of homiletics at the seminary. Newman took classes under Wilkinson as a student and developed a friendship with the professor after joining the faculty. He first mentioned the situation to his wife in a letter dated 7 March 1881.

> Dr. Wilkinson is having a good deal of trouble with the classes. The entire Junior class has been almost in a state of rebellion and the sentiment in the Senior class is very much against him....He is, I doubt not, in a great deal of trouble.[58]

Wilkinson's problems worsened as the semester progressed. While this transpired, Newman's friendship with the embattled professor grew stronger as they shared the same boarding house.[59] He also relied on the elder

55. Albert Henry Newman to Mrs. Newman, LS, 8 March 1881, Albert Henry Newman File, Baylor University 1. This letter is from a series of letters that Newman wrote to his wife during the spring, 1881. In early March of that year she moved back to her home in Alabama while Newman remained in Rochester. The reason she moved involved some type of health problem she experienced which made the winter especially dangerous for her. He wrote: "I really fear if you undertake to spend the next winter here you will have those dreadful pains again. I am afraid to have you here in cold weather until you have had a longer time in which to recover" (see letter dated 12 April 1881, 3). This may explain why she was away when Newman wrote her as a student at Rochester. See footnote # 47.

56. *Ibid.*, 2. Newman expressed his feelings about his purpose at Rochester in response to a letter he received from his mother-in-law in which she stated her desire that he move back to the south and rejoin his family.

57. *Ibid.*, 3.

58. Albert Henry Newman to Mrs. Newman, LS, 7 March 1881, Albert Henry Newman File, Baylor University, 1.

59. Albert Henry Newman to Mrs. Newman, LS, 17 March 1881, Albert Henry Newman File, Baylor University, 1.

professor for companionship. "What a comfort and help he is to me. He keeps me cheerful, happy and in a great many ways does me much good."[60] Some of their evenings were spent together reading literature for entertainment.[61]

Evidently, the problems between the students and Wilkinson had progressed for several years. Newman said of the situation:

> The fact that similar things have been happening almost every year since he began teaching in the seminary seems to have convinced those in authority that there is a radical defect somewhere. Dr. Strong says he has fought his battles for him heretofore, but that he will do so no longer...that Dr. W. was plainly told two years ago when a similar outburst of dissatisfaction occurred that the retaining of his position would depend on his getting on harmoniously with the students.[62]

Expressing his support for Wilkinson, Newman wrote, "[t]here is no man in the seminary...who more earnestly desires the well-being of the students...and no one that is capable of doing them more good."[63]

Eby said that Wilkinson's troubles at the seminary stemmed from his criticism of the students' lack of literary style and their poor delivery of sermons.[64] The account given by the seminary president, Augustus Hopkins Strong, sheds more light on the situation. He described how a conflict between Wilkinson and a student led to turmoil in the seminary:

> My friend [Wilkinson] made some fine point by way of criticism. The dull man could not see the point. The more blind he was, the more determined Wilkinson was to make him see. At last the man got angry; Wilkinson grew sarcastic; the man ended by losing all faith that his teacher was either a gentleman or a Christian. Incapacity to take another's point of

60. Albert Henry Newman to Mrs. Newman, LS, 15 March 1881, Albert Henry Newman File, Baylor University, 1-2.

61. For example see, Albert Henry Newman to Mrs. Newman, LS, 17 and 27 March 1881, Albert Henry Newman File, Baylor University, 1.

62. Albert Henry Newman to Mrs. Newman, LS, 27 March 1881, Albert Henry Newman File, Baylor University, 2.

63. *Ibid.*, 2-3.

64. Eby, *Newman the Church Historian*, 34.

view and to make friends of his students spoiled the professor's work as a teacher and at last roused the whole seminary to such a pitch of opposition that we had either to dismiss the seminary or dismiss him.[65]

Newman's position with the seminary became precarious when he became involved personally in the dispute by trying to play the role of mediator. He valued Wilkinson's friendship and respected him as a capable professor. But he also tried to convince Wilkinson that there were problems in his relations with the students.[66]

Newman realized however, that because of the student uproar, the seminary was suffering. He felt that under those circumstances, it would be best for Wilkinson to resign from the faculty.

> So we are in perplexity. Personally I believe that it would be better for the seminary–certainly better for some time to come, if Dr. W. would withdraw but I feel bound to do whatever I can do for him for the sake of friendship and because I believe him to be in the most respects a very extraordinary man.[67]

Newman moved into action attempting to mediate because he felt that the situation needed to be diffused and he did not want either side to be hurt. He delivered a speech concerning the situation to the Junior and Senior classes. Commenting on the reception of the speech he said:

> I rather think my address did me more benefit than it did Dr. W.; for the students appreciated it most highly, and considered it a priority to have an opportunity freely to discuss the matter with one whom they knew to be in sympathy with them while trying to defend the Professor.[68]

In spite of Newman's attempts to mediate, Wilkinson was forced to resign his position, though with a certain amount of animosity toward the

---

65. Crerar Douglas, ed. *Autobiography of Augustus Hopkins Strong* (Valley Forge: Judson Press, 1981), 229. Strong was a seminary classmate with Wilkinson and speaks very positively of him in the autobiography but admitted that a "great breach" existed between them, evidently because of Wilkinson's termination. For Strong's full discussion of Wilkinson, see 108-13.

66. Albert Henry Newman to Mrs. Newman, LS, 1 April 1881, Albert Henry Newman File, Baylor University, 2.

67. *Ibid.*, 2-3.

68. *Ibid.*, 1.

seminary during the weeks that followed. Apparently, Wilkinson appealed to the board of trustees but his attempt was fruitless.[69] Wilkinson left the seminary at the end of the semester.[70]

Newman first heard that his own job was in jeopardy in late April 1881. He expressed to his wife that the seminary was in financial trouble. Strong's plan was to change the makeup of the faculty by adding more preachers and removing some of the scholars and specialists. The president believed that this move would attract more students and financial contributions.[71] As a result, Newman discovered that he was to be replaced the next year.

> He [Strong] thinks that in order to make the faculty to correspond with the ideas of those whom he desires to please it will be necessary to make a change not only in the Homiletical department but also in the department of Church History. So it seems that we are likely to come sooner than we expected into something like Dr. Wilkinson's position, the only difference being that the students are unfriendly to him and friendly to me.[72]

The financial arrangement involved John D. Rockefeller and that did not please Newman. He said, "I have very little doubt but that the Seminary will in the long run be the worse for the Rockefeller influence."[73] What Newman exactly meant by this statement is hard to determine. Rockefeller could have promised to contribute money in return for a greater say in the control of the seminary and the selection of its faculty. Newman hinted at this by saying, "I think it altogether probable...that there was an

---

69. Albert Henry Newman to Mrs. Newman, LS, 27 April 1881, Albert Henry Newman File, Baylor University, 4.

70. Newman's respect and friendship for Wilkinson continued. See Albert Henry Newman, "A Higher Critic of Our Own Time: William Cleaver Wilkinson as Theologian and Critic," *Review and Expositor* 20 (April 1923): 138-55.

71. Albert Henry Newman to Mrs. Newman, LS, 22 April 1881, Albert Henry Newman File, Baylor University, 1. Newman said that Strong had just visited New York, not only to solicit contributions for the endowment, but to meet "with leading men in New York as to the internal affairs of the Seminary."

72. *Ibid.*

73. Albert Henry Newman to Mrs. Newman, LS, 6 May 1881, Albert Henry Newman File, Baylor University, 4.

understanding that in case such a man was made professor, such an amount of financial support would be forthcoming."[74]

In addition to the financial reason, Newman later felt that his dismissal was the result of a personality conflict with Strong. He suggested that the president harbored resentment because Newman proposed a change in the seminary curriculum the previous fall semester. This change would have made the Rochester curriculum similar to that of the Southern Baptist Theological Seminary.[75] Furthermore, Newman believed Strong had feelings of animosity concerning the speech given to the Junior and Senior classes in behalf of Wilkinson.

> This he took very much amiss, characterizing it as a gross breach of discipline which however he said he was not inclined to make much of owing to my good intentions in the matter. I have no doubt but that these things made him more willing to let me go than he would otherwise have been.[76]

Finally, with bitter feelings Newman said,

> I doubt whether there are many instances in history in which such an outrage has been perpetrated but S. has all the advantages and any attempt to set the matter right before the public would be misconduct and do more harm than good.[77]

The following week Newman had a conference with Strong in which the president was so cordial that Newman felt like taking back all that he had

---

74. *Ibid.*, 5. Strong discussed his personal involvement with Rockefeller and the millionaire's involvement with contributing money to the seminary in his autobiography. See Douglas, 237-39, 247-51. Of particular interest is Strong's account of how the money was secured for the building of Rockefeller Hall on the seminary campus. Rockefeller agreed to provide funds for the building totaling $38,000 if Strong could secure $100,000 for other needs in the seminary. Strong acquired the money from four other men: $25,000 from William Rockefeller (John's brother) for the library needs; $25,000 from Charles Pratt which served as an endowment for a Chair of Elocution; $25,000 from John B. Trevor for support of personnel; and $25,000 from Joseph B. Hoyt for a professorship in Hebrew. See p. 238. No mention is made about demands that certain individuals be chosen to fill the above mentioned positions.

75. Albert Henry Newman to Mrs. Newman, LS, 22 May 1881, Albert Henry Newman File, Baylor University, 1-2. The Southern Baptist Theological Seminary moved to Louisville, Kentucky in 1877.

76. Albert Henry Newman to Mrs. Newman, LS, 22 May 1881, Albert Henry Newman File, Baylor University, 2.

77. *Ibid.*, 3.

said about him previously.[78] However, two weeks later Newman's feelings of resentment were back as he presumed that "underneath that stereotyped smile of his I can see the hypocrisy and deceit. His ambitions and worldly mindedness he takes little care to conceal."[79] It is evident that Newman's feelings for Strong became less than cordial as the spring semester progressed. In the middle of June, Newman expressed more resentment toward Strong. "I believe it would be a tremendous strain upon charity to regard him as an earnest and honest Christian man."[80]

Strong's account of Newman's dismissal differs. In his autobiography, he reported that Newman lost his position for the same reasons that caused Wilkinson's termination.

> He [Newman] remained with us from 1877 to 1881. But his teaching ability was not equal to his learning. He could not command his classes. They rebelled against his instruction as minute and dull....The same wave of discontent among students which swept Professor Wilkinson from his professorship of homiletics dislodged Professor Newman from his professorship of church history.[81]

This explanation completely contradicts Newman who said on several accounts that he had the support of the students.[82] In addition to Newman's statement of student support, Strong himself spoke of Newman's rapport with

---

78. Albert Henry Newman to Mrs. Newman, LS, 31 May 1881, Albert Henry Newman File, Baylor University, 2-3.

79. Albert Henry Newman to Mrs. Newman, LS, 13 June 1881, Albert Henry Newman File, Baylor University, 1. In this letter there is an interesting revelation of another point of disagreement between Newman and Strong. Evidently, Strong had arranged a type of scholarship program for the most gifted students in the classes. Newman saw this as an attempt to buy students. "He discussed again with [me] the plan he has for buying students by paying them $300 a year apiece for submitting to be prepared for the ministry. To the three best (ablest) men in each class he would give $300.00 each, to those of less ability he would give either nothing at all or very little. There is Christianity for you with a vengeance! Imagine Paul conducting a Theological Seminary on such plans! It almost seems as if the man has gone deranged or at any rate has lost his sense not only of Christian morality, but even of common decency."

80. Albert Henry Newman to Mrs. Newman, LS, 13 June 1881, Albert Henry Newman File, Baylor University, 2.

81. Douglas, 229.

82. For instance see: Albert Henry Newman to Mrs. Newman, LS, 22 April 1881, 1; and 1 April 1881, 1; 22 May 1881, 2; 27 May 1881, 2-3, Albert Henry Newman File, Baylor University.

the students. In a letter from John H. Castle to Newman, Castle reported what Strong had said about the young church historian:

> Dr. Strong spoke of you when I was in Rochester in terms of the greatest respect and affection, with high appreciation of your scholarship and industry and your amiability in all your relations both with students and faculty.[83]

Finally in a formal letter of recommendation for Newman to Castle, Strong spoke of Newman being "personally a very popular man."[84] It would therefore seem that Strong made a mistake in his recollection of Newman as he reported it in the autobiography.

Perhaps the complete explanation for Newman's dismissal from Rochester cannot be recovered. However, it appears that the reason for his dismissal was due to three interlocking circumstances. First, there was a personality conflict, or at least a difference of opinion on certain things related to the seminary, between Newman and Strong. Second, his involvement in the Wilkinson affair served as a catalyst for causing a strained relationship between Newman and Strong. A third factor involves Strong's desire to change the faculty of the seminary in order to attract both money and students. Thus, the statement that Newman's dismissal from the seminary was due to student discontent similar to that of Wilkinson is an error on the part of Strong.

Toronto Baptist College and McMaster University

Transition Period

Newman's letters to his wife during the spring and early summer of 1881 exhibit a sense of optimism after his dismissal from Rochester. He said, "I think there is every reason to hope that some opening will occur before September."[85] He considered the pastorate, but seemed to dismiss the idea

---

83. John H. Castle to Albert Henry Newman, LS, 20 May 1881, Albert Henry Newman Papers, 1. Castle was president of the Toronto Baptist College.

84. Augustus H. Strong to John H. Castle, LS, 31 May 1881, Albert Henry Newman Papers, 4.

85. Albert Henry Newman to Mrs. Newman, LS, 23 April 1881, Albert Henry Newman File, Baylor University, 4.

because of a lack of confidence in his abilities in that area.[86] He expressed confidence that the providence of God eventually would secure a place of service where he would be content.[87]

During the weeks between his dismissal from Rochester and his acceptance of a position at the Toronto Baptist College, Newman received offers from two other schools for teaching positions. The first possibility was at the Norfolk College for Young Ladies, a female college in Norfolk, Virginia. The position was for a professor of Latin and English.[88] For some reason, by 13 June, Newman no longer included this position in his list of possibilities.[89] The second possible faculty position was the professor of Logic and Metaphysics at the Southwestern Baptist University in Jackson, Tennessee.[90]

Newman's main interest was in the possibility of a faculty position at the Toronto Baptist College. This could be attributed to the fact that the other two positions were not only out of his field of church history, but out of the field of religion altogether. He first revealed to his wife the possibility of the Toronto job in a letter dated 6 May 1881.

> I have within the last few days had an experience very decidedly calculated to set me all in a flurry again and to rob

---

86. Albert Henry Newman to Mrs. Newman, LS, 29 April 1881, Albert Henry Newman File, Baylor University, 1.

87. Albert Henry Newman to Mrs. Newman, LS, 29 April 1881, Albert Henry Newman File, Baylor University, 2. Other examples of Newman's trust in the providence of God are found in the letter to Mrs. Newman dated 1 May 1881, 3 and 22 April 1881, 2.

88. Albert Henry Newman to Mrs. Newman, LS, 25 May 1881, Albert Henry Newman File, Baylor University, 3. John A. Broadus of the Southern Baptist Theological Seminary wrote a letter of recommendation for Newman to the institution in Norfolk. John A. Broadus to Rev. R. M. Saunders, LS, 3 June 1881, Albert Henry Newman Papers. Crawford H. Toy also wrote a letter of recommendation to this institution for Newman. Crawford H. Toy to The Board of Trustees of the Norfolk College for Young Ladies, LS, 7 June 1881, Albert Henry Newman Papers.

89. Albert Henry Newman to Mrs. Newman, LS, 13 June 1881, Albert Henry Newman File, Baylor University, 1. Newman said, "I received a letter from you this morning. Of course you will know before you get this that it is no longer Norfolk that will probably be our home."

90. Albert Henry Newman to Mrs. Newman, LS, 6 June 1881, Albert Henry Newman File, Baylor University, 1.

me of my peace of mind and destroy my resolution not to care much.[91]

Evidently Newman had written to the president of the school, John H. Castle, a personal acquaintance of A. H. Strong, inquiring about the possibility of an open position on the faculty.[92] Castle visited Rochester during the first week of May 1881, talked with Newman, and even attended one of his lectures. Newman seemed excited about the possibility of a position in Toronto, but his excitement was guarded. The board of trustees was already examining one candidate. Though he was enthusiastic, Newman saw the situation in realistic terms.[93]

The possibility of Newman's election by the board of trustees to a faculty position at the Toronto Baptist College seemed to fade as the days went by. Castle wrote Newman on 17 May 1881 to inform him that the board had just about decided to elect D. M. Welton to the position. However, Castle told Newman that if the situation should change, Newman would be the next consideration and would probably get the job. Castle informed Newman that if he had applied for the position sooner, the situation may have been different.[94]

Later, Castle wrote Newman again to tell him that the board still wanted to hire Welton, but Newman was the alternate choice. However, he warned, "do not in the least depend on an appointment here for I have a pretty strong assurance that Dr. W. will come."[95]

Almost two months passed before Newman obtained a new teaching position. Despite whatever personality conflict existed between Strong and Newman, the Rochester president worked to secure Newman another place

91. Albert Henry Newman to Mrs. Newman, LS, 6 May 1881, Albert Henry Newman File, Baylor University, 2.

92. *Ibid.*

93. *Ibid.* Newman wrote Castle after the visit to Rochester. He included some of his class lecture notes and described his teaching method. Albert Henry Newman to J. H. Castle, LS, 6 May 1881, Albert Henry Newman Papers.

94. John H. Castle to Newman, LS, 17 May 1881, Albert Henry Newman Papers.

95. John H. Castle to Newman, LS, 20 May 1881, Albert Henry Newman Papers, 2.

of service. Strong wrote a very positive letter of recommendation for Newman to John H. Castle of the Toronto Baptist College.[96]

The situation remained without change for the remainder of May. On 10 June, Castle wrote Newman again informing him that the board of trustees was scheduled to meet on 21 June. Both Newman and Welton were expected to be suggested for the job. For some reason, Castle's positive outlook for Welton's election had diminished. Castle said that Welton still had the best chance of being elected, but it was not certain. By this time the Southwestern Baptist University in Jackson, Tennessee formally had offered Newman the position as professor of Logic and Metaphysics. They were awaiting Newman's response. Castle asked Newman if he could delay his answer to the offer until after the board of trustees met in Toronto.[97]

Why did Castle's positive outlook concerning Welton's election change? A clue may be found in the postscript to the letter to Newman:

> I see...that the Board of Governors of Acadia College have requested Dr. Welton to canvass for the endowment of a Theological Chair. They intend to protract the existence of the "Theological Dept." if possible.[98]

Welton served on the theological faculty of Acadia College. Castle evidently felt that there was a possibility that Welton would remain at the school instead of moving to Toronto. This would explain his change of attitude concerning Newman's prospects.

Newman responded to Castle and said that he would try to postpone his decision regarding the Southwestern Baptist University position until 21 June. He expressed in the letter that he preferred the Toronto position if it could be offered.[99] To his wife Newman said, "I shall await the decision of

---

96. Augustus H. Strong to John H. Castle. After Strong wrote the letter of recommendation for Newman to Castle, Newman wrote Castle to explain that he had not asked Strong to write the letter, but that the seminary president had done so out of his own initiative. Albert Henry Newman to John H. Castle, LS, 6 June 1881, Albert Henry Newman Papers.

97. John H. Castle to Newman, LS, 10 June 1881, Albert Henry Newman Papers, 1-2.

98. *Ibid.*, 2.

99. Albert Henry Newman to John H. Castle, LS, 11 June 1881, Albert Henry Newman Papers, 1-2.

the Toronto Board with entire calmness, for I have something certain to fall back upon in case that should fail."[100]

Newman wrote to his wife each day for the four days preceding 21 June. In those letters he expressed his anxiety about the upcoming vote of the board of trustees at Toronto. He compared both opportunities and speculated about which location would be most beneficial to both himself and his family.[101] Finally, late at night on 21 June, Newman received a telegram informing him of his unanimous election to the faculty of the Toronto Baptist College. His official title was Professor of Old Testament Exegesis (Hebrew) and Church History. The school offered Newman a salary of two thousand dollars per year.[102]

Newman still expressed uncertainty about which position to take. The climate in Tennessee would have been more beneficial for Mrs. Newman. Yet the Toronto position represented a challenge and was a position in the academic field for which he was best prepared. In addition, the salary in Toronto was more of a certainty whereas the salary at the Southwestern Baptist University would depend on crop prices and the number of students.[103] In spite of the advantages of both positions, Newman decided by the end of the week to accept the Toronto position.[104]

> I am *very, very* happy in consideration of my appointment to such a delightful position. I had become almost reconciled to throwing away in large measure the work of the last five years and to giving up plans which had become almost a part of my life. But now it is all bright again....[T]he earnest desire to do theological teaching and to carry foward [sic] my historical

---

100. Albert Henry Newman to Mrs. Newman, LS, 13 June 1881, Albert Henry Newman File, Baylor University, 2.

101. Albert Henry Newman to Mrs. Newman, LS, 17 June, 18 June, 20 June, 1881, Albert Henry Newman File, Baylor University. The letter dated 18 June contained information written on 19 June.

102. Albert Henry Newman to Mrs. Newman, LS, 21 June 1881, Albert Henry Newman File, Baylor University, 3-4.

103. Albert Henry Newman to Mrs. Newman, LS, 22 June 1881, Albert Henry Newman File, Baylor University, 1.

104. Albert Henry Newman to President J. H. Castle, LS, 23 June 1881, Albert Henry Newman Papers.

studies was not quenched and now it has come forth as strong and consuming as ever.[105]

Toronto Baptist College

Newman's experience at Toronto differed from his time at Rochester because the Toronto Baptist College was a newly organized school. Through the generosity of Senator William McMaster, a Baptist philanthropist, the funds were secured to establish the Toronto Baptist College.[106] The Baptists of Ontario and Quebec had attempted twice before to establish a theological school. The first venture, located in Montreal, failed. The second, located at Woodstock, "while it performed a glorious service, was soon recognized as a temporary expedient that could not entirely satisfy the needs of a growing, integrating denomination."[107] Two needs existed that prompted the idea of a new institution. The first was for a full college course, while the second was a desire for more scholarly training in the theological field.[108]

Students from the eastern provinces in Canada who desired to prepare for ministry usually attended Newton Theological Seminary in Massachusetts or one of the New York seminaries, either Rochester or Colgate. When the students graduated from these schools, they usually did not return to churches in Canada. Ontario students generally attended Woodstock for secondary education and then the University of Toronto for their college work. Their desire usually was not to return to Woodstock for theological training.

> Above every other impulse that animated the scattered Baptists of Canada was the desire for a theological seminary to train a ministry for the brotherhood for all parts of the broad Dominion.[109]

---

105. Albert Henry Newman to Mrs. Newman, LS, 23 June 1881, Albert Henry Newman File, Baylor University, 1.

106. For a biographical sketch of William McMaster see *Dictionary of Canadian Biography*, 1982 ed., s.v. "McMaster, William."

107. Eby, *Newman the Church Historian*, 36. For a description of the history of the Toronto Baptist College (which later became McMaster University) see: Charles M. Johnston, *McMaster University: The Toronto Years*, vol. 1 (Toronto: University of Toronto Press, 1976).

108. *Ibid.*

109. *Ibid.*, 37.

When Newman began work at the Toronto Baptist College in the fall of 1881, the faculty was very small.[110] Consequently he had duties in addition to teaching church history. The first task assigned to Newman was to develop a curriculum for the school. Newman described this task:

> Dr. Castle had me come, and asked me to write out a prospectus and curriculum for the Toronto Baptist College, which I did as well as I could. I adopted a somewhat new scheme of studies; I followed in general the scheme that was in force in the Southern Baptist Theological Seminary [which he had tried to implement at Rochester], and made each study independent, and allowed students to take as many or as few subjects as they could handle, without any regard to order except the natural order. I introduced also something I had not seen before, a systematic arrangement of subjects, Exegetical Theology, Historical Theology, Dogmatic Theology, and Practical Theology, and arranged the courses under those headings.[111]

In addition to designing the curriculum, Newman had a plethora of teaching duties, and he served as college librarian for several years.[112] He began by teaching Biblical Introduction, Old Testament Exegesis, and Church History. Later, he taught such courses as Hebrew, Greek, Comparative Religions, Historical Theology, Christian Ethics, and Homiletics. When Toronto Baptist College was incorporated into McMaster University in 1887, and an Arts department was added, Newman had to teach Political Economy and Civil Government.[113] He commented, "There's no telling what I didn't teach."[114] As the faculty grew, Newman was able to concentrate his energy more on church history.

---

110. J. L. Gilmour, "Albert Henry Newman," *The McMaster University Monthly* 10 (November 1901): 50 says that there were only three faculty members. A different account which names the faculty is found in a letter from E. J. Bengough to O. C. S. Wallace, TL, 30 November 1934, O. C. S. Wallace Papers, Canadian Baptist Archives, McMaster Divinity College, Hamilton, Ontario, 1. Bengough says that the faculty of the college during the term 1881-82 consisted of Newman, Castle, John Torrence, J. M. Hirschfelder, and W. H. Clarke. Special lecturers that year were R. S. McArthur, Warren Randolph, and H. E. Buchan.

111. Unpublished autobiographical speech delivered by Albert Henry Newman, 5 April 1929.

112. Bengough to Wallace, 30 November 1934.

113. Bengough to Wallace and Unpublished speech of Albert Henry Newman, 5 April 1929.

114. Speech, 5 April 1929.

McMaster University

William McMaster, the benefactor of the Toronto Baptist College, died in 1887. His will showed that he desired to further Baptist education in Canada. He left nearly $1 million to be used for the establishment of a Baptist institution of higher education. This new institution became McMaster University. The University incorporated both Toronto Baptist College and Woodstock College together. It opened its doors in 1890 in Toronto as an independent institution, after much discussion about the possibility of uniting with the University of Toronto.[115]

Newman's reputation increased as the university grew. He frequently submitted brief articles to *The Canadian Baptist* and from January through March of 1889, served as its editor.[116] Newman probably intended to continue in such capacity for a longer period of time but someone either on the board of trustees or the Senate of McMaster University objected to Newman's employment outside the university. Therefore he vacated the position after only three months.[117]

Newman's editorial experience in Canada was not confined to *The Canadian Baptist* alone. In 1891, he began and served as first editor of *The McMaster University Monthly*. A statement of the purpose of the journal appeared in the first issue:

> The best thought and the best literary gifts of our educational institutions and of the denomination should be made tributary to the pages of the Monthly. It will be equally hospitable to all departments, and there should be no lack of variety.[118]

Perhaps Newman's greatest contribution during the twenty years spent in Toronto was his literary output. There can be no question that the

---

115. Johnston, 45-68.

116. Newman had previously served as interim editor for a month in 1883, when the newspaper was purchased by William McMaster. Unpublished speech, 5 April, 1929.

117. Unpublished speech, 5 April 1929. In the editorial column of the final issue of *The Canadian Baptist* that Newman edited, he gave the following as his reason for leaving the position: "Owing to the pressure of other responsibilities, heavier now than when the position was assumed, the editor feels it to be his duty to relinquish the work entrusted to him by the Directors of the Standard Publishing Company." *The Canadian Baptist* 28 March 1889, 4.

118. "College News," *The McMaster University Monthly* 1 (June 1891): 40.

Toronto years represent the pinnacle of Newman's career. With the exception of his translation of Immer's *Hermeneutics of the New Testament* (1877), most of Newman's books were written during his employment at McMaster University. This includes *A History of Anti-Pedobaptism; From the Rise of Pedobaptism to A.D. 1609* (1897); *A History of Baptist Churches in the United States* (1894); *A Manual of Church History Vol. 1* (1899), Vol. 2 (1902). He also edited two other works: *A Century of Baptist Achievement* (1901) and *Memoir of Daniel Arthur McGregor* (1891).

Newman's literary output during this stage of his career was due in part to the schedule McMaster University allowed its faculty to keep. For almost five months in the summer the professors were free of teaching responsibilities. During these summer breaks Newman accomplished most of his research and writing. Not long after he came to Toronto he purchased an island in Lake Joseph, one of the Muskoka lakes, located about one hundred miles due north of Toronto. There he built a home where he would take his family during summer vacations. Other faculty members and pastors bought land in the area which resulted in the formation of a small community. According to Eby, in the summer Newman generally apportioned a certain amount of writing to be completed during the morning hours. The afternoon was then spent fishing or picnicking with the rest of the family.[119] Eby concluded that Newman's years in Toronto "were the most fruitful and, in many respects, the happiest years of his life."[120]

Twenty Years in Texas

Baylor University

In 1900, while at the height of his career, probably the last thing Newman thought about doing was moving to another sphere of service. During his twenty years in Canada he had seen the small Toronto Baptist College grow into McMaster University. Nevertheless, a major change in his career was imminent.

---

119. Eby, *Newman the Church Historian*, 48.
120. *Ibid.*, 49.

During that year, Benajah Harvey Carroll, a leading Texas Baptist and trustee of Baylor University in Waco, made the announcement that in 1901 the University would form a Theological Department for ministerial instruction. He invited Newman to come to Baylor and deliver the 1900 commencement address and lecture at the summer Bible school, sponsored by the University. The school also awarded Newman an honorary LL.D. degree at the graduation ceremonies.[121]

During his visit to Waco, Carroll made an appeal for Newman to join the faculty of Baylor. Newman was hesitant to leave his position in Canada. But Carroll persisted in his offer for the remainder of the year and during the spring of 1901. Unexpectedly on 21 March 1901, John S. Tanner, one of Baylor's most promising theological faculty members, died at the age of thirty-two. This made it even more imperative that Baylor secure someone of Newman's stature for the faculty.[122]

Newman agonized for several months over whether or not to move. Evidently, he wanted to make sure that a separate theological department would be formed at Baylor before he agreed to accept a position at the school. In a letter to her daughter, Mrs. Frederick Eby, Mrs. Newman wrote:

> Papa did not once think of going there until they were ready to begin the theological work sufficiently to offer a full course for the first year men, then to go on enlarging until they would cover the three years.[123]

Along with this, there was another setback to accepting the position at Baylor. Dr. Tanner had taught courses in Greek New Testament. Baylor wanted Newman not only to teach these courses, but also Hebrew and Church History. In addition, Samuel Palmer Brooks, who taught history, had asked for leave so he could study at Yale University. The school wanted Newman to assist in teaching courses in general history until the theological

---

121. Robert A. Baker, *Tell the Generations Following: A History of Southwestern Baptist Theological Seminary 1908-1983* (Nashville, Broadman Press, 1983), 115. Also see Eby, *Newman the Church Historian*, 49.

122. *Ibid.*

123. Mrs. Newman to Mrs. Frederick Eby, LS, no date, Albert Henry Newman Papers, 5.

department was organized completely.[124] Newman was willing to teach Greek New Testament, Systematic Theology, and Church History. However, he did not want to teach Hebrew because he had not worked with the language consistently for a number of years.[125] Also he did not want to teach the wide range of subjects at Baylor which he did when he first went to Toronto Baptist College. Finally, the salary offered at Baylor was only about sixty per cent of what he made at McMaster.[126]

Newman continued to struggle with the question of whether to move. Mrs. Newman in another letter to her daughter described his indecision:

> Since I wrote the first part of this letter, we got Dr. Carroll's letter and for the past two days Papa had almost decided to go, but then he got very unhappy about it when he began to think all it would mean especially to his prospects for writing in summers, and he could not think it right to go.[127]

Being unable to make a decision while in Canada, Newman journeyed to Waco to discuss the matter further. He set forth conditions which he thought would surely not be met. To his surprise, Baylor met all of the conditions, which evidently included the issues discussed above.[128] Newman pointed out that he lacked the type of zeal that he supposed Texas Baptists possessed and argued that he "was only a quiet scholar and teacher."[129] However, all his objections were met and he eventually agreed to accept the position offered at Baylor.[130] No doubt, the fact that Eby was on faculty at Baylor and the possibility of being close to his daughter and son-in-law influenced Newman's decision to move to Waco.

---

124. Eby, *Newman the Church Historian*, 53.

125. Mrs. Newman to Mrs. Frederick Eby, LS, 4 April 1901, Albert Henry Newman Papers, 2.

126. Eby, *Newman the Church Historian*, 54.

127. Mrs. Newman to Mrs. Frederick Eby, LS, May 1901, Albert Henry Newman Papers, 3.

128. Newman is listed as "Professor of Church History" in *The Round-Up* 1902-1907. This is the title of the Baylor annual.

129. Eby, *Newman the Church Historian*, 54.

130. *Ibid.* Interestingly, Newman changed his mind upon returning to Toronto. He tried to withdraw his acceptance. The press in Toronto even published that Newman had decided to stay at McMaster. But Baylor would not consider a release and Newman was forced to move. See pp. 54-55.

While at Baylor Newman seemed to be well-respected by the students. However, little is mentioned of him by the students in the yearbooks published by the senior classes. In the 1907 yearbook, a statement is written under each faculty members' name describing their character. The statement under Newman's name read simply "Thou art a scholar."[131]

The Southwestern Baptist Theological Seminary

The Theological Department of Baylor University officially became the Baylor Theological Seminary in 1905. This was largely due to the efforts and planning of B. H. Carroll. The idea of a new seminary to serve Southern Baptists west of the Mississippi River came to Carroll in the form of a "vision" as he described it.

> I was passing through the Panhandle on a Fort Worth and Denver train on my way to Amarillo to meet my wife and baby. I had read all day and my eyes were exhausted. My deafness made it impracticable for me to sustain a conversation with people on the train. So I fell to musing. As I looked out over those plains over which in my youth I had chased buffalo, there arose before me a vision of our Baptist situation in the Southwest. I saw multitudes of our preachers with very limited education, with few books and with small skill in using to the best advantage even the books they had....I saw here in the Southwest many institutions for the professional training of the young teacher, the young lawyer, the young doctor, the young nurse and the young farmer, but not a single institution dedicated to the specific training of the young Baptist preacher. It weighed on my soul like the earth on the shoulders of Atlas. It was made clear to me on that memorable day that, for the highest usefulness of our Baptist people, such an institution was an imperious necessity.[132]

---

131. *The Round-Up*, 1907, 25. From 1901-07 Newman taught such courses as Ancient Church History, Medieval Church History, Advance Research, Thr Protestant Reformation, History of Modern Denominations, History of Preaching, History of Doctrines, Historical Readings in Latin, German, and French. See *Baylor Catalogue*, 1901-07, as cited by Breazeale, 14.

132. Jeff D. Ray, *B. H. Carroll* (Nashville: Sunday School Board of the Southern Baptist Convention, 1927), 136-37.

The Seminary existed in conjunction with Baylor until 1908. On 14 March of that year, the charter of The Southwestern Baptist Theological Seminary was officially filed with the secretary of state in Texas.[133]

During the years 1908-09, Carroll became concerned that the seminary should be relocated. "He felt...that if the seminary remained at Waco it would either overshadow Baylor University or would be overshadowed by it."[134] The board of trustees designated Fort Worth as the new location for the seminary on 2 November 1909.[135] The school officially opened there on Monday, 3 October 1910.[136]

The situation at the seminary the first few years was far less than appealing, and one might question whether it caused Newman to regret leaving his comfortable position at McMaster to relocate in Texas. Describing these primitive conditions Lee Rutland Scarborough wrote:

> Some rooms were finished. The only roof we had on the building was the concrete floors above the first and second floors. We had no heating plant, no water system installed. We had to improvise our heat by putting stoves in the rooms and pipes out the windows. The story of sacrificing, doing without conveniences, waiting and working is a long, glorious one. Mrs. A. H. Newman was Superintendent of Fort Worth Hall. Her task was somewhat like Mrs. Noah's after the flood.[137]

During its first year the faculty numbered only seven. Carroll was President and Professor of English Bible. Newman was Professor of Church History and History of Doctrines. Charles Bray Williams served as Professor of Biblical Greek, Biblical Introduction and Bible Theology of the New Testament. Calvin Goodspeed was Professor of Systematic Theology, Apologetics, Polemics, and Ecclesiology. Jefferson Davis Ray taught

---

133. Baker, 136. Baker chronicles in detail the developments of the beginnings of Baylor Theological Seminary and its evolution into The Southwestern Baptist Theological Seminary. See 111-45.

134. *Ibid.*, 145.

135. *Ibid.*, 152. All of the events leading up to the selection of Fort Worth as the new location are described by Baker, 145-52.

136. *Ibid.*, 158.

137. L. R. Scarborough, *A Modern School of the Prophets* (Nashville, Broadman Press, 1939), 73.

Homiletics and Pastoral Duties and was Assistant in the English Bible. Lee Rutland Scarborough taught Evangelism and served as field secretary. Finally, James Josiah Reeve served as Professor of Hebrew, Cognate Languages, and Biblical Theology of the Old Testament.[138] Commenting on Newman's importance to the first faculty, W. R. Estep said:

> No member of that first faculty brought to Southwestern the background of experience in theological education that Newman possessed. Carroll could preach and teach, inspire and challenge, raise money and balance the books, but he had neither the education nor the academic learning of a Newman. It took a Newman to guide Southwestern's development into an institution of academic integrity. Perhaps, it is too much to say that Newman saved Southwestern from becoming merely a Bible institute, a trade school, or a degree mill, but he helped.[139]

Newman left the faculty of the Southwestern Baptist Theological Seminary in 1913. The circumstances surrounding his departure were unfortunate and somewhat similar to the reasons for his resignation at Rochester thirty-two years before. Newman became involved in a conflict with B. H. Carroll which led to his resignation. Eby said Newman's reason for leaving the seminary was due to theological differences caused by a more conservative atmosphere, which developed after Carroll's death. However this is somewhat incorrect as Newman left before Carroll's death.[140]

Newman and Carroll had probably been on a path leading toward conflict for a number of years due to several differences. Carroll had no formal education, while Newman had been well educated at several schools. Carroll was also a grand orator, able to arouse a congregation with his preaching. Newman was a scholar and had very little recognizable oratorical ability.[141]

---

138. *Ibid.*, 188.

139. W. R. Estep, "A. H. Newman and Southwestern's First Faculty," *Southwestern Journal of Theology* 21 (Fall 1978): 91-92.

140. Eby, *Newman the Church Historian*, 59. Eby says that Carroll died in 1913 which is incorrect. B. H. Carroll died on 11 November 1914.

141. *Ibid.*, 56-57.

There was one further difference between these two men which may have been the primary point of contention between them. At the time that Newman was connected with Southwestern, B. H. Carroll's brother, James Milton Carroll another Baptist historian, was busy delivering a popular series of lectures in Texas and Oklahoma with the title of the "Trail of Blood." These lectures sought to prove the Landmark Movement claims of Baptist successionism by tracing Baptists back through the history of the church to Jesus and the disciples.   This viewpoint supported the Baptist view of apostolic succession, held by James Robinson Graves, the instigator of the Landmark Movement. Newman disagreed with this view, knowing that it had no historical reputability. However, B. H. Carroll was partial to successionism, and Newman's position conflicted with Carroll's views.[142] Dr. William Wright Barnes, who succeeded Newman at the seminary reported:

> Dr. C. was an ardent successionist; Dr. N. did not believe any denomination can be traced historically to Jesus and the Apostles. Dr. C. told his wife that Dr. N. with his learning and his reputation could undo all that Dr. C. stood for.[143]

The situation became critical in the spring of 1911. In a letter to the president dated 2 May 1911, Newman resigned his position as Professor of Church History.[144] However, after a trip to Dallas to speak with James Bruton Gambrell, chairman of the seminary's board of trustees, he evidently reconsidered.   When he returned, he wrote Carroll another letter which said:

> I had a long talk with him [J. B. Gambrell] on my relations with the Seminary. He assures me in the most emphatic way that he will discountenance the raising of any issue in the reappointment of a professor or in the appointment of a new professor on such points of church history as those involved in my case, and that if you will take the same stand and hold firmly to it he will support you to the full measure of his strength and influence. He feels assured that Dr. Truett will

142. W. R. Estep, "Newman of McMaster and Southwestern," *Theodolite* 8 (Issue Number 2, 1987): 27-28.

143. This statement is from a handwritten note by W. W. Barnes on the back of an envelope just two years before his death. The note is located in the Newman file, A. Webb Roberts Library, Southwestern Baptist Theological Seminary, Fort Worth, Texas.

144. Albert Henry Newman to B. H. Carroll, LS, 2 May 1911, B. H. Carroll Papers, A. Webb Roberts Library, Southwestern Baptist Theological Seminary.

take the same position. He thinks it could be disastrous to allow the Seminary Board to commit itself to the requirement in its professors of a particular way of interpreting the facts of history.[145]

Therefore, Carroll did not accept Newman's resignation in 1911. But two years later, the church historian was forced to resign. This time the issue involved an attempted change in the seminary curriculum.

During most of 1912 and the spring of 1913, B. H. Carroll became seriously ill. His "pride and joy" at the seminary was a course based on his thirteen volume commentary, *An Interpretation of the English Bible*. This was a required course for all seminarians, and it was Carroll's desire that the course should remain in the curriculum of the seminary forever.[146]

Because Carroll was ill, the responsibility fell to Newman as dean of the faculty to provide leadership in administrative duties. The faculty minutes of 2 January 1912 reported that Newman raised a question about students not being able to earn the required eight hours credit in English Bible while Carroll was ill. The decision of the faculty present then was that if a student could not complete those courses with Carroll in two years, he could substitute courses in New Testament and Old Testament and thereby fulfill the English Bible requirements.[147]

The trend of revising the curriculum continued at Southwestern, no doubt with Newman's approval. The faculty appointed Professors Williams and Reeve to form a committee on curriculum revision on 4 April 1912. Six days later, the committee reported back to the faculty. It recommended several revisions. First, the committee recommended that the two year requirement in Evangelism should be lessened. But when Professor Scarborough protested, this requirement was restored. Second, the committee made a recommendation that since President Carroll was ill and unable to teach, the curriculum should be revised so that English Old Testament could be taught in conjunction with Hebrew and Old Testament

145. Albert Henry Newman to B. H. Carroll, LS, 16 May 1911, B. H. Carroll Papers, A. Webb Roberts Library, Southwestern Baptist Theological Seminary, Fort Worth, Texas.

146. Estep, "Newman of McMaster and Southwestern," 28.

147. Faculty Minutes, Southwestern Baptist Theological Seminary, Fort Worth, Texas, 2 January 1912, as cited by Baker, 166.

Theology and that English New Testament be taught in conjunction with Greek and New Testament Theology. The committee noted that this was the method of instruction in all seminaries and that men trained in the Biblical languages were better prepared to interpret the English Bible than those who did not know the languages.[148]

Evidently, the process of curriculum revision continued until the late spring of 1913. W. W. Barnes later reported the events that caused Newman's resignation.

> During the severe illness of Dr. C. in April and May 1913 Dr. C. B. Williams led Dr. N. and R. [Newman and Reeve] to plan with him the partition of Dr. Carroll's Department (Interpretation of Eng. Bib.), giving Dr. W. [Williams] NT Interpretation with his Greek and NT Theology; giving Dr. R. [Reeve] OT Interpretation with his Hebrew and OT Theology. Upon Dr. C.'s unexpected recovery (partial) he notified Dr. N. and R. that they would not be elected for another year. (Members of the faculty were elected annually in those yrs.). Dr. Wm. [Williams] escaped by denying part in the scheme.[149]

Evidently Carroll interpreted the efforts by Newman and Reeve to revise the curriculum as subversive. No doubt, much of Carroll's actions could be interpreted as resulting from his sickness. In a letter to a friend, W. C. Taylor, Newman reported what Mrs. Carroll had said to him about the president's condition. Carroll

> would not have interfered with me had it not been that in his illness the thought pressed itself upon him that if he left me in the Faculty and as Dean of the Faculty my influence might result in the destruction of the chair of English Bible...and that if he had continued in health he would not have taken the step he did.[150]

Once again, now at age sixty-one, circumstances forced Newman to find another teaching position. Thus, he returned to Baylor University where he taught church history until 1921.[151]

---

148. Baker, 166.

149. Barnes, Handwritten Statement

150. A. H. Newman to W. C. Taylor, 8 June 1913, as quoted by Baker, 167.

151. Eby, *Newman the Church Historian*, 59.

Mercer University

Newman spent seven of the last eight years of his teaching career at his *alma mater*, Mercer University. In the spring of 1921, he attended the Mercer graduation exercises for two reasons. First, the school awarded him an honorary Doctor of Laws degree at the commencement.[152] Second, his own graduating class met that year for a reunion and a semicentennial celebration of their graduation from Mercer.[153]

While Newman was at Mercer for this occasion, President Rufus C. Weaver offered him the Chair of Church History in a newly organized seminary at the school which provided a two year course of study comparable to the Southern Baptist Theological Seminary in Louisville, Kentucky.[154] Newman decided to accept the position and began work there in the fall of 1921.[155]

While he seemed content with his work at Mercer, Newman's experience there was somewhat shortened by financial problems within the university. By 1928, the school had accumulated an indebtedness of approximately $100,000. The Georgia Baptist Convention assumed the debt but instructed its Executive Committee to take the responsibility of formulating a plan to make the university debt-free. The plan decided upon would lift the debt by applying a fixed sum of $5,000 annually with interest, from the yearly endowment income until the debt was retired.[156]

This plan resulted in the university being forced to readjust its budget in several areas. One such area affected was the Theological Seminary. In its meeting on 24 February 1928, the Mercer board of trustees made five important decisions designed to improve the efficiency of the university. The decisions concurred with the results from a study of the university conducted

---

152. Newman had received an honorary Doctor of Divinity degree from Mercer in 1885. See Dowell, 404.

153. Eby, *Newman the Church Historian*, 61.

154. Dowell, 267.

155. *Ibid.*, 62.

156. *Ibid.*, 295.

one year earlier by a trustee-appointed committee from outside the school. The decision regarding the Theological Seminary read as follows:

> That the Theological Seminary be adjusted to the status of a pre-theological school, its work being correlated with that of the Southern Baptist Theological Seminary and other standard schools.[157]

With the change in the status of the seminary, the school determined that it no longer needed Newman's services. Dr. Andrew Philip Montague, vice-president of the university, informed Newman of the decision by letter.

> For some weeks it has been a matter of uncertainty how many members of the theological faculty could be retained for the next academic year, since the financial condition of the university demands stern retrenchment....To my deep regret it was found that but two of the theological faculty could be retained....While the trustees, Dr. Dowell and I would have found joy in your retention, it came evident that the condition of Mercer University forbade an increase of debt....Most of all of those who will not be kept I regret your leaving.[158]

Newman responded without bitterness. "I do not feel at all inclined to be contentious about the matter."[159] However, there were some of the Mercer supporters who did not like the decision to release Newman. The Mother's Bible Class of the First Baptist Church of Macon, Georgia submitted a resolution to the Mercer trustees protesting the decision and appealing to the board to reconsider its decision.[160] The teacher of the class said:

---

157. Hugh M. Willet, "The Meeting of the Mercer Trustees," *The Christian Index*, 1 March 1928, 23. The other four decisions were (1) the president should be the executive head of the university responsible only to the trustees; (2) the School of Liberal Arts should become the central element within the university; (3) the Law School should continue as a regular law school and improvements should be made; and (4) each department in the university should submit a budget and its spending should be limited to that budget.

158. A. P. Montague to A. H. Newman, LS, 24 March 1928, Albert Henry Newman File, Baylor University, 1-2.

159. Albert Henry Newman to Mrs. Judith Gambrell Wiley, LS, 30 March 1928, Albert Henry Newman Papers, 2. In this letter, Newman indicated that he believed the decision may have been the result of an assumption by the trustees that he was ready to retire from active service as a professor and that financially he did not need the salary that he was making. He also indicated that since he was only teaching part-time, he was deemed more expendable.

160. Judith Gambrell Wiley to A. H. Newman, LS, 10 April 1928, Albert Henry Newman File, Baylor University.

> You have been a great inspiration to me and to our class and
> as the mothers of sons who are prospective students at Mercer
> and who we hope to see grow up loyal and intelligent Baptists,
> we feel justified in making this protest.[161]

In spite of their protest, the end of the spring semester of 1928 found Newman at age seventy-five, with fifty-one years of teaching experience, unemployed.

Visiting Professor

After leaving Mercer, Newman occupied the position of visiting professor at McMaster University beginning in the fall of 1928. The death of Dr. J. S. Brown, professor of church history at McMaster, left the school in need of someone to occupy the position until a new professor could be found. After twenty-seven years, Newman now returned to the place where he had experienced the peak of his career and where he had been held in very high esteem.[162] Mrs. Newman expressed their feelings near the end of Newman's work there:

> We ought to be very thankful...we are so much appreciated by
> so many friends. This year the last one of teaching, back in the
> institution papa had so much to do with getting started, we
> have heard from various sources how much they have
> appreciated papa being here this year.[163]

The 1928-29 experience as visiting professor at McMaster was not the first time Newman served in such capacity. In the summer of 1906, Newman taught four courses and delivered several lectures at the University of Chicago. During the first term of the summer he taught "Schisms and Controversies of the First Six Centuries," and "Anti-Catholic Parties of the Middle Ages." During the second term he taught "The Era of Modern Denominationalism," and "The Anabaptists of the 16th Century." In August of that same summer, Newman delivered several lectures which were open to the public: 7 August, "Thomas Munzer;" 8 August, "Andrea Bodenstein von

---

161. *Ibid.*, 1.

162. Eby, *Newman the Church Historian*, 62.

163. Mrs. Newman to Mrs. Eby, LS, no date, Albert Henry Newman Papers, 2.

Karlstadt;" 9 August, "Melchior Hofmann;" 10 August, "Johannes Campanus;" 14 August, "Michael Cervetus;" and 15 August, "Faustus Socinus."[164]

Newman returned to the University of Chicago in the fall quarter of 1926 and taught two courses. The first was "English Church History during the Eighteenth and Nineteenth Centuries." The second course was entitled "The Protestant Revolution of the Sixteenth Century."[165]

Another opportunity as visiting professor came during the academic year 1917-18. Vanderbilt University invited Newman to teach church history and comparative religions as a replacement for one of their religion faculty members who engaged himself in work for the war effort during the first world war. During this year Newman became closely acquainted with Dr. Wilbur F. Tillett, who was dean of the school of religion and vice-chancellor of the university.[166] Concerning that year, Tillett said: "Dr. Newman rendered the School of Religion of Vanderbilt University important and much appreciated service during the trying years of the World War."[167]

Personality

Family Life

The marriage between Albert Henry Newman and Mary Augusta Ware lasted to within one month of sixty years. Their life together was happy and productive. Eby described the complementary relationship between Newman and his wife:

> Dr. and Mrs Newman were a marital team remarkable for their complementary abilities. He was decidedly circumscribed in his manual activities and interests. Other than fishing in Muskoka he had no hobby. To all intents and purposes he was an introvert, reflective, somewhat absentminded, and absorbed in scholarly pursuits. Mrs. Newman, on the other hand, was an

164. Letter from Richard L. Popp, 29 October 1989, Archives Assistant, Special Collections, The University of Chicago Library, Chicago, Illinois.

165. *Ibid.*

166. Eby, Unpublished biographical sketch of Newman written April, 1926, Albert Henry Newman Papers, 15-16.

167. Wilbur F. Tillett to Rufus W. Weaver, TL, 5 January 1927, Albert Henry Newman Papers.

extrovert, extremely versatile, energetic to the last degree, a born manager and executive.[168]

Four children were born to the Newman family. The first child, Horatio Hackett Newman was born 19 March 1875. He earned a Ph. D. in zoology at the University of Chicago and remained there for a career in teaching. The second child, Elizabeth Nuckolls Newman, was born 31 July 1877. Henry Ware Newman was the third child, born in 1878.[169] He was a medical missionary for thirteen years then returned to practice medicine in the United States. Albert Broadus Newman was the fourth child born 3 May 1888. He earned a Ph. D. in chemistry and enjoyed a career in both teaching and chemical engineering. At the time that Eby wrote *Newman the Church Historian*, Albert Broadus Newman was the chief of the Chemical Industry Section of the United States Office of Military Government in Berlin, Germany.[170]

Eby described the Newman home life as reverent with family worship held every day. Church attendance was regular every week. The family found many ways to amuse themselves. During the summer months in Toronto when the family went to the summer home in Muskoka, hunting, fishing, boating, and swimming occupied the leisure time. Another form of leisure enjoyed by the family was the practice of reading books and stories aloud in the family circle.[171]

Religious Convictions

Worship for Newman was always a vital part of his life. He was active in a local Baptist church from his childhood until his death. Though never ordained as a minister, Newman did serve as a deacon in the Bloor Street

---

168. Eby, *Newman the Church Historian*, 105.

169. At least three dates can be located for Henry Ware Newman's birthdate: 4 February 1878, 12 December 1878, and 3 December 1878. These dates are found in a biographical file contained in the Albert Henry Newman Papers. However, the date of birth on Henry Newman's tombstone, located in Austin, Texas, is 4 December 1878.

170. Eby, *Newman the Church Historian*, 107 and *Ibid*.

171. Eby, *Newman the Church Historian*, 108.

Baptist Church in Toronto, Canada and in the First Baptist Church of Waco, Texas.[172]

Evangelical Christianity could best describe Newman's expression of his faith. He believed that Christianity consisted of more than simple assent to a creed.

> The ritualistic, the institutionalistic, the conventional and rationalistic forms of worship did not satisfy his spiritual cravings. For him, Christianity meant a genuine religious experience that produced a profound ethical life in constant communion with God.[173]

The New Schaff-Herzog Encyclopedia of Religious Knowledge describes Newman's theological position as a moderate conservative.[174] He seemed to be able to work amiably with both sides of any issue. For instance, his own view concerning the millennium was postmillennialism. Yet he worked comfortably with those who advocated premillennialism. When the higher critical methods of Biblical study began to become popular, Newman maintained a moderate position repudiating both Fundamentalism and Modernism.[175]

There is little information concerning Newman's feelings toward some of the early Fundamentalist and Modernist leaders. However, Mrs. Newman expressed her disagreement with the Fundamentalists, particularly with T. T. Shields of Toronto, and this may shed light on what Newman's feelings were.

---

172. *Ibid.*, 123. Newman was known to deliver church history lectures to the laity within the church to which he belonged. For instance, in 1895 he delivered a series of lectures in Baptist history to the youth of the Bloor Street Baptist Church. Another church in Toronto, the Lansdowne Avenue Baptist Church heard about the series and asked Newman to deliver the lectures there also. O. C. S. Wallace, "Toronto Letter," *The Watchman* 7 March 1895, 27.

173. *Ibid.*, 119.

174. *The New Schaff-Herzog Encyclopedia of Religious Knowledge*, 1953 ed., s.v. "Newman, Albert Henry."

175. Eby, *Newman the Church Historian*, 140-43. Newman maintained a high regard for the Scriptures, yet he was willing to admit that they were to be read for the purpose of attaining spiritual understanding and not scientific or philosophical truth. Futhermore, they provided spiritual truth to the people of the times in which they were written primarily, and then secondarily, to the following generations. See Newman, "Up With the Times," *The Canadian Baptist* 19 April 1883, 4. (This article is not signed by Newman. But someone has written his name across the column in the issue of *The Canadian Baptist* that was read for this study).

We have heard from various sources how much they have appreciated Papa being here this year. They say it has given them such advantage over Shields to have Papa tell of the beginnings [of McMaster University].[176]

Rapport With Students

Newman's teaching career lasted more than fifty years. During that time he encountered a large number of students in his classes. How was Newman evaluated by his students? Eby quotes some of the testimony given about Newman by his former students. Dr. Isaac George Matthews, who graduated from McMaster University in 1897 wrote:

Dr. Newman, as a teacher left varied impressions. I well remember a college mate, a lordly senior, saying "Dr. Newman is the most inspiring lecturer in the University." Other students might have had other ideas, but all would agree that Dr. Newman in the classroom was a gentleman of the old school. To me he now remains one of the most clean-cut figures in the classroom of those early days.[177]

Much of the testimony of former students indicates that Newman's shy personality prohibited him from being popular with a large number of students. "His mannerism of shyness somewhat robbed him of that inspiration which more direct face-to-face instruction might have created."[178] At Baylor University, except for the captions under his photograph, he is seldom mentioned in the Baylor Round-up, the student yearbook. One former student of Newman's at Baylor candidly described her impressions of Newman as a teacher.

He was a learned man but uninteresting to me as a professor. He wrote the textbook and sat there and read the book and did

---

176. Mrs. Newman to Mrs. Frederick Eby, LS, no date, Albert Henry Newman Papers, 2. While at Baylor, Newman taught J. Frank Norris, who later became one of the most colorful of the early Fundamentalists. Eby recalled an interesting encounter between Newman and Norris. It seems that Norris was "called on the carpet" by B. H. Carroll after complaining that a textbook used by both Eby and Newman was "liberal." The textbook was *A Study of Ethical Principles*, by James Seth. See Breazeale, 102. Breazeale received this information from a personal interview with Eby.

177. Eby, *Newman the Church Historian*, 63.

178. *Ibid.*, citing Dr. H. E. Stillwell, a former student, 64.

not want to be disturbed if someone wanted to start a discussion. He said he needed that time for the lecture.[179]

It may be added that the student's major at Baylor was not religion. She only signed up for Newman's class because she heard from another student that it was an easy class. She revealed that because Newman did not stimulate any discussion and read his lectures from his textbook, the students in the class occupied their time writing letters or studying for another class while he lectured.[180]

Regardless of their feelings about Newman as a teacher, his students recognized that he was a learned scholar. "We knew that even in our day his fame as a historian was international."[181] Another former student, Dr. John D. Freeman, who graduated from McMaster in 1890, said, "Dr. Newman inspired his students with awe for the Encyclopaedic range of his knowledge while he won their profound regard for his shining Christian character."[182]

No evidence can be located that any student harbored resentment against Newman. On the contrary, even though some found his lectures boring, all regarded him as a Christian gentleman who treated his students with respect and fairness.[183] Eby summarized the general attitude toward Newman by his former students by saying:

> As a teacher, Dr. Newman belonged to the university rather than to the college level of instruction. He was primarily a research scholar and author, a graduate professor....His method of exposition was always clear and incisive rather than superficial, brilliant, and catchy. In a present day institution he would be most at home as a research professor, with ample opportunity to pursue investigation and to confine his lecture to advanced students.[184]

---

179. Miss Martha Emmons, personal interview by author, 8 March 1989.

180. *Ibid.*

181. Eby, *Newman the Church Historian*, quoting Stillwell.

182. Eby, *Newman the Church Historian*, quoting Dr. John D. Freeman, 65.

183. Eby, *Newman the Church Historian*, 63-69. In this section, Eby quotes from letters of other former students who agree to the fact that Newman's kindness and gentleness were always evident in the classroom.

184. *Ibid.*, 69.

How did Newman spend the last days of his life? The final section of this chapter will attempt to answer that question.

Final Years

Special Honors

In the last years of his life, Newman received several important honors. Probably the most important was a celebration of the fiftieth anniversary of his teaching career. This event occurred at Mercer University on 14 January 1927. A meeting in the college chapel comprised the morning session of the celebration. Dr. Frederick Eby, Newman's son-in-law, delivered an address entitled "Life and Work of Albert Henry Newman." Dr. George Cross, a close friend, former student, and Professor of Theology at Rochester Theological Seminary, spoke on the topic "The Contribution Made to Theological Education in America by Albert Henry Newman." Other speakers on the program in the morning activities included Edward Bagby Pollard from the Crozer Theological Seminary in Chester, Pennsylvania and William Owen Carver of the Southern Baptist Theological Seminary in Louisville, Kentucky.[185]

The University sponsored a banquet honoring Newman in the evening as a second part of the celebration. A program consisted of the above speakers with two additions: Dr. Arch C. Cree from the Georgia Baptist Convention, and Louie D. Newton from *The Christian Index*. Telegrams from friends and dignitaries who could not attend the celebration were read during the evening. Newman responded to this honor with a short speech appealing to "some generous friend to endow a chair in this institution [Mercer University], perhaps the chair of church history."[186]

Another honor that came to Newman during his last years related to his graduating class from the Rochester Theological Seminary. At the 1925 graduation ceremonies, the seminary celebrated its seventy-fifth anniversary. That year also marked the fiftieth anniversary of Newman's graduation from

---

185. Copy of the Program from the celebration contained in the Albert Henry Newman Papers. Also Eby, *Newman the Church Historian*, 175.

186. Eby, *Newman the Church Historian*, 179. Newman donated his personal library which consisted of 1,126 volumes to Mercer University. See Breazeale, x.

the institution. The seminary extended an invitation to Newman to attend the ceremonies and to deliver an address at the annual meeting of the alumni which met during the week of graduation ceremonies.[187] Newman agreed to attend and delivered an address entitled "Baptist Ministerial Education Seventy-Five Years Ago."[188]

Newman retired from service as a teacher in 1929, after a year as visiting professor at McMaster University. Upon his retirement, the university sponsored a banquet in his honor. The event occurred on 5 April 1929. The highlight of the evening was a speech given by Newman in which he recounted the highlights of his career, especially his service to McMaster and to the Baptists in Canada.[189]

Death

After leaving McMaster in 1929, Dr. and Mrs. Newman retired to Austin, Texas. Here they resided with their only daughter and son-in-law, the Ebys. Newman's days were occupied with many activities such as automobile rides into the country and church involvement. The American Baptist Publication Society requested Newman to revise the *Manual of Church History*, a task which he completed in late 1932.[190]

During his leisure time Newman became especially fond of a little five year old girl who lived across the street. Newman enjoyed her visits and when the visit was over he would guide her across the street safely to her home. One evening, after leaving the little girl at her house, a car struck Newman as he attempted to return to his home. His son, Dr. Henry Newman, gave immediate medical attention. The injuries did not seem severe at first, as the X-rays did not reveal anything significant. However,

---

187. Clarence A. Barbour to Albert Henry Newman, TL, 29 November 1924, Crozer Rochester Divinity School alumni files, Samuel Colgate Historical Library, Rochester, New York.

188. *Ibid.*, 23 December 1924. This address was published in *The Rochester Theological Seminary Bulletin*, 76 (July 1925): 345-61.

189. This information is from a transcript of the evening's activities. It was located in the Canadian Baptist Archives, McMaster Divinity College, Hamilton, Ontario. Also see Eby, *Newman the Church Historian*, 181-84.

190. Eby, *Newman the Church Historian*, 185-86.

after a few weeks, Newman began to lose control of his fingers, and he began to lapse into unconsciousness. This eventually resulted in a coma. Eby says that the accident evidently injured the brain more severely than realized and caused the tissues to degenerate. Newman finally died on 4 June 1933 at age eighty. Mrs. Newman died seven months later on 16 January 1934.[191]

---

191. *Ibid.*, 186-87, 91-92.

CHAPTER II

ALBERT HENRY NEWMAN AS A
GENERAL CHURCH HISTORIAN

Introduction

Church history in America grew into a professional discipline during the late nineteenth century.[1] New ideas about the nature and method of history gradually became the working model for church historians. It was a period which marked "a watershed in American thought, a transition from historical sensitivity, at once patriotic and hagiographical to a discipline selfconsciously...tied to documentary evidence."[2] The purpose of this chapter is to chronicle the changes in the discipline of church history and determine

---

1.   There have been several major interpretations of this development. Most important are the works by Henry Warner Bowden: *Church History in the Age of Science*; "Science and the Idea of Church History, An American Debate," *Church History* 36 (September 1967): 308-26; Charles H. Lippy and Peter W. Williams, eds. *Encyclopedia of the American Religious Experience* (New York: Charles Scribner's Sons, 1988), s.v. "The Historiography of American Religion," by Henry Warner Bowden; and Henry Warner Bowden, ed., *A Century of Church History: The Legacy of Philip Schaff* (Carbondale, IL: Southern Illinois University Press, 1988).

In addition to Bowden, *see* David W. Lotz, "Changing Historiography: From Church History to Religious History," in *Altered Landscapes: Christianity in America: 1935-1985*, ed. David W. Lotz (Grand Rapids: William B. Eerdmans Publishing Company, 1989), 312-39 and George Hunston Williams, "Church History," in *Protestant Thought in the Twentieth Century*, ed. Arnold S. Nash (New York: The Macmillan Company, 1951), 147-78. *See also:* Sydney E. Ahlstrom, "The Problem of the History of Religion in America," *Church History* 39 (June 1970): 224-35 and Winthrop Hudson, "Shifting Trends in Church History," *Journal of Bible and Religion* 28 (April 1960): 235-38.

2.   Bowden, "Science and the Idea of Church History," 308.

what part Albert Henry Newman played as a church historian working in that era. The first section of the chapter will discuss the development of history as a professional discipline in the nineteenth century. The second part of the chapter will discuss the rise of church history as a discipline, locating three different schools of historiographical thought and describing how Newman related to each expression. The final section of the chapter will evaluate Newman's *A Manual of Church History*.

The Rise of History as a Professional Discipline

Early Historical Methods

Prior to the last quarter of the nineteenth century historians could be grouped into two basic categories.[3] The first group included men such as George Bancroft, William Prescott, John Motley, and Francis Parkman. They attempted to present history from a literary perspective, thereby assuming history to be one of the literary arts.[4]

> They concentrated on literary technique...and effect not only because they had been literary men before they became historians, but also because they believed that the recreation of the Past requires imaginative and literary skill.[5]

In addition to the presentation of history in literary form, the romantic historians retained certain ideas about the progress of history. "History was the unfolding of a vast Providential plan, and the laws of the moral world were the links between the ages."[6]

A second group of historians, served as "collectors" of historical source materials. They attempted to collect and arrange the historical materials with a view that "no later spokesman could measure up to eyewitnesses and no interpretation could equal the unembellished reproduction of authentic records."[7] Peter Force, a journalist and printer by trade, in 1822 began to

---

3.   Bowden, *Church History in the Age of Science*, 4-6.

4.   John S. Bassett, *The Middle Group of American Historians* (New York: The Macmillan Company, 1917), 221.

5.   David Levin, *History as Romantic Art* (Stanford: Stanford University Press, 1959), 9. *See* pages 4-45 for a general discussion of the work of Romantic historians in America.

6.   *Ibid.*, 26.

7.   Bowden, *Church History in the Age of Science*, 5.

collect historical materials concerning the American Revolution.[8] So important was his work as a collector that "[t]here was hardly a man in the country then engaged in research who did not write to Peter Force."[9] Another representative of this group was Jared Sparks. His first major accomplishment was a study of the letters of George Washington, followed by those of Alexander Hamilton, Lafayette, and John Jay.[10] Sparks' work is characterized mainly by the attention he gave to biography. From 1834-1838, he edited a ten volume series called *The Library of American Biography*. "Sparks's great interest in biography came from his belief...that a nation's history can be told through biographies of its leading men."[11]

There was a marked difference between these two groups concerning the way they interpreted historical evidence. The romanticists believed it was permissible to survey material, and then produce accounts which "glorified heroic contests, excoriated deceit and tyranny, or lauded the democratic process."[12] The archivists considered such practice a violation of their task.[13]

In Germany, prior to the last quarter of the nineteenth century, names such as George Niebuhr, Theodore Momsen, Heinrich von Sybel, and Heinrich von Treitschke, dominated the study of history.[14] But Leopold von Ranke is probably the best remembered of the nineteenth century German historians. Ranke's work provided the foundation for the rise of scientific historiography. Herbert Baxter Adams called him the "father of scientific

---

8.   Michael Kraus, *A History of American History* (New York: Farrar and Rinehart, 1937), 173.

9.   Bassett, 275. *See* pages 233-302 for a full discussion of Force's life and work.

10.   Kraus, 203.

11.   *Ibid.*, 209. For a full discussion of Sparks' contributions *see* pages 200-15.

12.   Bowden, *Church History in the Age of Science*, 6.

13.   *Ibid.*

14.   For a discussion of nineteenth century German historians *see*: Antoine Guilland, *Modern Germany and Her Historians* (Westport, CT: Greenwood Press, 1970) and Georg G. Iggers, *The German Conception of History: The National Tradition of Historical Thought From Herder to the Present* (Middletown, Conn.: Wesleyan University Press, 1968).

history."[15] Ranke attempted to study the past *"wie es eigentlich gewesen,"* ("as it really had been") thereby relying totally on the sources for historical conclusions.[16] Around 1830 Ranke began to apply the seminar method to historical study at the University of Berlin. These seminars began as private sessions for a few students. The students studied various medieval documents belonging to Ranke's personal library. Not only did the students study the documents but Ranke drilled them in their analysis of sources and taught them how to evaluate fragmentary sources. By the 1860s most of the major German universities offered history seminars and those who traveled to Germany from the United States to study history invariably encountered this method of instruction.[17]

The study of church history was developing in nineteenth century Germany as well, largely through the influence of Johann August Wilhelm Neander. Neander interpreted the history of the church as the history of the divine life of Christ as it permeates humanity. Every Christian, therefore, portrays the life of Christ in his or her own peculiarities. No person has the divine life of Christ entirely. Consequently, Neander's historiography concentrated on individual Christian lives. "He honored the individual as no other historian before him."[18] In Neander's historiography, the biographical element is dominant.

The Rise of Scientific Historiography

During the last quarter of the nineteenth century the study of history changed due to the rapid advances in the natural sciences. Gradually, professional historians began to apply the methods of science to their work.

---

15. Herbert Baxter Adams, "New Methods of Study in History," *Johns Hopkins University Studies in History and Political Science* 2 (1884): 65, cited by Iggers, 63.

16. For a good discussion of Ranke's historiography and its effect on American historiography *see* Georg Iggers, "The Image of Ranke in American and German Historical Thought," *History and Theory* 2, no. 1 (1962): 17-40.

17. Bowden, *Church History in the Age of Science*, 10-11.

18. *The New SchaffHerzog Encyclopedia of Religious Knowledge* 1953 ed., s.v. "Neander, Johann August Wilhelm."

The Universities

The development of scientific historiography parallels the rise of the universities in America. Johns Hopkins University, which opened in 1876, became the first American institution committed primarily to graduate education. Shortly thereafter, graduate schools formed at the University of Michigan and Cornell University.[19] Prior to this time, American historians were clergymen, judges, or independent writers who pursued a study of history only in their leisure moments. With the rise of the university and graduate school, history became a profession as historians in the 1880s and 1890s began to occupy professorial chairs and produce writings from their own research.[20]

The seminar, an idea taken from the German universities, provided the setting for this new group of historians to disseminate their ideas to students. Charles Kendall Adams, at the University of Michigan in 1869, conducted the first history seminar in the United States following the German method. Ten years later Moses Coit Tyler began another seminar at the University of Michigan, transferring the idea to Cornell University in 1881. Though Charles K. Adams developed the first seminar in America, Henry Adams initiated the first seminar composed entirely of graduate students at Harvard University in 1874.[21]

These early pioneers were notable in the development of history as a scientific discipline, but Herbert Baxter Adams became the most influential figure to espouse and propagate the new scientific historical method. "Herbert B. Adams not only witnessed the process but played a larger part than any other one man in America in the establishment of the historical profession."[22] He completed a Ph.D. degree from the University of Heidelberg in 1876. That same year he received a fellowship in history at the Johns Hopkins University. Adams' training and Ph.D. were in the area of

---

19. Bowden, "Science and the Idea of Church History," 308.

20. W. Stull Holt, *Historical Scholarship in the United States and Other Essays* (Seattle: University of Washington Press, 1967), 15.

21. Bowden, *Church History in the Age of Science*, 9-13.

22. Holt, 5.

political science, but he saw no difficulty relating that background to the study of history. Upon assuming the position at Johns Hopkins he declared his career intention:

> It is my aim to pursue historical researches and to contribute something to Political Science. I would like to write the History of American Political Literature and to help organize the Sources of American History.[23]

Through his teaching Adams popularized the ideas of scientific historiography.[24]

Defining Scientific Historiography

The development of the study of history occurred during a period in American intellectual thought which was increasingly concerned with scientific accuracy. As the universities began to offer history as a separate course of study, it became associated with the study of science, and historians began to strive for historical accuracy through use of the scientific method. This new method of historical study favored the inductive method of reasoning and eschewed the work of earlier historians who practiced their craft with preconceived notions.[25] "In a large sense, the new historical movement was part of the turn in American culture from romanticism to realism."[26] The new historians adopted the scientific method to their history

---

23. Letter from Herbert Baxter Adams to Daniel Coit Gilman, 21 May 1876, in W. Stull Holt, ed. "Historical Scholarship in the United States, 1876-1901: As Revealed in the Correspondence of Herbert Baxter Adams," *Johns Hopkins University Studies in Historical and Political Science*, 56 (1938): 31-32, cited in Bowden, *Church History in the Age of Science*, 13.

24. Holt emphasized Adams' strengths as a teacher. So committed was Adams to his students that he once planned to write a history of the relationship between church and state. However, upon realizing that the project would take away from his time with students, he chose to forego the project. "He had in rare proportions some of the qualities most desirable in a teacher. He always took a personal and generous interest in his students. A natural enthusiast himself, he imparted to them his enthusiasm for scholarly work. He seemed to have the faculty of bringing out the best that was in them." *See* Holt, *Historical Scholarship in the United States and Other Essays*, 14.

25. Bowden, "Science and the Idea of Church History," 312.

26. John Higham, Leonard Krieger, and Felix Gilbert, eds., *History* (Englewood Cliffs: Prentice Hall, 1965), 92.

seminars with the attitude that it was "of as much consequence to teach a young person *how* to study history as to teach him history itself."[27]

According to Bowden, the scientific historians had at least three common characteristics. First, they exhibited an "iconoclastic" attitude toward earlier historical writing.[28] They considered it their task to rewrite history using only the facts found in the documents. Stressing the importance of revising the past record, Moses Coit Tyler declared that "every fact of American history for the last century has to be re-examined."[29]

The scientific historians displayed an emphasis on "objective empiricism" as a second characteristic.[30] They used the seminar room like a science lab with the purpose of excluding all *a priori* assumptions which they believed weakened the earlier historical accounts. Describing the similarities with the science lab Herbert Baxter Adams said: "For the beginners in history concrete facts are quite as essential as clams or earthworms for beginners in biology."[31] When the Johns Hopkins history seminar began to use a suite of rooms in the biology department, Adams noted the symbolic connection:

> The influence of the newly acquired environment had, perhaps, some effect upon the development of the seminary. It began to cultivate...the laboratory method of work and to treat its book collections as materials for laboratory uses. The old tables which had once been used for the dissection of cats and turtles were planed down, covered with green baize, and converted into desks for the dissection of government documents and other materials for American institutional history.[32]

---

27. Herbert Baxter Adams, "Special Methods of Historical Study," *Johns Hopkins University Studies in Historical and Political Science*, second series 1-2 (January-February 1884): 12, as cited in Bowden, *Church History in the Age of Science*, 16.

28. Bowden, *Church History in the Age of Science*, 16-19.

29. Howard Mumford Jones, *The Life of Moses Coit Tyler* (Ann Arbor: The University of Michigan Press, 1933), 153.

30. Bowden, *Church History in the Age of Science*, 19-23.

31. Herbert Baxter Adams, "New Methods of Study in History," *Journal of Social Science* 18 (May 1884): 213, cited in Bowden, *Church History in the Age of Science*, 20.

32. Herbert Baxter Adams, "Seminary Libraries and University Extension," *Johns Hopkins University Studies in Historical and Political Science* 5 (1887): 455, cited by Bowden, *Church History in the Age of Science*, 25.

Though they attempted it, the scientific historians did not think of themselves as able to achieve complete objectivity. "They taught the inexactness of history with the intention and expectation of attaining an ever increasing precision."[33]

A third characteristic of the new historians was their "naturalistic bias."[34] They attempted to remove all metaphysical values from their work unlike the earlier romantic historians. "That spirit was impersonal, collaborative, secular, impatient of mystery, and relentlessly concerned with the relation of things to one another instead of their relation to a realm of ultimate meaning."[35] This inclination toward naturalism caused the scientific historians to identify closely with the natural sciences. Adams said,

> before a student has advanced very far in carrying on his investigations, he will almost inevitably arrive at the conclusion that the historical seminary is to the study of history, what the laboratory is to the study of the natural sciences.[36]

The founding of the American Historical Association officially marks the emergence of history as a professional discipline. Herbert Baxter Adams, along with men such as Charles K. Adams, Moses Coit Tyler, and Justin Winsor, officially convened the organization on 9 September 1884. At its preliminary business meeting, Winsor greeted the participants and announced the controlling historiographical principles:

> We have come, gentlemen, to organize a new society, and fill a new field. We are drawn together because we believe there is a new spirit of research abroad, a spirit which emulates the laboratory work of the naturalists....This spirit requires for its sustenance mutual recognition and suggestion among its devotees.[37]

---

33. Higham, 101.

34. Bowden, *Church History in the Age of Science* , 23-26.

35. Higham, 94.

36. Herbert Baxter Adams, "On Methods of Teaching History," in *Methods of Teaching History*, ed. G. Stanley Hall (Boston: Ginn, Heath and Company, 1885), 176, cited in Bowden, *Church History in the Age of Science*, 24.

37. Justin Winsor, "Secretary's Report of the Organization and Proceedings," *Papers of the American Historical Association* 1 (1885): 11.

Church History as a Professional Discipline

Scientific historians displayed much impatience toward many church historians who spoke of providential acts in history. Windsor summarized the attitude by saying:

> God in history...appears to be a noble phrase, but the ways of Providence are no less inscrutable to the historian than laws of the natural world that are not understood. What seems providential in history is but the reflex of the mind that contemplates it, and depends upon the training and sympathies of that mind.[38]

In spite of this attitude, scientific historians did not disregard church history. Herbert Baxter Adams taught a church history course at Johns Hopkins for a number of years. However, instead of defending theological doctrines or searching for God's activity in various stages of the church, Adams saw the church as "a human phenomenon capable of being dissected in seminar laboratories."[39]

How did church historians respond to the changes occurring in the field of history in the late nineteenth century? At least three distinct modes of thought in church historiography can be identified: scientific, theological, and sectarian. From about 1880-1900 they disagreed as to how church history should be studied, until the scientific method eventually won the debate.[40]

The only essay that mentions Albert Henry Newman's position within the broad spectrum of nineteenth century historiography is by George Hunston Williams. He classifies Newman as a mediator between the conservative older school of church historians and those committed to the scientific method.[41] Williams cites the introductory essay in Newman's first edition of *A Manual of Church History* as evidence of this mediating position. In the essay, Newman specified several reasons why church history should be studied, one of which is that church history provides a commentary on Scripture, showing that every instance of divergence from the New

---

38. Justin Windsor, "Perils of Historical Narrative," *The Atlantic Monthly* 66 (September 1890): 294, as cited in Bowden, "Science and the Idea of Church History," 313.

39. Bowden, "Science and the Idea of Church History," 313.

40. Lotz, 318-21.

41. *See* Williams, 151-52.

Testament model of Christianity, "has resulted in evil-the greater the departure the greater the evil."[42] Williams correctly identifies this concept as relating to the older historiographical concern. However, interpreting Newman further he says, "the study of Church history...increases charity and mutual understanding, thus promoting Church unity."[43] Here, Williams contends that an interdenominational interest is revealed, thus identifying him with the new breed of nineteenth century historians.[44] Neither Bowden nor Lotz attributes interdenominational interest or propagation of church unity to the new breed of historians. While they shared ideas together within the American Historical Association and the American Society of Church History, interdenominational unity was not their stated goal.

In relation to Newman's historiography, the third school of sectarian historians should be included. Consequently, a new appraisal of Newman's work is needed.

Scientific Church History

Ephraim Emerton

Ephraim Emerton, Professor of Ecclesiastical History at Harvard University, best represents the school of church historians which accepted the scientific methodology.[45] Emerton, a co-founder of the American Historical Association, was a layman and secular historian who made church history his area of specialization.

Emerton wanted church history separated from historical theology. He criticized curricula in which church history was subsumed under historical

---

42. Albert Henry Newman, *A Manual of Church History*, Vol. 1, (Philadelphia: The American Baptist Publication Society, 1899), 18.

43. Williams, 152

44. *Ibid.*

45. Emerton studied with Henry Adams at Harvard (A.B. 1871) then pursued graduate work at Berlin and Leipzig (Ph.D. 1876). He was professor of Ecclesiastical History at Harvard Divinity School from 1882 to 1918. *See Ibid.*, 320; Bowden, *Church History in the Age of Science*, 94-114; Lotz, 319-22; Williams, 150. Other spokesmen from this new school of church history who became well known at the beginning of the twentieth century include: Williston Walker (Yale), Arthur Cushman McGiffert (Union), Frank Hugh Foster (Oberlin), Shirley Jackson Case, and William Warren Sweet (University of Chicago).

theology "as if history were no independent subject by itself, but only a form or mode of theological speculation."[46]

In his inaugural address at Harvard as Winn Professor of Ecclesiastical History, Emerton set forth his appraisal of the study of church history. He defined church history as "the record of the life of men together, under the form of the Christian Church."[47] He invited his students to join him in studying "the history of the Christian Church as a great human institution."[48] Church History must be divested of all theological presuppositions according to Emerton, because theology and history are two entirely different areas of study.[49]

An example given by Emerton concerning the coming of the Holy Spirit in Acts 2 illustrates his approach to church history.

> I should consider myself trespassing beyond my own limits, if I should say that on a certain day the gift of tongues descended upon the disciples of Jesus, and gave that impulse from which the Church as an organization derives its origin.[50]

He had no difficulty claiming that the historical documents show that on a particular day a group of disciples began to preach the ideas they received from Jesus. As to whether the disciples of Jesus received a gift from God on that day, Emerton said, "you must inquire of a professed theologian, not of me."[51]

Newman and Scientific Church History

Since the early part of Newman's career as a church historian (1877-1900) coincided with the rise of scientific church historiography, one might logically inquire as to how much influence the new methods had on Newman and whether he agreed with this type of historiography. Bowden identified three attributes of the scientific historians, while Lotz identified six. These

46. Ephraim Emerton, "The Study of Church History," *Unitarian Review and Historical Magazine* 19 (January 1883): 8.

47. *Ibid.*, 2.

48. *Ibid.*, 16.

49. *Ibid.*, 7 and Lotz, 320.

50. Emerton, 18.

51. *Ibid.*

will serve as a guide to evaluate Newman's similarities and differences with the scientific historians.

Division Between History and Theology

The first of Lotz's characteristics describing the scientific church historians concerns their attempt to provide a strict division between history and theology. These historians sought to eschew any blending between the empirical and speculative and wanted to eliminate all metaphysical suppositions from their work.[52]

Newman, on the other hand, disagreed. In an extended review of Augustus Hopkins Strong's *Systematic Theology*, he noted that Strong divided the discipline of theology into four areas: Biblical, Historical, Systematic, and Practical. Newman thought that a better division would be Exegetical, Historical, Theoretical (which includes dogmatics and ethics), and Practical. He continued saying, "Historical Theology includes not only Church History and the History of Doctrines...but Biblical and inter-biblical history and Biblical and inter-biblical Theology as well."[53] Furthermore, Newman wrote that church history is the "Historical Theology of the Christian religion in its most comprehensive sense."[54] Clearly, Newman was not willing to divorce history from theology, but instead wanted church history subsumed under historical theology.

Naturalism

A second characteristic of the scientific church historians was that they sought to interpret the history of the church in naturalistic terms without reference to the providence of God or miracles. For their work, this presupposition was "a necessary methodological atheism."[55]

Newman's historiography differed here also. Expressing his idea about the movement of God in history, Newman clearly showed his unwillingness to

---

52. Lotz, 320. *See also* Bowden, *Church History in the Age of Science*, 19-23.

53. Albert Henry Newman, "Strong's Systematic Theology," *The Baptist Review and Expositor* 2 (January 1905): 43.

54. *Ibid.*, 44.

55. Lotz, 320. This corresponds to what Bowden calls a "naturalistic bias." *See* Bowden, *Science and the Idea of Church History*, 17.

interpret history from a naturalistic standpoint. He said there were three different ways to approach the Reformation. The first seeks to trace the course of events leading up to the Reformation and to analyze the cause and effect relationships of certain events. A second way is to see the personalities involved, their motives, and the effects of their work, and "test everything by the eternal principles of right and wrong, as determined by the conscience and the written Word."[56] Newman affirmed the legitimacy of these two methods, but also advocated a third method.

> We may view the movement as a link in the chain of the accomplishment of the divine purposes, knowing that the Almighty is able to make evil forces to cooperate with good thereunto. This last process...[is] so essential...to the proper understanding of the ways of God to men.[57]

While he advocated the third view, Newman was quick to say that the historian should not neglect the first two methods. Accepting the idea that God has ruled over a particular course of events for the purpose of accomplishing good "by no means bars criticism of the actors."[58] Neither does it modify the idea "that this series of events is itself the product of antecedent evil commingled with antecedent good."[59]

Newman's definition of history as "the setting forth in literary or oral form of the development in time of the divine plan of the universe,"[60] also provides proof that he was not willing to remove the purpose of God from history. Continuing, he said that this definition recognizes the fact that "the universe was planned and created and has been continuously sustained and ordered by an infinite God."[61] Furthermore, "[u]niversal history is best understood when Christ is regarded as the central figure."[62]

---

56. Albert Henry Newman, "The Reformation From a Baptist Point of View," *The Baptist Quarterly Review* 6 (January 1884): 47.

57. *Ibid.*

58. *Ibid.*

59. *Ibid.*

60. Newman, *Manual*, vol. 1, 3.

61. *Ibid.*

62. *Ibid.*, 17.

*Division Between Church History
and Secular History*

A third characteristic of the scientific church historians, cited by Lotz, concerns their opinion that church and secular history should be combined into one discipline, thereby rejecting the older notion of subordinating the latter to the former. The new church historians wanted to see the church "as only a part of the great story of humanity."[63]

While Newman included the providence of God in his definition of history, he went further by saying that human history tells all that was known about humanity "in all its aspects and under all circumstances."[64] Sacred history adds the influence of the "providential, inspiring, and self-revealing presence of God."[65] Church history more specifically "is the narration of all that is known of the founding and the development of the kingdom of Christ on earth."[66] This includes the history of organized Christianity, as well as the movement of the Christian religion itself and all of the influences that Christianity has exerted throughout the world.[67] Newman maintained the divine element in his definitions of both history and church history. But he clearly distinguished between the two disciplines.

Objectivity

The scientific church historians sought to use a vocabulary of detachment. They attempted to use vernacular which was impartial and objective ("language about faith") instead of a rhetoric of commitment ("language of faith").[68]

Scientific church historiography advocated pure disassociation from the topic of study. Newman accepted this concept partially, at least regarding the treatment of sources. He believed "that in the process of investigation he [the church historian] should deal as impartially with his materials as does

---

63. Lotz, 320-21.

64. Newman, *Manual*, vol. 1, 3-4.

65. *Ibid.*, 4.

66. *Ibid.*

67. *Ibid.*

68. Lotz, 321. This is similar to Bowden's notion of "objectivity."

the chemist with his specimens."[69] The end result of historical work should be derivation of facts so that the truth might become manifest. The historian should guard cautiously against letting his judgement be influenced "by the supposed bearing of the facts on the traditions of his denomination or his own individual opinions."[70] Always conscious of the dichotomy between objectivity and subjectivity, Newman advocated the fair treatment of all sources regardless of one's predisposed ideas. He thought it was inconceivable that a person who claimed to be a follower of Christ "should seek to advance the cause of Christ by the suppression of facts or by the suggestion of falsehood."[71] Therefore, the church historian who loves the truth, "will seek to be as scrupulously just to individuals and parties from whom he fundamentally differs as to those with whom he fundamentally agrees."[72]

Yet, on the other hand, the church historian should not be indifferent to the subject, or "so destitute of convictions as to form no moral judgments on the parties and individuals whose history he studies."[73] In this respect Newman differed from the pure detachment idea of the scientific church historians. Critiquing the scientific historical spirit he declared:

> It is not the scholar who is without personal interest in Christianity and who studies its history in a purely scientific spirit, that is likely to enter into the fullest appreciation of the facts of church history; but the scholar who is most profoundly imbued with the spirit of Christianity, rejoices in all that is Christlike and heroic, laments the corruptions and perversions

69. Newman, *Manual*, vol. 1, 5.

70. *Ibid.*

71. *Ibid.*, 6.

72. *Ibid.* On another occasion Newman declared, "For years it has been a maxim by which I have guided my own historical studies, and sought to guide those of others, to read what both sides in every controversy have to say. It is astonishing to what an extent the personality of a controversial writer, apart from any conscious and deliberate perversion of facts, colors the representation." *See* Albert Henry Newman, "A Review of Dr. Christian's Articles," *The Western Recorder*, 25 May 1899, 3.

73. *Ibid.*

of the past, and is most deeply concerned for the honor and purity of the Christianity of the present and the future.[74]

Newman urged impartiality with reference to the sources. However, he remained unwilling to call for complete detachment of the historian's faith from the topic to be studied.

Legitimacy of Church History

Lotz identified, as a fifth characteristic of the scientific church historians, their desire to vindicate church history as a legitimate discipline within the university curriculum. They wanted equal treatment of church history by all the other divisions of history on the basis that church historians use the same methods as their peers.[75] With this characteristic Newman agreed.

In an editorial comment contained in *The McMaster University Monthly*, Newman showed his agreement with Henry M. McCracken, who presented a paper at the 1890 meeting of the American Society of Church History entitled, "The Place of Church History in the College Course of Study." McCracken argued for the legitimacy of church history within the curriculum of the university. After quoting excerpts from the paper, Newman concluded the editorial remark by saying:

> The authorities of McMaster University have been among the first to give to the Bible and to Church History alike, full recognition as a valuable and a necessary means of culture, and to accord to each a prominent place in the Arts curriculum.[76]

Newman believed that church history was of such importance to universal history, that "the history of humanity would be incomplete and unintelligible without it."[77]

---

74. *Ibid.*, 5-6.

75. Lotz, 321.

76. Albert Henry Newman, "Editorial Notes," *The McMaster University Monthly* 1 (January 1892): 181. Newman was professor of church history at McMaster University when he made this comment.

77. Newman, *Manual*, vol. 1, 17.

Iconoclasm.[78]

Does Newman exhibit an iconoclastic attitude toward previously written church history as is characteristic of the scientific church historians? Though Newman rarely critiqued deficiencies in previous historical writing, one indirect comment may have a bearing. In a letter to John H. Castle in 1881, Newman commented that he hoped to

> fill up some lamentable gaps in our denominational literature. It really seemed to me that I had been set apart as it were by Divine Providence for the work of writing an exhaustive history of the Baptists.[79]

Continuing, Newman quoted from a recently received letter written to him by John A. Broadus. Broadus said:

> I hope you may see your way to continue your studies in Church History....We have no American Baptist but you and Whitsitt...who is really making researches in that great subject. Our denomination is becoming a good deal interested in CH. Hist., and the wiser men see that after the fusillade of popular books we have had there must be real work done.[80]

The fact that Newman would quote this statement in the context in which he was writing would seem to indicate that he agreed with Broadus that some newer, more scholarly work needed to be done.

In summary, it is clear that Newman had little in common with the scientific church historians. He agreed with them concerning the importance of studying church history. He also urged the fair treatment of sources, though he was unwilling to call for complete detachment in keeping with the scientific methodology. He exhibited somewhat of an iconoclastic attitude, but his primary point of departure is centered in his understanding of the nature of history. His definition of church history was more in keeping with that of the theological church historians.

---

78. This characteristic of scientific historiography comes from Bowden. Lotz gives the scientific historians a sixth feature in his list: "A confidence that church history, though not itself a theological discipline, is of material importance for the work of theological construction and...is of indispensable service to vital religion." *See* p. 321. Since Newman believed that church history was a theological discipline, Lotz's sixth feature is not applicable to him.

79. Albert Henry Newman to John H. Castle, LS, 6 June 1881, Albert Henry Newman File, 1.

80. *Ibid.*, 1-2.

Philip Schaff

There is little doubt that Philip Schaff was the most eminent church historian of the nineteenth century in America. The sheer volume of Schaff's literary output coupled with his high academic standards of scholarship place him above others of his era. Born in Switzerland (1819) and trained in Germany (Tübingen, Halle, Berlin), Schaff lived in the United States from 1844 until his death in 1893.[81]

Schaff's theological schooling came during a time in Germany in which three streams of thought were prevalent. The first, New Lutheranism, was intent on returning the church to the confessional stance it occupied in the sixteenth and seventeenth centuries. The second, rationalism (sometimes called radicalism), attempted to use critical techniques in the study of Christianity's beginnings and sought to challenge supernaturalistic interpretations. The third current of thought, led by August Neander, was a mediation, which provided an evangelical/romantic approach to history and theology. Schaff, a student of Neander, became an advocate of the mediating school of thought.[82]

Schaff maintained some common characteristics with the scientific historians, namely his prolific literary output, attention to primary sources, and the value he placed on history.[83] But his concept of the church made it impossible to classify him as scientific historian. Schaff viewed the church as an organic institution, the presence of the body of Christ on earth. "In the

---

81. For the life of Schaff *see*: David Schaff, *The Life of Philip Schaff* (New York: Charles Scribner's Sons, 1897) and George H. Shriver, *Philip Schaff: Christian Scholar and Ecumenical Prophet* (Macon, Georgia: Mercer University Press, 1987). For the purposes of this discussion *see also*: Bowden, *Church History in the Age of Science*, 31-68; "Science and the Idea of Church History," 313-20; Lotz, 318-19; and James H. Nichols, *Romanticism in American Theology: Nevin and Schaff at Mercersburg* (Chicago: University of Chicago Press, 1961), 107-39.

82. Shriver, 3-4.

83. Bowden, "Science and the Idea of Church History," 314. Schaff's value of church history can be seen in the following statement: "How shall we labour with any effect to build up the Church, if we have no thorough knowledge of her history, or fail to apprehend it from the proper point of observation?" Philip Schaff, *What is Church History? A Vindication of the Idea of Historical Development* (Philadelphia: J. B. Lippincott and Company, 1846), 5.

Church, Christ carries forward, so to speak, his divine human life."[84] Therefore it is more than just an institution created by humans, as the scientific church historians claimed. While Schaff emphasized the importance of the church's history, he was more concerned with its essence.[85]

> Such a conception tended to raise his evaluation of church history to a level on which the church, because of its essential nature, was not entirely a human institution and could not be fully understood in naturalistic terms.[86]

To understand church history in Schaff's estimation, one must first approach the topic from within the church.

> He who would know the truth, must himself stand in the truth; only the philosopher can understand philosophy; only the poet, poetry; only the pious man, religion. So also the church historian, to do justice to his subject must live and move in Christianity.[87]

A proper understanding of the history of the church was the key to its future progress for Schaff. If the great forces at work in the past could be identified, they possibly could be used for future development.[88]

Just as secular history gained professional status with the organization of the American Historical Association, the discipline of church history gained professional status through the American Society of Church History.[89] Schaff was concerned for his theological concept of church history as the scientific historians began to flourish in the last quarter of the nineteenth century. His ideas increasingly found less value among the secular historians

---

84. Schaff, *What is Church History?*, 37.

85. *Ibid.*, 315.

86. Bowden, "Science and the Idea of Church History," 314.

87. Philip Schaff, *History of the Apostolic Church With a General Introduction to Church History*, trans. Edward D. Yeomans (New York: Charles Scribner, 1853), 35. In an earlier writing he said: "A right conception of the Church is indispensable for a living apprehension and satisfactory exhibition of its history. This is itself indeed, in one respect, the product of a thorough insight into its actual development,...but in another respect, it is the *spiritus rector*, the conducting genius of the Church historian." *See What is Church History?*, 37.

88. Bowden, *Church History in the Age of Science*, 43.

89. An important recent essay describing the history of the American Society of Church History can be found in Henry Warner Bowden, "The First Century: Institutional Development and Ideas About the Profession," in *A Century of Church History*, ed., Henry Warner Bowden, 294-328.

within the American Historical Association. Thus, in 1888, Schaff organized
the American Society of Church History with the intention of preserving a
place for theological historians to practice their approach. But upon his
death in 1893, the scientific historians gained control of the organization and
united it with the American Historical Association, thereby signaling that the
scientific method had gained superiority in church history.[90]

Newman and Theological
Church History

Philip Schaff was nearing the end of his career when Newman began
teaching at the Rochester Theological Seminary in 1877. The first contact
between the two historians came after Newman wrote a review of Schaff's
History of the Christian Church. He criticized the work on several points,
including superficiality, but his respect for Schaff was obvious.

> In a work of such magnitude, performed amidst a multiplicity
> of engagements, it could hardly be expected that even gross
> blunders should be absolutely avoided.[91]

Schaff saw the review and wrote Newman, challenging him in a friendly
manner for being too critical. Eby notes that this initial contact between
Schaff and Newman proved to be beneficial for the latter. "For the first time
Schaff's attention was called to the exceptional ability and sound learning of
the rising young scholar."[92] Newman always maintained respect for Schaff
and on one occasion said:

> Dr. Schaff is one of the most genial and amiable of men, to
> know him is to love him. The writer [Newman] esteems the
> personal friendship of Dr. Schaff as one of the most precious of
> his possessions.[93]

---

90. *Ibid.,* 58-67. There were no feelings of antagonism between the two groups. The
American Society of Church History separated from the American Historical Association in
1906 and has remained independent ever since.

91. Albert Henry Newman, review of *History of the Christian Church*, by Philip Schaff, in *The
Baptist Quarterly Review* 7 (July 1885): 379.

92. Eby, 72. This initial letter from Schaff is not located in the extant Newman papers. Eby
mentions it on p. 71.

93. Albert Henry Newman, "Editorial Notes," *The McMaster University Monthly* 2 (April
1893): 341.

Newman's admiration of Schaff is clear. Concerning their basic approach to church history, there exists both similarities and differences.

Definition of History

Newman and Schaff both adhered to what Lotz refers to as a "salvation history" approach to defining church history.[94] Both historians saw the history of the church as the history of the redemptive work of God in the universe. Schaff said that church history is

> the progressive execution of the scheme of the divine kingdom in the actual life of humanity; the outward and inward development of Christianity; the extension of the church over the whole earth, and the infusion of the spirit of Christ into all the spheres of human existence.[95]

Newman's understanding of church history as being the recounting of all that is known about the progress of the Kingdom of Christ on earth is in virtual agreement with Schaff.[96] This salvation history approach to church history saw the church as a divine organism which grows as history progresses.[97]

Newman presupposed that the human race was alienated from God and needed redemption. The goal of Christianity is the restoration of humanity to a state of obedience. Therefore, the "history of the church should show...the progressive accomplishment of this divine purpose through the centuries."[98]

Another point of agreement between Newman and Schaff, concerning the study of church history, was that of rejecting the scientific historiography notion of pure detachment. Both historians believed that only the Christian historian, who practiced the faith, could adequately understand church history. Schaff, a pupil of Neander here undoubtedly demonstrated his teacher's influence. Neander said, *"pectus est quod facit theologum"* ("it is the heart that makes the theologian"). Newman made note of this in an article

---

94. Lotz, 318.

95. Philip Schaff, *History of the Apostolic Church*, 16.

96. *See above. Also*, Newman, *Manual*, vol. 1, 4.

97. Schaff liked to use the parables of Jesus concerning the mustard seed and leaven (Matthew 13) to describe this organic development. *See:* David Schaff, *The Life*, 236.

98. Newman, *Manual*, vol. 1, 5.

where he mentions the German historian.[99] Though it is conjecture, Newman may have been influenced by Neander in this respect as well. Eby relates that during Newman's tenure as church history professor at Rochester, the seminary library acquired a collection of source materials from Neander's library. He said that Newman's linguistic abilities gave him access to the materials. Through a study of these materials Newman's historiography may have been influenced by Neander's.[100]

Ecumenism

Schaff may be best remembered for his ecumenical activity. He divided the history of the church into three ages. The first embraced the initial six centuries of Christianity, extending until the reign of Gregory the Great (590). The second encompassed the Middle Ages, extending from Gregory the Great until the Reformation (1517). The final age encompassed the modern period, from the Reformation until present.[101]

The first age, according to Schaff, was a positive time for the church. It successfully overcame opposition from heretical groups and formed the theological foundation for the future of the church. The second period exemplifies a negative period within the history of the church. During this era the church lost sight of its apostolic beginnings resulting in the development of legalism and church authority. The third age, commencing with the Reformation, signals a new beginning for the church, a glorious period which Schaff hoped would combine the best elements of Protestantism and Catholicism into *"a higher union of Protestantism and Catholicism* in their pure forms, freed from their respective errors and infirmities."[102]

---

99. Albert Henry Newman, "Fifty Years of Progress in Church History," *The Review and Expositor* 7 (January 1910): 67.

100. Eby, *Newman the Church Historian*, 32. *Also see* Chapter 1 of this study: pp. 15, 27-28.

101. Philip Schaff, *History of the Christian Church*, vol. 1, (Grand Rapids: William B. Eerdmans, 1867), 14-18.

102. Schaff, *History of the Apostolic Church*, 36-45, quote from 45. The emphasis is Schaff's.

The goal of achieving the reunion of Christendom became for Schaff "the supreme task of church history."[103] Yet, in spite of the fact that they agreed on a theological definition of church history, Newman did not agree with Schaff on the idea of ecumenism. Newman believed that there were only two ways by which Christianity may be united. The first way, used in the Middle Ages by the ruling hierarchy, attempted to suppress all dissent from the state form of religion. The other method:

> is for all believers...*to accept the Scriptures as the only rule of faith and practice*....Christians will never unite on the Canons of the Council of Trent, on the Augsburg Confession, on the Heidelberg Catechism, on the Thirty-Nine Articles and the Prayer Book, on the Confession of the Westminster Assembly of Divines, on the Book of Discipline, or any other human statement of doctrine and practice that has been or ever will be made.[104]

Since Newman believed that Baptists followed the New Testament pattern for Christianity, reunion of Christendom would be achieved if all Christians came to the same conclusion.[105]

Newman had little use for compromise among the denominations for the purpose of attaining Christian union. Near the beginning of his career (1883) he reviewed a series of articles written by Washington Gladden which advocated ecumenism. They were entitled "The Christian League in Connecticut." Newman countered that surrendering certain distinctive principles within one's own denomination for the sake of union signals that the denomination has become "so feeble that they no longer care for anything but to have a good, quiet, comfortable home."[106] The opposition to ecumenical ideas continued later in Newman's career. Two years after

---

103. Philip Schaff, *Amerika*, 2d ed. (Berlin: Wiegandt and Grieben, 1858), 262, cited by Klaus Penzel, "The Reformation Goes West: The Notion of Historical Development in the Thought of Philip Schaff," *Journal of Religion* 62 (July 1982): 229.

104. Albert Henry Newman, "Wiclif and the Mendicant Friars," *The McMaster Monthly* 4 (November 1895): 66. The emphasis is Newman's.

105. Albert Henry Newman, ed., *A Century of Baptist Achievement* (Philadelphia: American Baptist Publication Society, 1901), 1-2.

106. Albert Henry Newman, "A New Scheme of Christian Union," unsigned article, *The Canadian Baptist*, 18 January 1883, 4. On the copy of this issue which was photographed for the microform, someone wrote Newman's name across the column identifying him as author.

Schaff died, Newman spoke directly about Schaff's ecumenicity. He could not agree with "the breadth of his charity" toward other denominations, but he was still appreciative of a man with such a Christlike manner who could value and provide theological literature for all groups of Christians.[107] Newman could not agree with the ecumenical ideas because of his belief in the absolute correctness of the Baptist position. Therefore, any compromise for the purpose of unity with other denominations would dilute the Baptist position.

> The great inferiority of English Baptists in point of prospects to American is due in great measure to this compromising spirit and the great prosperity of American Baptists is due to uncompromising fidelity to principle. If this practice is correct nothing is gained in the long run by the union efforts that are becoming so common. These are a snare to Baptists and are designed in great measure to destroy Baptist consistency.[108]

In spite of differences between Newman and Schaff concerning ecumenism, the two men worked together within the American Society of Church History and on a major project called "The American Church History Series." This project, an ecumenical effort, attempted to provide a series of denominational histories. Each volume was written by a representative historian from that denomination. Newman, before 1890, had the idea for this series because he thought that there should be some publication which would continue Schaff's *History of the Christian Church* beyond the middle of the seventeenth century. He wrote to Schaff with this idea and in the reply learned that Schaff had contemplated the same notion sometime before, but had abandoned it because of the inability to secure a publisher for the

---

107. Albert Henry Newman, "Heimgegangen – Philip Schaff," *The McMaster Monthly* 2 (November 1893): 83.

108. Albert Henry Newman, Unclassified lecture notes, "Lectures on Church History: Seniors Volume II," Albert Henry Newman Papers, 87. Newman believed that modern denominationalism was a positive factor within modern Christianity because it fosters the idea of liberty of conscience. He said, "modern denominationalism is one of the most important products of the gradual recognition of the right of Christians of all shades of belief." *See,* Albert Henry Newman, "Toleration and Liberty of Conscience," *The Western Recorder* 31 October 1901, 1.

project. Together, Schaff and Newman planned to ask the endorsement of the American Society of Church History for the project, which both men felt would aid in securing a publisher.[109]

Originally, Newman was a part of the editorial committee for the project. However, the committee chose him to write the volume on the Baptists and Schaff convinced him to resign his position because it was felt that this committee "should have nothing to do with the preparation of any volume, but confine itself to the work of selecting the writers and examining their manuscripts."[110] The project took four years to complete (1893-97). Newman described the irenical nature of the project to the American Society of Church History:

> While each writer would have every inducement to exhibit his denomination in the most favorable light that the facts of history would warrant, it would be impossible for him to write in complete disregard of the rights of other denominations to favorable consideration. Thus the character of the readers addressed would minister to fairness of treatment in matters of controversy, and could scarcely fail to secure the production of works decidedly irenical in spirit.
>
> As the circumstances under which such a series should be prepared would be favorable to the production of peculiarly valuable works, so also might large irenical results be expected in the readers....A wide reading of histories of all the denominations...could not fail to be promotive, in a high degree of truth and peace.[111]

Though Schaff did not live to see its completion, the project has been termed "the most valuable literary achievement in an ecumenical vein."[112]

---

109. Albert Henry Newman, "Report on a Proposed Series of Denominational Histories to be Published Under the Auspices of the American Society of Church History," *Papers of the American Society of Church History*, First Series, 3 (1890): 209-11.

110. Philip Schaff to Albert Henry Newman, LS, 7 February 1891, Albert Henry Newman Papers, 2.

111. Newman, "Report," 210.

112. Bowden, *Church History in the Age of Science*, 64. Schaff proposed six guidelines for each volume: (1) each volume was to be written by representative writers from that denomination "who combine loyalty to their own Church with comprehensive culture and a liberal, catholic spirit;" (2) each denomination should be traced to Europe and presented as a member of the "Church universal;" (3) footnotes were to be kept to a minimum, but the sources were to be identified; (4) the volume should be written in a scholarly style, yet still be able to reach the

Schaff saw this project as a means to promote Christian union, the "evangelical Catholicism" he so desired.[113] If Newman was so opposed to ecumenism, why did he participate in this endeavor? Perhaps the answer lies in the fact that Newman saw it as an opportunity to expose Baptist ideas and history to the other denominations. Also, it was a cooperative affair and advocated no formal union. Newman worked willingly with other denominations throughout his career with the idea in mind that those groups would eventually see the Baptist position as the only true one in accordance with scripture.[114]

Approach to Church History

Another historiographical difference that existed between Newman and Schaff was their basic approach to church history. Newman identified four different ways that historians might approach the topic. The "Romanist"[115] could not be objective because he would write church history from a hierarchical perspective as determined by the authority of the church. Similarly, the Anglo-Catholic historian could not be objective because he "will inevitably write church history with a view to establishing the identity of his own church with the church of the Fathers."[116] The third view, held by those who advocated ecclesiastical development, insisted that there was no prescribed form of church organization that should be forever binding. They believed instead that Christianity in its organization adapted to varying circumstances throughout its history. The fourth option concerns the church historians who see the apostolic church order as authoritative.[117]

---

interest of the laity and ministers of that denomination; (5) the size of the volume is limited to approximately 500 pages; (6) one or more editors should have responsibility for the project as selected by the American Society of Church History. *See* Newman, "Report," 212.

113. *See* Shriver, 96-97.

114. This idea will be discussed fuller later but for example *see*: Albert Henry Newman, "The Early Waldenses," *The Baptist Quarterly Review* 7 (July 1885): 322.

115. Newman used this term frequently to identify the Roman Catholic Church. This exemplifies his aversion toward that expression of Christianity.

116. Newman, *Manual*, vol. 1, 6-7.

117. *Ibid.*, 7-9.

Because of his Hegelian emphasis on the development of Christianity, Schaff's inclination was to approach church history from the perspective of the third view mentioned above. Of the historians holding this position Newman said,

> Freed from the necessity of defending any particular form of Christianity as exclusively valid, he will be in a position to treat sympathetically, with reference to the circumstances of their times, even the most corrupted and distorted forms of Christianity, and especially will he be interested in all efforts, however misguided, to bring about reforms.[118]

Newman, on the other hand, tended to elevate the apostolic norm as the goal for modern Christianity. He argued that any departure from the apostolic standard was "obnoxious to the spirit of Christianity."[119] He admitted that apostolic church order was given only in outline, and that much was open for later development as long as the believers "organized in the apostolic way, practice[d] apostolic ordinances, and [were] subject continually to the guidance of the Holy Spirit."[120]

With the apostolic standard as revealed in the New Testament in mind, Newman believed that church history itself provided a commentary on scripture showing how any deviation from the principles set forth in the New Testament has resulted in error.[121] Therefore, Newman's historiography revolved around this vision of the New Testament pattern. He sought not only to identify the apostolic norm, but also to analyze the history of Christianity and discover the places where these principles were most evident. He then attempted to address the modern church situation using the apostolic pattern.[122]

---

118. *Ibid.*, 7.

119. *Ibid.*, 8.

120. *Ibid.*

121. *Ibid.*, 18. and Mark Steven Fountain, "A. H. Newman's Appropriation of the Spiritual Kinship Theory of Baptist Origins as a Historiographical *Via Media*" (Th.M. thesis, Southern Baptist Theological Seminary, 1986), 24. Fountain's work is particularly insightful concerning how the spiritual kinship theory affected Newman's historiography.

122. Fountain, 25.

The point where this difference between approaches to church history is most readily seen in Newman and Schaff is in their appraisals of the Reformation. Schaff saw the Reformation as the inauguration of a great period in church history. He said, "The course of church history has thus far evidently lain through the colossal counter-movements of Catholicism and Protestantism; the chronological turning point being the sixteenth century."[123]

For Schaff, the future of all Christianity was initiated in the Reformation. He was able to appreciate the positive and negative factors of Protestantism and Catholicism, because his idealistic historiography saw church history progressing around the conflict between the two expressions of Christianity. Schaff was able to maintain the Christian quality of Catholicism, while at the same time garrison the catholic quality of Protestantism.[124]

Newman viewed the Reformation in a somewhat different manner. His appraisal of the Magisterial Reformers was negative because they failed to complete their original intention when they decided to retain infant baptism, thereby rejecting the principle of regenerate church membership. He said that almost all of the leading reformers were brought to the realization that infant baptism was without scriptural support, but they were forced ultimately to defend it as a "practical necessity."[125] As a result they united themselves with the civil rulers, which drove them further away from the apostolic norm, Newman's aspiration for Christianity.[126] Therefore, the Magisterial Reformers did not really produce reform of the church in Newman's opinion.

The highlight of the Reformation era for Newman was the rise of the Anabaptist movement. He believed that they represented the best

---

123. Schaff, *History of the Apostolic Church*, 676.

124. Penzel, 229-30.

125. Albert Henry Newman, "The Opponents of Infant Baptism and Related Errors In the Reformation Time," *The Baptist Standard* 8 August 1901, 1.

126. *See* Albert Henry Newman, "Liberty and Creed," *The Southwestern Theological Review* 1 (January 1904): 148. Newman lacked respect in particular for Martin Luther. For his impression of Luther's character *see Manual*, vol. 2, 84-90.

expression of apostolic Christianity since the third century. The Anabaptists carried out the concepts first proposed by the Magisterial Reformers, thereby becoming the true reformers of Christianity.[127]

Sectarian Church History

A third group of historians in the nineteenth century made their presence known on a much less professional basis. These sectarian historians concentrated most of their work within the individual Protestant denominations of which they were a part. Though the theological and scientific historians began to replace their work after the Civil War, they nevertheless continued to make their presence known even into the twentieth century. James Hastings Nichols described the prevalent atmosphere out of which came their labors:

> The prevailing habit of thought in both American Protestantism and Roman Catholicism...was unhistorical. Each sought to claim the support of historical evidence for his dogmatic position, but neither would admit the force of inconvenient evidence.[128]

The *a priori* assumption of this older breed of historian was that their particular confessional stance descended from the original expression of Christianity in the first century. Therefore it was their duty to recover the history of their denomination and show how it linked directly to Jesus and the Apostles.[128]

---

127. Albert Henry Newman, *A Manual of Church History*, vol. 2, (Philadelphia: The American Baptist Publication Society, 1902), 151. See also Fountain, 50-51.

128. Nichols, 107.

128. Hudson, "Shifting Trends in Church History," 235. Hudson maintains that the emphasis in the nineteenth century was predominantly Evangelicalism which concentrated on religious experience and not on history. Therefore, before the Civil War "[d]enominational histories...were written to give sanction and support to continuing denominational activity, and some attention was given to the first two or three centuries of the Christian era in an effort to prove the validity of various denominational emphases by the norm of the Apostolic Church. But this historical interest was peripheral and largely incidental.

Successionist Historiography

Several examples of this successionist historiography in the nineteenth century are evident.[129] When Philip Schaff began his American teaching career at Mercersburg Seminary in Pennsylvania, he encountered opposition to his views from Joseph F. Berg, pastor of the First German Reformed Church in Philadelphia. The Eastern synod of the German Reformed Church convened on 17 October 1844 officially to accept Schaff as a member. On that day, Berg preached the opening sermon. He declared that the German Reformed church could trace its existence to the first century through the persecuted ancient and medieval sects, therefore denying the Catholic Church a part in the true Christian tradition.[130]

David Lipscomb, leader in the Church of Christ denomination also exhibited this type of historiography. He said that the true church of Christ had existed since the day of Pentecost and that all through the Dark Ages these congregations continued to exist. These congregations are not to be confused with the Protestant denominations, which emerged from the Catholic Church and could not trace their origin back to Jesus and the day of Pentecost.[131] Libscomb wrote, "I believe as firmly as any one in an unbroken descent of congregations and ordinances from the days of the apostles to the present time."[132]

Perhaps the most visible expression of sectarian historiography is found within Newman's denomination, the Baptists of the nineteenth century. The successionist ideas became most evident with the rise of the Landmark Movement in the middle of the nineteenth century and culminated in the Whitsitt Controversy at the Southern Baptist Theological Seminary

---

129. Morgan Patterson, *Baptist Successionism: A Critical View*, (Valley Forge: Judson Press, 1969), 70074. Patterson mentions successionism in the Baptist and Mennonite denominations.

130. Shriver, 21-28.

131. David Lipscomb, "Church of Christ in the Dark Ages," *Gospel Advocate* 8 (21 August 1866): 533-36, as cited by Myer Phillips, "A Historical Study of the Attitude of the Churches of Christ Toward Other Denominations" (Ph.D. diss., Baylor University, 1983), 84.

132. David Lipscomb, "The Baptists," *Gospel Advocate* 8 (12 June 1866): 373; cited by Phillips, 84.

(1890s).[133] James Milton Carroll best summarized this Baptist view of history in *The Trail of Blood*, published posthumously in 1931.[134] It speculated that dissenting groups during the history of the church represent an unbroken organic connection of historical Baptist churches, which were called by other names depending on the historical period.[135] Other representative expressions of this position included: Adam Taylor, *The History of the English General Baptists* (1918); G. H. Orchard, *A Concise History of Baptists in England in 1838* (1855); and David Burcham Ray, *Baptist Succession: A Handbook of Baptist History* (1883).[136]

Newman and Sectarian Historiography

Newman shared a similar interest with the sectarian historians, particularly of his own denomination, though he rejected their claims of succession. He would not allow himself to go any further in his conclusions than the facts would warrant. Furthermore, though avidly a Baptist, he counseled that historians should accomplish their work without any denominational coloring. "The historian should seek to rise above partisanship of every kind and should make it his business to discover and to bring forward the truth."[137]

Though not a lineal successionist, Newman's interest in apostolic Christianity and his desire to find traces of it throughout the history of the church, produced a viewpoint which found a measure of similarity with succession. Robert Torbet, in his *History of the Baptists*, identified this view as

---

133. The successionist idea was only one aspect of the Landmark Movement although a vital one. For a discussion of the Landmark Movement *see* James E. Tull, "A Study of Southern Baptist Landmarkism in Light of Historical Baptist Ecclesiology" (Ph.D. diss., Columbia University, 1960). For a discussion of the Whitsitt Controversy, *see* Rosalie Beck, "The Whitsitt Controversy: A Denomination in Crisis" (Ph.D. diss., Baylor University, 1984).

134. James Milton Carroll, *The Trail of Blood* (Lexington, Kentucky: Ashland Avenue Baptist Church, 1931). Carroll popularized the ideas in this book during his career in the nineteenth century while speaking in various churches.

135. *See* H. Leon McBeth, *The Baptist Heritage* (Nashville: Broadman Press, 1987), 58-60.

136. *Ibid.*, 60.

137. Albert Henry Newman, "The Whitsitt Controversy," in *A Review of the Question*, ed. George Augustus Lofton, (Nashville: University Press Company, 1897), 161.

the "Spiritual Kinship Theory."[138]   Instead of advocating an unbroken succession of Baptist churches throughout church history, this view postulated instead an unbroken succession of evangelical or apostolic principles.[139]

The sectarian historians sought to trace their denomination through the dissenting sects. Newman became an expert on these dissenting sects and analyzed their beliefs to see how closely they resembled the Baptists of his day, but throughout this process he found no justification for the successionist claims. At the conclusion of an article on the Paulician sect, he delivered a caustic comment to those among the Baptists who supported the idea of succession.

> If the reader is disposed to lay a good deal of stress upon Baptist apostolic succession, as I am not, he will find in the Paulicians by far the best support for this contention. If one can fellowship their Adoptionism, their seeming belief that the remission of sins takes place only in baptism administered by a duly qualified minister, their rather strong language regarding the eating of flesh and the drinking of the blood of Christ in the Supper, their connectional rather than congregational form of church government, their designation of their entire brotherhood as the Holy Catholic Apostolic Church, their attribution of authority and holiness to their ordained ministers, I think he is reasonably warranted in claiming Baptist apostolic succession as an established historical fact.[140]

Newman was not concerned with finding a direct lineal succession of Baptist churches throughout church history. He felt that "it is of vastly more importance to feel assured that vital evangelical Christianity has persisted and will persist."[141]   He wrote *A History of Anti-Pedobaptism* with the

---

138. Robert Torbet, *A History of the Baptists*, (Valley Forge: Judson Press, 1950), 17-21.

139. This theory was a major part of Newman's historiography. Consequently, it will be discussed in each of the subsequent chapters as it applies.

140. Albert Henry Newman, "An Antipedobaptist Holy Catholic Apostolic Church," *The Crozer Quarterly* 1 (October 1924): 394-95. This statement reflects a change of opinion on the part of Newman concerning the Paulician sect. In 1898 he referred to the Paulicians as "in nearly every particular Baptists of the strictest and staunchest sort," except for their adoptionist Christology. *See* Albert Henry Newman, "The Opportunity For Baptists in the Present Religious Progress," *Proceedings of the Baptist Congress* 16 (1898): 53.

141. Albert Henry Newman, "The Significance of the Anabaptist Movement in the History of the Christian Church," *The Goshen College Record*, Review Supplement 27, No. 4 (1926): 15.

purpose of studying the dissenting sects to see how close to the apostolic standard they came, particularly regarding the issue of baptism.[142]

One area in which Newman had definite identity with the sectarians of his denomination regarded a bias toward the Baptists. Related to the apostolic norm, one of the central tenets of Newman's historiography was his appraisal that the Baptist denomination alone exhibited this type of Christianity. "Baptist churches are Apostolical, alike in spirit and form."[143]

The structure and traditions of the Baptist expression of Christianity caused Newman to accept this appraisal, not any inherent perfection within the denomination itself. Fountain notes that for Newman "no particular value was found in simply being Baptist *per se.*"[144] The most important aspect for Newman was always obedience to New Testament Christianity. The Baptists could be judged as any other group for violation of this principle and at times the principle had been violated in Newman's estimate.[145]

A Manual of Church History

Newman's most lasting contribution to general church history was the two volume *A Manual of Church History.* The first volume appeared in 1899, followed by the second volume in 1902. The purpose of this section is to provide a critique of the *Manual,* to compare it with other contemporary works, and to evaluate its durability.

Purpose

In the preface to the first volume of the *Manual,* Newman related that it was the product of over twenty years of labor in the study of church history and that it grew out of his own endeavors as a teacher. Newman's primary intention was that the book would serve "as a textbook for theological seminaries and universities," but he believed that it could also serve to meet

---

142. Albert Henry Newman, "Traces of Baptist Teaching During the First Sixteen Christian Centuries," *The Baptist Standard* 17 October 1901, 1.

143. Albert Henry Newman, "Baptist Churches Apostolical," in *Baptist Doctrines*, ed. Charles A. Jenkens (St. Louis: C. R. Barns Publishing Company, 1892), 236. This will be discussed further in subsequent chapters.

144. Fountain, 24.

145. Newman, "Baptist Churches Apostolical," 279-81.

the requirements of ministers as well as laymen "throughout our great Baptist constituency."[146]   One reviewer, commenting on this quality said, "The reader...will soon come to believe that church history is really a very easy subject that may be understood by all people of average intelligence."[147] In addition to his desire that Baptists find the work useful, Newman hoped that other denominations would find it a worthwhile tool as well because he sought to "record the facts...without distorting them...in favor of any particular view of history, or any peculiar tenets of his denomination."[148]

The first volume of the *Manual* met a hearty reception. Newman attested to this in the preface to the second volume.

> The unanimous and hearty commendation of the first volume by professors of church history and other scholars of the various evangelical denominations on both sides of the Atlantic, and the extent to which it has been adopted as a textbook in theological seminaries and universities of different denominations has stimulated the author to endeavor to make the present volume even worthier of acceptance.[149]

In addition to Newman's statement concerning the reception of the volume, Mrs. Newman commented on the book's popularity in a letter to her son-in-law, Frederick Eby, "The...Manual has been *so very* favorably received abroad and everywhere. He continues to hear of various leading teachers in other denominations who are introducing it in their classes."[150]

Organization

Newman provided a rather clever organizational scheme to the *Manual*. Evidently, the work was an expansion of his class lecture notes.[151]

---

146. Newman, *Manual*, vol. 1, vii.

147. J. W. Moncrief, review of *A Manual of Church History*, by Albert Henry Newman, In *The American Journal of Theology* 4 (October 1900): 852.

148. *Ibid.*

149. Newman, *Manual*, vol. 2, v.

150. Mrs. Newman to Frederick Eby, 8 April 1901, as cited by Eby, 202.

151. This becomes evident when reading the lecture notes and comparing them with the *Manual*. For instance *see* Newman, *Manual*, vol. 2, 350-89 on "The Counter Reformation" and compare it with the same section in the miscellaneous lecture notes "Lectures on Church History, Seniors, Vol. II," 29-47. Most of the major section headings are the same or similar. Newman expanded the material in the *Manual*.

The organizational pattern allows easy note taking on the part of the reader. This was beneficial to both the student using the *Manual* as a textbook as well as to the professor who desired to use it to prepare lecture notes.[152]

The introductory section of the *Manual* discusses the study of church history, then provides a description of the Ancient Near East before the time of Christ. The history of Christianity is then divided into six periods: (1) The birth of Christ until A.D. 100; (2) from 100 until the conversion of Constantine in 312; (3) 312 until the coronation of Charlemagne in 800; (4) from 800 until the initiation of the Protestant Reformation in 1517; (5) 1517 until the end of the Thirty Years War in 1648; (6) the modern period which extends from 1648 until the present.[153] The division between the first and second volumes of the *Manual* occurs at the beginning of the Reformation.

Strengths and Weaknesses

Besides the organizational scheme which makes the *Manual* easy to study and use, there are other positive factors in the work. First, the *Manual* is comprehensive, yet brief, which made it a popular work. Other histories of the time were often multi-volume works. For instance Philip Schaff's *History of the Christian Church* (1882-94) filled seven volumes and ended with the Reformation.[154] Henry Clay Sheldon used five volumes in his work (1894).[155] George Herbert Dryer also used five volumes for his history (1896-1903).[156] George Park Fisher produced a one volume *History of the Christian Church*, published twelve years before Newman's first volume

---

152. Note the interview with Miss Martha Emmons, Chapter I, above. She reported that Newman read his text for the class lectures.

153. *See* the tables of contents in both volumes of the *Manual. Also see* vol. 1, 17.

154. *See* Schaff, *History of the Christian Church*.

155. Henry Clay Sheldon, *History of the Christian Church* (New York: Thomas Y. Crowell and Co., 1894).

156. George Herbert Dryer, *History of the Christian Church* (Cincinnati: Jennings and Pye, 1896-1903).

appeared.[157]   John Fletcher Hurst's work was two volumes but was substantially longer than Newman's.[158]

A second positive factor related to Newman's *Manual* regarded the sources he used and the way he cited them. Instead of appending a long bibliography at the end of the work, Newman included a list of sources at the beginning of most of the major sections.[159] This allowed the student to have bibliography at hand for further study relating to each subject contained within the *Manual*. Though the work is short on footnotes, it is replete with bibliography.   The reader is aware from a perusal of the bibliographic sections that Newman retained almost an encyclopedic knowledge of the field of church history of works which were most trustworthy for various topics.

Showing no partiality to theological persuasion but interested only in the best scholarly works on the topic to be discussed, Newman included names of academicians from Europe as well as America. Particularly noticeable were the names of the German scholars that he deemed important.   Adolph Harnack, Albert Hauck, Ferdinand Christian Baur, Johann Lorentz Von Mosheim, Johann August Neander, Johann Josef Döllinger, and Johann Loserth were only a few names of German scholars Newman included.   Among American scholars recognized as important included Ephraim Emerton, Arthur Cushman McGiffert, and Philip Schaff.

Though there are positive features about the *Manual*, it has weaknesses as well.   Perhaps its most glaring fault is its anti-Catholic sentiment. Newman tried to be impartial in the *Manual*. For the most part this goal was achieved in relation to the Protestant denominations. However, there are instances of anti-Catholicism interspersed throughout the work.   For example, the word "popish" is used frequently relating to Roman

---

157. George Park Fisher, *History of the Christian Church* (New York: Charles Scribner's Sons, 1887).

158. John Fletcher Hurst, *History of the Christian Church* (New York: Eaton and Mains: 1897-1900). Fletcher's work totaled 1867 pages of text while Newman's first edition was comprised of 1334 pages.

159. For example *see Manual*, vol. 1: 3, 20, 34, 67.

Catholicism.[160] John Winthrop Platner, a Congregationalist and assistant professor of ecclesiastical history at Harvard University and later at Andover Theological Seminary, provided a private critique of the *Manual* in a personal letter to Newman. Chastising Newman Platner said, "I feel that no historian of the church ought ever to employ the term 'popish.'"[161] Another example of Newman's aversion toward Roman Catholicism relates to the Catholic victory over the Bohemian Protestants during the Thirty Years War. Newman commented, "Roman Catholicism had an opportunity here to exhibit itself in its true character."[162]

Another characteristic of the *Manual*, which may be regarded as a weakness, concerns the fact that Newman used the method of biography for much of his analysis of church history. Instead of a social history approach, which analyzed the social aspects of various periods of history, or a political history approach which examined how political currents affected the church, Newman chose to relate the church's history from the perspective of the important personalities. The weakness of this method is that many of the forces affecting church history are precluded, or only mentioned as they relate to individuals. Not all of the *Manual* is written with this approach but it is obvious in certain places. For example, in the second volume, Newman devoted an entire chapter to a discussion of the Roman Catholic Church during what he terms the modern era (1648-1932). But instead of analyzing

---

160. *See* Newman, *Manual*, vol. 1, 447. Referring to the spurious "Donation of Constantine," Newman said, "Here again we see the popish doctrine that the end justifies the means, while not formulated, yet consistently acted upon." This is just one example among many others of the use of the work "popish."

161. John Winthrop Platner to Albert Henry Newman, TL, n.d., Albert Henry Newman Papers. This is a fragment of a letter. This page of the letter is all that survives in the Newman Papers.

162. Newman, *Manual*, vol. 2, 401. In addition to these examples, Newman had negative comments about the Roman Catholic institution of monasticism. *See Manual*, vol. 1, 319. He said the institution had positive effects such as resistance to worldliness; attraction of pagans to Christianity; promotion of theological study; providing refuge for those cast out from society. But the negative factors included: taking large numbers of good Christians from the churches; causing spiritual pride to develop; providing the church with wrong ideas concerning morality and theology; abusive practices; causing the development of the hierarchy within the structure of the church. He classified monasticism among the evils resulting from the union of church and state under the rule of Constantine.

the church in relation to political efforts or social movements, he examined the period by a discussion of each pope who served during that era.[163] This approach to writing history did not originate with Newman. Yet, he considered biography an excellent method of relating history.

> Biography is a department of history...the history of individuals directly, and for the most part indirectly of the time, in so far as it reflects the genius, the institutions, the thought of the time. Whatever importance, then attaches to history in general, attaches to biography, or the history of prominent and representative individuals. But apart from the importance and interest that attach to history as such, I do not hesitate to affirm that biography is the most *inspiring* of all literature.[164]

Comparison With Contemporaries

The *Manual* appeared during a time in the late nineteenth century when writing entire histories of the church was in vogue. "Most of these general church histories were designed to relate a particular denominational tradition to the history of the Christian movement as a whole."[165] However,

> To say that the universal Church histories of these older men had been disguised expansions of denominational histories reaching for larger perspectives would be inexact, but the anchorage of their authors had been the denominational fellowship more than the academic community.[166]

While the *Manual* is not blatantly biased, Newman does seem to show partiality toward the dissenting sects throughout church history. This was, no doubt, due to his Spiritual Kinship Theory, which placed more value and emphasis on these sects than on the mainstream of orthodox Catholicism.

> In keeping with his denominational origin and sponsorship, the *Manual* gives prominence...to the dissenting tradition down through the centuries, a survival of an older denominational

---

163. Newman, *Manual*, Vol. 2, 425-518.

164. Albert Henry Newman, "A Biographical and Bibliographical Account of Dr. H. A. W. Meyer," *Baptist Quarterly* (Philadelphia) 8 (October 1874): 438.

165. Hudson, "Shifting Trends in Church History," 235.

166. Williams, 154.

objective within the framework of German ecclesiastical historiography.[167]

It is helpful to compare the *Manual* with other church histories written during the same period. George Park Fisher's work, *History of the Christian Church*, is similar to the *Manual* in its approach. Fisher was a Congregationalist and professor of ecclesiastical history at Yale University who retired in 1901. He wrote from a denominational perspective, and also sought to be fair with the sources much as Newman did. Yet his work "preserves something of the older denomination based theological and apologetic interest in the subject."[168]

Methodist Henry Clay Sheldon, like Newman, wrote his *History of the Christian Church* for both the academician and layman. Because he had written a history of theology in 1887, Sheldon felt that a detailed treatment of the history of doctrine was unnecessary in his church history. Three out of five of the volumes comprise a discussion of the modern church because of the lack of comprehensive works on the subject and because of what he considered the complexity of the topic.[169]

John Fletcher Hurst, also a Methodist, was trained in Germany and then was professor and later president of Drew Theological Seminary. His *History of the Christian Church* represents "the new historiography, situated within the denominational context but keenly conscious of the universal Church and thoroughly committed to...the German methodology."[170]

George Herbert Dryer's five volume *History of the Christian Church* differed from Newman's *Manual* in that Dryer's stated purpose was to appeal to the layperson rather than the student of church history. "This book has been written for popular use. It is hoped it will have interest for those who only hear it read aloud."[171] Therefore Dryer's history is more of a popular work, aimed at church libraries and family reading.

---

167. *Ibid.*, 152.

168. *Ibid.*, 153.

169. Sheldon, iii-iv.

170. Williams, 152.

171. Dryer, 3.

Durability

The final question concerning the *Manual* relates to its popularity and usage over the years since its publication and how it compares to modern church history texts. The revision of the work occurred just before Newman's death in 1933. Volume two received the first revision in 1931, followed by volume one in 1933. The major changes in the revised work involved updating sources and the history of the church itself. Volume one offered a new chapter entitled "The Oriental Churches from the Great Schism to the Close of the Middle Ages," which concerned the Eastern Orthodox church. Volume two offered a new chapter entitled "Twentieth Century Supplement," which described the progress of Christianity from the beginning of the century. This chapter included a section on Russian Orthodoxy from the sixteenth century, but emphasized the dissenting sects more than the Orthodox Church.[172]

Interestingly, the *Manual* continued as a popular textbook for several decades after Newman's death. The highest royalty paid by the publisher occurred during the year 1953-54, when the Newman family received $1062.95.[173] From then the popularity of the work declined as the book became more outdated.

Williston Walker's *History of the Christian Church*, published in 1918, competed with Newman's *Manual* throughout the middle decades of the twentieth century and still continues to be one of the most popular texts. It was revised in 1959 by Cyril Richardson, Wilhelm Pauck, and Robert T. Handy, again in 1970 by Robert T. Handy, and most recently in 1985 by Richard A. Norris, David W. Lotz and Handy. Walker's *History of the Christian Church* represented the only significant general history to appear in the period from 1900 to 1920, an era dominated instead by efforts to produce specialized monographs.[174]

---

172. Newman, *Manual*, Volume 2 (1931 edition), 714-81.

173. These figures are found in the Albert Henry Newman File, Baylor University. They are the receipts from the amount paid by the American Baptist Publication Society.

174. *Hudson, "Shifting Trends in Church History,"* 236.

Walker's work is compact, occupying only one volume, which contributes to its lasting popularity over the *Manual*. "It is comprehensive without being unmanageably long, terse without loss of clarity, and notably lacking in eccentricities of emphasis."[175] It also differs from the *Manual* in that it exhibits the scientific historiographical approach similar to that of Ephraim Emerton.[176] Unlike the *Manual* and the general church histories mentioned above, Walker's work "conveyed no sense of writing from within the church. He had no confession to make, no thesis to defend."[177] Because of its neutrality, it appealed to a wider variety of readers, thereby causing it to outlive the *Manual's* popularity.

There are specific differences between the *Manual* and the *A History of the Christian Church* which illustrate Walker's detachment from the topic as opposed to Newman's bias. For example, Newman offered a judgement concerning the authenticity of Constantine's conversion to Christianity:

> In general, it may be said, that while his character compares favorably with that of pagan despots, and had many admirable and amiable traits, he can hardly be supposed to have exercised a saving faith.[178]

Walker, on the other hand, refused to make a judgement but still gave essentially the same information:

> He was, thenceforth, in all practical respects a Christian, even though heathen emblems still appeared on coins, and he retained the title of Pontifix Maximus.[179]

Another difference in the two texts concerns Martin Luther. Newman included an entire section on Luther's morality entitled, "Some Demoralizing

175. B. A. Gerrish, review of *History of the Christian Church*, by Williston Walker, rev. ed., In *The Journal of Religion* 40 (January 1960): 55.

176. Williams, 153-55. Walker earned a Ph. D. from the University of Leipzig in 1888. *See* Bowden, *Church History in the Age of Science*, 115.

177. Hudson, 236.

178. Albert Henry Newman, *Manual*, Vol. 1, 306.

179. Williston Walker, *A History of the Christian Church* (New York: Charles Scribner's Sons, 1918), 111.

Elements in Luther's Teachings and Life."[180]   Walker's work contains no such appraisal of Luther's life.

As the *Manual* was losing popularity in the middle of the twentieth century, another text, Kenneth Scott Latourette's *A History of Christianity*, provides a convenient watershed by which to separate the era accepting Newman's work with the era of modern church history texts.[181]   Latourette attempted to tell the story of the history of Christianity recognizing that "he who would survey the history of Christianity must strive to view it in its global setting."[182]   This aspect distinguishes Latourette from either Walker or Newman. *A History of Christianity* provides ample discussion of Christianity in the East, while both Walker and Newman concentrate on the West and do not devote as much attention to the Eastern church.[183]   Differing from Walker, Latourette confessed at the beginning of *A History of Christianity*, that the work was not written from a purely "objective" approach.

> If it is complained that this is not an "objective" approach, it must be remembered that pure objectivity does not exist, even in the natural sciences.   One is either for or against Christianity: there is not neutral or strictly "objective" ground.[184]

Latourette's *A History of Christianity* remains a popular text today.   It was revised and divided into two volumes in 1975.

Roland Bainton's *Christendom* appeared in 1964.[185]   As the subtitle implies, this work is much shorter than Newman, Walker, or Latourette although it consists of two volumes.   The strength of *Christendom*, in addition to its brevity, is the vast amount of illustrations which included art from the

---

180. Albert Henry Newman, *Manual*, Vol. 2, 84-90.

181. Walker's *A History of the Christian Church* remained popular along with Latourette because of its revisions beginning in 1959.

182. Kenneth Scott Latourette, *A History of Christianity* (New York: Harper and Brothers, 1953), xvii.

183. *See* W. E. Garrison, review of *A History of Christianity*, by Kenneth Scott Latourette, In *The Christian Century* 70 (19 August 1953): 941.

184. *Ibid.*, xxi.

185. Roland Bainton, *Christendom: A Short History of Christianity and Its Impact on Western Civilization* (New York: Harper and Row, 1964).

history of the church. This quality adds to the appeal of using the book as a text for an introductory class in church history.

The appearance of two new texts in the last decade has challenged both Walker and Bainton in popularity. Kurt Aland's *A History of Christianity* was published in German in 1980 with the English translation following in 1985.[186] Like the works mentioned above, Aland divides the history of the church at the Reformation, which begins the second volume. Aland sought to narrate the history of Christianity with the presupposition that "[i]t is not the knowledge of historical details which is important, but understanding the contexts in which they belong."[187] Aland's work is unique in that he includes a detailed chronological table of the major events within the history of the church at the back of each volume. Therefore, the text is not filled with the endless names and facts that Newman's *Manual* contains. Aland's work shows a development along this line. Modern texts are more concerned with "telling the story" of the development of Christianity, rather than detailing the history of the church on the basis of names and events, as texts in the era of the *Manual* were prone to do.

Justo Gonzalez's *The Story of Christianity* is another church history text which has recently gained popularity.[188] Similar to Bainton's *Christendom*, Gonzalez's work is well illustrated. Though it consists of two volumes, *The Story of Christianity* is nonetheless a brief overview of the history of Christianity which is in keeping with the current trend. Also, Gonzalez begins the second volume of his work with the Reformation which is the convenient division for most of the popular church history texts. Similar to Aland, Gonzalez provides a chronological table of events at the beginning of each major division in the work.

---

186. Kurt Aland, *A History of Christianity*, trans, James L. Schaaf (Philadelphia: Fortress Press, 1985).

187. *Ibid.*, xiii.

188. Justo L. Gonzalez, *The Story of Christianity*, 2 Vols. (San Francisco: Harper and Row, 1984).

Conclusion

During the nineteenth century, the study of history underwent a dramatic shift evolving into a professional discipline. The rise of scientific historiography is largely responsible for this change. In the area of church history at least three distinct types of historiography can be identified: scientific, theological, and sectarian. By the beginning of the twentieth century, the scientific historians largely dominated the field of church history.

Though Newman was not a representative of any of the three schools of church historiography, he most nearly identified with the ideas of the theological approach to church history while simultaneously maintaining a degree of identification with sectarian historiography. Newman was not an exponent of scientific church history. Because he lacked identification with the scientific church historiography, his work became obsolete as the twentieth century progressed. The decreasing popularity of *A Manual of Church History* compared with the increasing approval of Williston Walker's *History of the Christian Church* serves as evidence that Newman's work became antiquated.

CHAPTER III

ALBERT HENRY NEWMAN AND ANABAPTIST
HISTORIOGRAPHY

Introduction

Before the nineteenth century, Anabaptist historiography exhibited an essentially negative bias. The historians who studied Anabaptism tended to base their analyses and conclusions on the treatises written by the enemies of the movement. These works generally viewed all Anabaptists as fanatic radicals in light of the Münster debacle and the Peasants' War. Because Anabaptism was censured, the writings of the Anabaptists themselves remained in virtual obscurity. Those scholars who treated the Anabaptists in a positive light generally were met with rejection.[1]

Though the field of Anabaptist studies began to blossom in Europe in the nineteenth century, very little work was accomplished in the United States. Albert Henry Newman was among the first American scholars to contribute to Anabaptist research.[2] Newman's first significant works

---

1. Harold S. Bender, "The Historiography of the Anabaptists," *The Mennonite Quarterly Review* 31 (April 1957): 88-90. Bender cites Gottfried Arnold's *Unparteyische kirchen-und Ketzer-Historie*, (Frankfurt, 1699) as the first work to make a complete break with the traditional view of the Anabaptists, but it took a long time before it found its deserved recognition. *See* pp. 90-91.

2. Harold S. Bender and C. Henry Smith, eds. *The Mennonite Encyclopedia* (Scottdale, Pennsylvania: Mennonite Publishing House, 1957), s.v. "Newman, Albert Henry," by Harold S. Bender. Bender states that Newman, along with Henry S. Burrage, Henry C. Vedder, and William J. McGlothlin were the only American historians besides the Mennonites who made a significant contribution to the field.

concerning the Anabaptists appeared in the early 1880s. His *magnum opus* in Anabaptist historiography was the classic *A History of Anti-Pedobaptism: From the Rise of Pedobaptism to A.D. 1609*, published in 1897.[3]

The purpose of this chapter is to examine Newman's Anabaptist historiography. The first section will consider the reasons why Newman developed an interest in the Anabaptists. The second section will examine some of Newman's specific conclusions about Anabaptist history. The third section will discuss Newman's work in light of other Anabaptist scholars.

Newman's Interest in Anabaptist History

The previous chapter provided a discussion of sectarian historiography prevalent in the United States in the second half of the nineteenth century. Cognizant of this type of historiography and even identifying with it to a certain extent, Newman spent his career as a historian within the Baptist denomination that was permeated by lineal successionist claims. The prevailing attitude of succession combined with his strong Baptist bias and the Spiritual Kinship Theory, served to foster Newman's interest in the Anabaptists.

Baptist Bias

Newman's favorable bias toward the Baptist denomination not only gave him identity with sectarian historiography but it also helped generate his interest in the Anabaptists. One of the guiding principles of his historiography was that Baptists practiced Christianity in complete accordance with the principles set down by the New Testament. This idea seems to have been with him from the beginning of his career. Eby said:

> Quite early in life he reached the very positive conclusion that Baptist doctrines are in accordance with the teachings of the New Testament; that they are also rationally defensible; that scholarly theologians of other faiths are gradually becoming convinced that the Baptist position on all fundamental issues is correct; and that these doctrines are ultimately to be universally accepted by all unprejudiced minds and hearts.[4]

---

3.   Albert Henry Newman, *A History of Anti-Pedobaptism: From the Rise of Pedobaptism to A. D. 1609* (Philadelphia: The American Baptist Publication Society, 1897).

4.   Eby, 154.

In an 1883 letter Newman conveyed the thought that to distance oneself from the Baptist position places that person in opposition to Scripture, reason, and the lessons of history. He declared that "the Baptist position is the only one that Protestants can consistently hold."[5] Furthermore, Newman believed that the Baptist position was completely logical. In fact, the only other logical system he could identify was that of Roman Catholicism, which he contended was neither true nor in accordance with Scripture.[6]

Coupled with his conviction that Baptists practice New Testament Christianity, Newman was optimistic about the future progress of the denomination. On several occasions he expressed the belief that other denominations gradually were realizing that the Baptist ideal was the only true expression of Christianity. He told his students during classroom lecture that history shows "the Baptist cause is the gaining cause."[7] This is evident, he said, from the fact that greater respect was shown to Baptists of his day as opposed to the early Baptists who had to endure persecution, and that Baptist ideas were increasingly gaining recognition from non-Baptist groups.[8] At the Baptist Congress in 1898 he said, "If Baptists are right in their distinctive views the profounder study of the Scriptures will confirm them in their views...and will bring others nearer and nearer to the Baptist position."[9] Another example of Newman's feeling that other denominations were moving to a recognition of the correctness of Baptist ideas is found in the

5.   Albert Henry Newman to Dr. Murdoch, LS, 2 June 1885, Albert Henry Newman Papers, 1. This quote is from a rather caustic letter in which Newman chides Dr. Murdoch (not identified further) for apparently having left the Baptist denomination for another. Eby quoted this letter on 120-21. He said that he found the letter folded as if it were in an envelope and that Newman may have never sent the letter, opting instead to send a less caustic one. If Newman did send the letter, he may have made a copy for himself.

6.   Albert Henry Newman, *Liberty of Conscience: A Fundamental Baptist Principle* (Toronto: Standard Publishing Company, 1883), 24.

7.   Albert Henry Newman, Unclassified lecture notes, 88.

8.   *Ibid.* On another occasion he told his students: "The doctrine of religious liberty brought out clearly by Anabaptists in the Reformation time and maintained continuously in the Netherlands and in England from the beginning of the 17th century, found comparatively little acceptance until the present century; yet it has been constantly making way and seems likely at no very remote time to become universal." *See* Unclassified lecture notes, 49.

9.   Albert Henry Newman, "The Opportunities of Baptists in Present Religious Progress," 52.

conclusion of an article entitled "The Early Waldenses." With a swell of Baptist pride he said:

> It is the writer's conviction that even now Baptist principles are latent in evangelical Pedo-baptist churches, being logically involved in the evangelical principles professed, and that under favoring circumstances we shall soon see them asserting them selves with irresistible power. The great Baptist movement which showed such vitality and power during the mediaeval and Reformation times, and which has so far revolutionized the religious thinking of the world within the last two hundred and fifty years, will sooner or later sweep away the last vestiges of Popery from the doctrines and practices of the great evangelical denominations.[10]

The Baptist ideas that Newman believed were surfacing in non-Baptist groups were: a decrease in infant baptism, a common recognition of liberty of conscience, a tendency in the non-Baptist groups to require regenerate membership, and a general feeling against union of church and state.[11]

Newman provided some specific evidence for his claim that non-Baptist groups were gradually acquiring Baptist principles. An article for *The Canadian Baptist* entitled "The Decline of Infant Baptism," may serve as one example. Here Newman cited an article written by another Baptist historian, Henry C. Vedder.[12] Vedder, in an elaborate statistical analysis, concluded that the number of infant baptisms in various denominations over the previous fifty years had declined. Newman attributed this to Baptist influence.[13] Vedder also attributed the decline to Baptist influence.[14] However, the decline in the number of infant baptisms may be due to a

---

10. Albert Henry Newman, "The Early Waldenses," 322. Other examples of this optimistic attitude concerning the spread of Baptist ideas are found in Albert Henry Newman, "Baptist Progress and Prospects," *The Canadian Baptist*, 8 February 1883, 4 and "Editorial Notes: The Decline of Infant Baptism," *The Canadian Baptist*, 14 March 1889, 4 (unsigned article).

11. Albert Henry Newman, Unclassified lecture notes, 88.

12. Henry C. Vedder, "The Decline of Infant Baptism," *The Baptist Quarterly Review* 4 (April 1882): 173-89.

13. Albert Henry Newman, "The Decline of Infant Baptism," *The Canadian Baptist*, 11 May 1882, 1.

14. Vedder, 188-89.

decline in the birthrate. Or it may simply be the result of indifference on the part of parents belonging to those denominations. Though the decrease may have been real, Newman gave no evidence for his conclusion that it was due to Baptist influence.

Newman provided further evidence for his optimism concerning Baptist principles. In "Traces of Baptist Teaching and Practice During the First Sixteen Christian Centuries," Newman quoted prominent scholars such as Adolf Harnack and Albert Hauck who concluded that Christians of the Apostolic era did not baptize infants. He deduced that these scholars supported the Baptist claims of being congruent with the Apostolic Christians.

> There is almost a consensus of opinion among scholars of the highest rank of all the leading denominations that in matters that differentiate Baptist churches from others, Baptists are in accord with apostolic precept and example.[15]

Newman however, did not cite any specific evidence that the scholars he named made such a statement. They may have believed that infant baptism was not a part of apostolic Christianity, but that does not necessarily mean they believed that nineteenth-century Baptists practiced apostolic Christianity. In this instance, Newman simply cited scholars who agreed with his conclusions that infant baptism was not practiced in apostolic times. He then exhibited this as evidence that modern scholarship was gradually moving to affirm the Baptist position.

From early childhood until his death Newman remained a Baptist. His partiality toward Baptist ideas remained throughout his career. At times his denominational pride was blatant. On one occasion he said, "The world does not yet begin to know what Baptist principles have achieved. It is time it was learning."[16] This favorable bias toward the Baptists encouraged Newman's Anabaptist work because he believed that the Anabaptists were the forerunners of the seventeenth-century Baptists.

---

15. Albert Henry Newman, "Traces of Baptist Teaching and Practice During the First Sixteen Christian Centuries," 24 October 1901, 5.

16. Albert Henry Newman, *Liberty of Conscience: A Fundamental Baptist Principle*, 34.

98

Spiritual Kinship

A second factor in Newman's historiography, the Spiritual Kinship Theory, combined with his Baptist bias to produce his interest in the Anabaptists. With his impression that Baptist churches are identical to apostolic Christianity, Newman began to study the apostolic era. He identified what he considered to be the distinguishing marks of the apostolic churches in an article entitled "Baptist Churches Apostolical:" (1) ascription to the absolute lordship of Christ; (2) regenerate church membership; (3) independence of each local church; (4) equality of all members in rank and privilege; (5) no union of church and state; (6) each church's leaders chosen from among their own ranks for the performance of certain tasks; (7) believer's baptism and the Lord's Supper as the only two ordinances.[17] He then compared Baptist principles with those identified from the apostolic period, concluding that Baptist churches were almost identical with the churches of the first century. Newman conceded that the Baptists of his day were not synonymous with the apostolic Christians on two minor points: the practice of the Love Feast and the fact that apostolic churches had no buildings or musical instruments.[18] What Newman failed to account for in his appraisal of apostolic Christianity is how external forces such as sociological factors caused similarities and differences between nineteenth-century Baptists and apostolic Christians.[19]

With Newman's conclusion that a congruence existed between apostolic Christianity and nineteenth-century Baptists, the task before him was to investigate what happened to the apostolic principles between the first and the nineteenth centuries. Apostolic Christianity continued until the second

17. Albert Henry Newman, "Baptist Churches Apostolical," 236-70.

18. *Ibid.*, 273-74.

19. Newman defined apostolic Christianity on another occasion as well. In "the apostolical and immediately post-apostolical times the churches were composed of those who had been baptized upon a personal profession of faith; that in them the Supper was restricted to church members; that churches were organized on a congregational basis with a plurality of elders or bishops; and that each church of Christ embracing usually the baptized believers of the entire community, was independent in respect to every other." *See* Albert Henry Newman, "Traces of Baptist Teaching and Practice During the First Sixteen Christian Centuries," 17 October 1901, 1.

century according to Newman. "If the apostolic churches were Baptist churches, the churches of the second century were not. Still less were those of the third and the following centuries."[20] The introduction of infant baptism, an innovation Newman believed to be totally unwarranted by scripture, was evidence of the corruption of Christianity. Therefore he investigated the history of Christianity in order to find traces of apostolic principles and identify their location. This became the stated goal of *A History of Anti-Pedobaptism: From the Rise of Pedobaptism Until A.D. 1609*. "The problem in the work...was to trace and account for the protests against incoming perversions of apostolic precept and example regarding the subjects of baptism."[21] Newman believed that even though apostolic Christianity experienced corruption in the second century, traces of it continued to exist through the history of the church. "It is our firm belief that from the apostolic age to this good day the religion of Christ has persisted in its saving and sanctifying power."[22] Newman located these traces of genuine apostolic Christianity in the dissenting sects throughout church history. He cautioned, however, that the early dissenting sects were far from what could be termed the apostolic norm, even though they did subscribe to some of its principles.[23] Here Newman's Spiritual Kinship is distinguished from the type of lineal successionism found in James Milton Carroll's *The Trail of Blood*. Carroll identified the dissenters as Baptist churches. Newman refused to go this far. Instead, he saw in them various Baptist principles, and he proposed "to present as strongly as the facts seem[ed] to him to warrant...the persistence of Baptist principles from the apostolic age onward."[24]

---

20. Albert Henry Newman, *A History of Anti-Pedobaptism: From the Rise of Pedobaptism to A.D. 1609*, 3.

21. Albert Henry Newman, "Traces of Baptist Teaching and Practice During the First Sixteen Christian Centuries," 17 October 1901, 1.

22. *Ibid.*

23. Albert Henry Newman, *A History of Anti-Pedobaptism: From the Rise of Pedobaptism to A.D. 1609*, 15-29.

24. *Ibid.* For other statements that Newman made against lineal successionist claims *see*: Albert Henry Newman, "The Significance of the Anabaptist Movement in the History of the Christian Church," 15 and *Manual*, Vol. 2, 178 concerning successionist claims among the Mennonites.

Newman pointed to the Middle Ages as a time when the apostolic form of Christianity gradually began to resurface. Though traces of the apostolic norm were evident throughout church history, it became more pronounced in the Middle Ages.[25] With the Petrobrusians and Arnoldists in the twelfth century, Newman found a form of Christianity he believed could be regarded as "measurably conformable to the apostolic standard."[26] After the Petrobrusians and the Arnoldists came the Waldenses and their related groups, followed by Wycliff and Hus. But Newman noted that apostolic Christianity still had not come to complete fruition in the Middle Ages. For instance, he noted that Wycliff and the Lollards still retained the practice of infant baptism.[27] He said, "Even those who rejected infant baptism and practised [sic] rebaptism had much in their doctrine and practice that present-day Baptists would not fellowship."[28]

Newman placed great emphasis on the medieval dissenting groups because they set the stage for the Protestant Reformation. The Reformation did not begin with Luther, the Humanists, Wycliff, or even Hus according to Newman. It began with the "so-called heretical...parties protesting with terrible earnestness against the corrupt hierarchy."[29] These groups became the seed from which later sprang the Anabaptist movement.

> It is not denied that most of the phenomena of the Anabaptist movement could be accounted for without the supposition of the persistence in it of mediaeval types of evangelical life and thought; but it seems more reasonable to postulate the perpetuity of the older types than to suppose that so many varieties of teaching had independent origin in the two periods and that the older types that can be traced to the Reformation

---

25. For instance *see Manual*, Vol. 1, 374-76 concerning the Jovinianist Controversy. Newman believed that this group kept the evangelical witness alive and that it influenced the rise of the Arnoldists, Petrobrusians, and Henricians in the twelfth century.

26. Albert Henry Newman, *A History of Anti-Pedobaptism: From the Rise of Pedobaptism to A.D. 1609*, 30.

27. *Ibid.*, 55.

28. *Ibid.*, 61.

29. Albert Henry Newman, "The Reformation From a Baptist Point of View," *The Baptist Quarterly Review* 6 (January 1884): 52.

time should have suddenly become extinct to give place to similar parties newly originated.[30]

Newman believed the Reformation provided the best expression of apostolic Christianity since the first century. The evangelical witness progressed through the centuries and produced an air of expectancy at the beginning of the sixteenth century.

> A spirit of revolution was abroad. Enough of evangelical light and enough of the spirit of freedom had been diffused among the masses to insure an enthusiastic reception for any movement that should give fair promise of relief from priestcraft and of social amelioration.[31]

But Luther and the magisterial reformers proved to be a disappointment. They turned their backs on the old evangelical Christianity when they retained infant baptism thereby uniting church and state. The Anabaptists, however, continued the course of medieval evangelical life. Regarding the Swiss Anabaptists, Newman said, "Anabaptists of this type superadded to what was best in medieval evangelical life and thought."[32] He concluded that the Anabaptist movement simply completed the process of reform started by the magisterial reformers.[33]

Because Newman believed the Baptists to be the full expression of apostolic Christianity, and because he saw the Anabaptists as the group that came the closest to that apostolic standard, it was left to him to determine all that he could about their movement and their influence on the rise of the Baptists in the seventeenth century. Eby referred to this lifelong process as Newman's mission.

> To trace the history of the Baptists and their doctrines became his life mission. This mission he pursued with unswerving fidelity and singleness of purpose, because of fixed confidence that every man who wants to know the truth and is willing to

30. Albert Henry Newman, *Manual*, Vol. 2, 151.

31. Albert Henry Newman, *A History of Anti-Pedobaptism: From the Rise of Pedobaptism to A.D. 1609*, 63.

32. Albert Henry Newman, "Some Biblical Anabaptists," *The Baptist Standard*, 19 September 1901, 5.

33. Albert Henry Newman, *Manual*, Vol. 2, 151. Newman went so far as to say that "Lutherans had no sooner thoroughly overthrown Scholasticism than they introduced an era of Protestant Scholasticism, with the same deadening and despiritualizing effect as had marked that of the Middle Ages." *See* "The Reformation From a Baptist Point of View," 61.

follow after the truth with absolute sincerity must come to the Baptist position."[34]

Since the study of the history of the Baptists was Newman's lifelong task, he naturally wanted to investigate any group with similar distinctives. This explains his interest in studying the history of the Anabaptists. He admitted that there were differences between the Anabaptists and Baptists.[35] But he saw in the Anabaptist movement the antecedents of the Baptists, and the recovery of apostolic Christianity in its infancy. They were not regular Baptists, but they were thoroughly imbued with Baptist principles, and were...the forerunners of all that was best in Puritanism and in the great modern Baptist movement.[36]

Newman's Conclusions About the Anabaptists

Different Types of Anabaptists

Harold S. Bender noted that Newman was the most prominent of the Baptist historians who made a contribution to Anabaptist studies as he was "the first historian writing in the English language who assigned to the Anabaptist movement its proper position, free of doctrinaire distortion."[37] Newman was able to provide such an accurate appraisal of the Anabaptists partly because he was able to distinguish their differences.

The foundation of the Anabaptist movement for Newman was not the rejection of infant baptism, although that was a definite result. The concept of regenerate church membership gave the Anabaptists their distinctive quality. He believed that this characteristic identified the Anabaptists with the apostolic form of Christianity.[38]

Although the foundation of the movement was regenerate church membership, Newman sought to identify different kinds of Anabaptists. This classification changed slightly during his career. In his first published article

---

34. Eby, *Newman the Church Historian*, 123.

35. Newman, "The Significance of the Anabaptist Movement in the History of the Christian Church," 22.

36. Albert Henry Newman, "The Whitsitt Controversy," 173.

37. *The Mennonite Encyclopedia*, "Newman, Albert Henry."

38. Albert Henry Newman, "Baptist Churches Apostolical," 276.

concerning the Anabaptists, Newman concluded that there were three basic categories of Anabaptists. The "Fanatical Anabaptists" included Thomas Münzer and the Zwickau Prophets, as well as Melchior Hoffman and the Münster radicals. The "Baptist Anabaptists" were comprised mainly of the Swiss Anabaptists. Newman called them Baptist because they were the closest to what he considered the Baptist ideal. The "Mystical Anabaptists" included Faustus Socinus, Michael Servetus, and Casper Schwenkfeldt, who were concerned about infant baptism but not as much as they were about other doctrinal matters.[39]

About twenty years later, when Newman published the second volume of the *Manual*, he provided different Anabaptist categories. His earlier category of "Fanatical Anabaptists" became the "Chiliastic Anabaptists," whose primary concern was speculation about the coming of the millennial kingdom. His basic definition of the group corresponded to that of the earlier category.[40]

The second group of Anabaptists specified in the *Manual* corresponds to the earlier category of "Baptist Anabaptists." However, he changed the name of this group to the "Soundly Biblical Anabaptists." In this classification Newman included the early Swiss Anabaptists as well as those from Moravia.[41]

The group Newman identified as "Mystical Anabaptists" in the earlier list is divided further in the listing of groups in the *Manual*. In the *Manual* he still used the same terminology to describe this group. He included the names Hans Denck and Casper Schwenkfeldt with the Mystical Anabaptists.[42] The difference in the earlier and later category of Mystical Anabaptists is that in the later list Newman divided the group further, creating a fourth and fifth category of Anabaptists. This was obviously the result of twenty more years of research.

---

39. William Cathcart, ed. *The Baptist Encyclopedia* (Philadelphia: Louis H. Everts, 1883), s.v. "Anabaptists," by Albert Henry Newman.

40. Albert Henry Newman, *Manual*, Vol. 2, 156-68. Newman said that this group's main concern was speculation about the coming of the millennial kingdom.

41. *Ibid.*, 168-81.

42. *Ibid.*, 181-85.

104

The fourth group Newman called the "Pantheistic Anabaptists." Here he cited only two names, David Joris and Heinrich Niclaes, neither of whom is a well known Anabaptist. Without explaining clearly his understanding of pantheism, Newman called both of these men pantheists because they each claimed to receive visions from God and developed large followings as a result.[43]

The fifth Anabaptist category that Newman specified in the *Manual* is that of the "Anti-trinitarian Anabaptists." In this category Newman included Johannes Campanus and Michael Servetus as well as the Polish Brethren (Socinians) and the Italian Anabaptists.[44]

Though he recognized differences within the Anabaptist movement, Newman also identified certain characteristics common to all Anabaptists: (1) tendency toward communism and rejection of possessions; (2) regenerate church membership; (3) rejection of infant baptism; (4) separation of church and state; (5) refusal to allow a Christian to be a magistrate; (6) prohibition of oaths; (7) pacifism; (8) rejection of capital punishment; (9) a conviction that they had been divinely commissioned to set up a theocratic kingdom; (10) opposition to an Augustinian system of doctrine; (11) a Christian life similar to the medieval sects, which bordered on asceticism; (12) belief that the Lord's Supper was only for the baptized and that it was the most solemn act in which a Christian could participate; (13) extreme separatism from other religious groups; and (14) whenever free of persecution, the formation of a system of connectional church governments similar to the Waldenses and Bohemian Brethren.[45]

The Münster Affair

Newman asserted that "No episode in history has done so much to impede the progress of Baptist principles as that of Münster."[46] Therefore he took it upon himself to study the incident and discover its cause as well as

---

43. *Ibid.*, 185-87.

44. *Ibid.*, 187-200.

45. *Ibid.*, 153-56.

46. Albert Henry Newman, *A History of Anti-Pedobaptism: From the Rise of Pedobaptism to A.D. 1609*, 292.

its relevance to the Anabaptist movement. He was among the first historians to provide an accurate description of the Münster debacle and discover that the characters involved differed from mainstream Anabaptism.[47] He expressed this conclusion in his tract called *Liberty of Conscience*. "No more connection is there between English Baptists and the furious Fifth Monarchy Men of the Commonwealth period than between Anabaptists of the Baptist type and the wild men of Münster."[48]

Newman identified two causes of the Münster tragedy. First, he attributed the event to the oppression of the working classes and to the institutions that made that oppression possible. This set the stage for fanatical leaders to capture the support of the people by promising them emancipation. Here, Newman blamed Luther for contributing to the situation. Initially, Luther's writings aroused the hopes of the common people for liberation. His teaching convinced the people that their treatment was unjust. The ideas of liberation did not die with the suppression of the Peasants' War. Instead they resurfaced during the Münster affair.[49] Newman may have been influenced here by the German historian Karl Kautsky. Kautsky, a socialist, believed that the principle of communism was the original Christian economic system. Newman had a favorable impression of Kautsky's book *Communism in Central Europe in the Time of the Reformation*.[50] He provided an extended review of the book in three

---

47. *The Mennonite Encyclopedia*, s.v. "Newman, Albert Henry."

48. Albert Henry Newman, *Liberty of Conscience*, 17.

49. Albert Henry Newman, *A History of Anti-Pedobaptism: From the Rise of Pedobaptism to A.D. 1609*, 292. Newman directly attributed the cause of the Peasants' War to Luther: "It has been proved beyond question that from 1517 to 1522 Luther's doctrinal views were almost identical with the old evangelical views with which the peasants had long been familiar, and that after the latter date a marked change for the worse appears in his teachings. There can be no doubt, therefore, that the bold evangelical utterances of Luther during these years constitute an important factor among the influences that led to the great peasant's revolt." *See* Albert Henry Newman, "The Peasants' War," *The Baptist Quarterly Review* 11 (January 1889): 56-57.

50. Karl Kautsky, *Communism in Central Europe in the Time of the Reformation*, trans. J. L. and E. G. Mulliken (London: T. Fisher Unwin, 1897).

different articles, indicating his desire to relate its ideas to American readers.[51]

A second reason for the Münster disaster, which Newman considered the more immediate cause, was fanatical eschatology. "The bane of the peasants' movement, just as a little later it became the bane of the Baptist movement of the sixteenth century...was millenarianism."[52] The prophetical mysticism found in leaders such as Nicholas Storch and Thomas Münzer was continued by Hans Hut, Melchior Rinck, and Melchior Hoffman. According to Newman, the rigorous persecution of the Anabaptists put the people in such a frame of mind that they were willing to believe these prophetic proclaimers who taught that a new era was about to begin in which the persecutors of the people of God would be destroyed.[53]

Balthasar Hubmaier

Newman's Anabaptist writings clearly reveal that his favorite Anabaptist personality was Balthasar Hubmaier. While delivering an address before a group of Mennonites, Newman expressed his personal thoughts about Hubmaier as being "the foremost antipedobaptist of his age and one of the heroes of our common faith."[54]

Newman regarded Hubmaier as the most respectable of the sixteenth-century reformers. His comparison between Luther and Hubmaier found Luther somewhat lacking. "Hubmaier made, with divine help, self-sacrificing

---

51. *See* Albert Henry Newman, "Some Recent Literature on the Anabaptist Movement," *The Southwestern Theological Review* 1 (1903): 2-8; Albert Henry Newman, "An Important Work on the Anabaptists and Their Predecessors," *The Western Recorder*, 27 September 1900, 1; and Albert Henry Newman, "Kautsky on Thomas Münzer and the Anabaptists," *The Western Recorder*, 25 October 1900, 1.

52. Albert Henry Newman, "The Peasants' War," 64.

53. Albert Henry Newman, *A History of Anti-Pedobaptism: From the Rise of Pedobaptism to A.D. 1609*, 293.

54. Albert Henry Newman, "The Significance of the Anabaptist Movement in the History of the Christian Church," 19. On another occasion Newman expressed his opinion that "[i]f there ever was a man that more earnestly sought to know God's will, and was more ready to sacrifice everything for what he believed to be the truth than Balthazar Hubmaier, I have yet to read the history of that man." *See* Albert Henry Newman, *Liberty of Conscience*, 10.

Christians. Luther made self-indulgent Protestants!"[55] His ideas about the Reformation and Luther in particular, are evident here. Newman regarded Luther as a repulsive individual, not only because of his failure to carry out his reform plans by retaining infant baptism, but also because of the moral character of his life.

> Hubmaier or Luther–which? The man that, at the very beginning of his career, could write the ablest plea of the age for liberty of conscience, who showed forth an apostolic faith and suffered an apostolic martyrdom, or the man who put himself at the head of a politico–religious movement, who drove to despair and to death such as refused to yield to his *ipse dixit*, whose controversial language was more becoming to a fish woman than to a theologian, who did not blush to hold out the most unworthy inducements to those whose alliance he would gain, whose arrogance was equaled only by his exceeding bitterness of spirit?[56]

In addition to being the most appealing reformer, Newman attributed to Hubmaier another important characteristic. He discovered that Hubmaier differed from the other Anabaptists in his appraisal of oaths, the magistracy, warfare, and the right of Christians to attain private property. Therefore, he was similar to the Baptists of the seventeenth century. "Except in his practice of affusion as the act of baptism his position is hardly distinguishable from that of modern Baptists."[57] He had great appreciation for Hubmaier's tract *Von Ketzern und ihren Verbrennern*, and considered Hubmaier a pioneer of the Baptist idea of liberty of conscience.[58] For Newman, Hubmaier seemed to represent a bridge between the Anabaptists of the sixteenth century and the Baptists of the seventeenth century.[59]

---

55. Albert Henry Newman, "The Reformation From a Baptist Point of View," 49.

56. *Ibid.*, 67.

57. Albert Henry Newman, *Manual*, Vol. 2, 174. Newman made a similar statement in "Balthasar Hubmaier and the Moravian Anabaptists," *The Goshen College Record*, Review Supplement 27, Number 10 (1926): 11.

58. Albert Henry Newman, "Baptist Pioneers in Liberty of Conscience," *The Review and Expositor* 6 (April 1909): 242.

59. Albert Henry Newman, "Liberty and Creed," *The American Journal of Theology* 2 (January 1898): 43-44.

Distinction Between Baptists and Anabaptists

The terminology Newman used in his Anabaptist writings is somewhat confusing. Clearly, he used the term "Anti-pedobaptist" to refer to all parties in opposition to infant baptism from the apostolic period until the Reformation. That is reflected in the title, *A History of Anti-Pedobaptism: From the Rise of Pedobaptism to A. D. 1609.* The terms "Baptist" and "Anabaptist" are somewhat more obscured in his writings.

Newman distinguished between the two terms in his earliest Anabaptist writing for *The Baptist Encyclopedia* (1881) as well as in an article written toward the end of his career entitled "The Significance of the Anabaptist Movement in the History of the Christian Church" (1926).[60] This would seem to indicate that he understood the differences between the two groups. Yet in another article called "The Moravian Baptists," (1887) he consistently used the term "Baptist" to refer to the Anabaptists.[61] If Newman understood the difference between the two groups, what could account for his occasional confusing of the terms?

One explanation may be that Newman simply utilized the terminology that the persecutors of the Anabaptists used. The terms "Anabaptist," "Catabaptist," and "Baptist" were all common terms of derision used by the enemies of the Anabaptist movement.[62]

Another explanation may be found in the way Newman viewed the Anabaptists. He recognized that some of the Anabaptist groups were very similar to the later seventeenth century Baptists. In fact, he included the Moravian Anabaptists in the category of Anabaptists he called "Baptist Anabaptists" or later, "Soundly Biblical Anabaptists."[63] Also, he said that Anabaptists such as Balthasar Hubmaier, Hans Denck, Conrad Grebel, Menno Simons, and their followers "had not yet fully attained to the Baptist

---

60. *The Baptist Encyclopedia*, s.v. "Anabaptists," and Albert Henry Newman, "The Significance of the Anabaptist Movement in the History of the Christian Church," 22.

61. Albert Henry Newman, "The Moravian Baptists," *The Baptist Quarterly Review* 9 (January 1887): 41-62.

62. Albert Henry Newman, *A History of Baptist Churches in the United States* (Philadelphia: The American Baptist Publication Society, 1898), 1.

63. *See* the discussion above concerning Newman's classification of the Anabaptists.

position, [but] were Baptist in spirit."[64]   Because he seemed to think that these Anabaptists were so similar to the seventeenth-century Baptists, he may have interchanged the terms in order to stress the similarity, while at the same time recognizing the difference. Newman's use of the term "Baptist," therefore, could have two different meanings. He used it to refer to the seventeenth-century movement out of which came modern day Baptists. But he also used it in an adjectival sense occasionally to distinguish groups that had Baptist-like qualities, but did not fully share all of the Baptist distinctives.[65]

Mark Steven Fountain reasoned that Newman's understanding of the Anabaptists evolved, which, in turn explains the different uses of the terms. Fountain said that in Newman's earlier writings he had a generalized use of the term "Baptist." His *A History of Anti-Pedobaptism* (1897) title shows him moving away from this generalization.[66]   While Newman's work on the Anabaptists did show development concerning particularly the classification of different Anabaptist groups, from his earliest writings he had an understanding concerning their difference from the Baptists.[67]

Newman and Other Anabaptist Historians

Newman's work as an Anabaptist historian may be better evaluated after a comparison with other Anabaptist historians. The first part of this

---

64. Albert Henry Newman, *Liberty of Conscience: A Fundamental Baptist Principle*, 17. Newman made a similar statement in *The Baptist Encyclopedia*, s.v. "Anabaptists."

65. For another example of the use of "Baptist" to refer to Anabaptists *see*: Albert Henry Newman, "The Peasant's War," 64. Here he mentioned the "Baptist movement of the sixteenth century." This may be interpreted as the movement in the sixteenth century which brought forth "Baptist" like ideas.

One specific difference noted by Newman between the Baptists and Anabaptists concerned Christology. He said, "Most of the early antipaedobaptists of Switzerland, Germany, Austria, and the Netherlands whose writings or confessions have been preserved show either by avoidance of orthodox trinitarian formulae or by using language inconsistent therewith their tendency toward Arian or Adoptionist Christology." *See* Albert Henry Newman, "Adam Pastor: Antitrinitarian Antipaedobaptist," *Papers of the American Society of Church History*, Second Series, (1917): 78. He pointed to Menno Simons as exemplary of this Christology. *See Manual*, Vol. 2, 179 and *A History of Anti-Pedobaptism: From the Rise of Pedobaptism to A. D. 1609*, 302.

66. Fountain, 64.

67. *See The Baptist Encyclopedia*, s.v. "Anabaptists."

section will discuss Newman in relation to two scholars contemporary with him, followed by a section which will evaluate the durability of Newman's work in relation to modern Anabaptist historiography.

Ludwig Keller

Ludwig Keller (1849-1915) was one of the earliest nineteenth-century Anabaptist scholars. Keller was not an academician, but rather an archivist in the city of Münster. A member of the German Reformed Church, his work as state archivist in Münster gave him access to documents related to the Anabaptists and led him to certain conclusions about their place in church history.

His first book, *Geschichte der Wiedertäufer und ihres Reich zu Münster* (1880), attempted to show that the Anabaptist tragedy in Münster was an aberration and was not exemplary of the true characteristics of Anabaptism.[68] He concluded that the Anabaptist movement needed a new examination. "It is not possible to penetrate further into the so-called Baptist movement unless one sharply distinguishes its different epochs and directions, and examines each one separately and with scientific thoroughness."[69] Keller divided the Anabaptist movement into three parties, each centered around a strong leader. These three leaders were John Denck, Melchior Hoffmann, and Menno Simon.[70] "This type of analysis was perhaps his most enduring achievement, having since become an integral commonplace feature of later Anabaptist studies."[71]

Keller highlighted the characteristics he considered to be the essence of Anabaptism. These included: voluntarism, rather than denominational formalism; a system that emphasized free thought instead of rigid doctrine; a

---

68. Mary Sprunger, "Anna Brons and Ludwig Keller," *Mennonite Life* 40 (June 1985): 13.

69. Ludwig Keller, "An Apostle of the Anabaptists," trans. Henry S. Burrage, *The Baptist Quarterly Review* 7 (January 1885): 36.

70. Keller, 34. It should be Hans Denck and Menno Simons. Keller tended to concentrate on Denck and the Spiritualist wing of the Radical Reformation. *See* Fountain, 53-54. One of Keller's earliest works was a life of Denck entitled, *Ein Apostel der Weidertäufer*, (1882).

71. Fountain, 53.

life of discipleship based on biblical faith; Christian charity; and discipline through use of the ban.[72]

> Whereas up to that time Anabaptism had been interpreted chiefly through the distorting glasses of official church historiographers with their disparaging concept of "heretical enthusiasm," this was now gradually changed as a result of Keller's labor. It was largely through him and others stirred by him that a fair picture and a full vindication of the Anabaptist movement was achieved.[73]

In addition to his discoveries concerning the essence of Anabaptism, Keller sought to connect the Anabaptists to earlier dissenting groups through a line of successionism. This successionist theory, which is similar to Newman's, linked the Anabaptists to dissenting groups he called *altevangelische Brüdergemeinden*, ("old evangelical brotherhoods"). For example, he postulated a direct connection between the Waldenses and the Anabaptists and believed that their distinctive ideas had always been present from the apostolic era throughout the history of the church.[74]

Keller's conclusions concerning the Anabaptists were not received enthusiastically. Some people in Münster called him *Wiedertäufer-Apostel*, smashed his windows and "attempted still worse persecution."[75] For fifteen years he endured literary attacks and hostility from his colleagues. In a letter to Anna Brons in 1886 he said, "I have quietly endured all the falseness and defamation that one person possibly could."[76]

Keller and the Mennonites

In addition to his academic endeavors to discover the truth about Anabaptism, Keller embarked on a mission for the reinstitution of the old evangelical brotherhood and its principles. He said to John Horsch:

> Just as in the "Evangelical Alliance" Lutherans, Methodists, Baptists, etc., meet from time to time, the Mennonites of

---

72. Sprunger, 13.

73. Robert Friedmann, "John Horsch and Ludwig Keller," *The Mennonite Quarterly Review* 21 (July 1947): 161.

74. *The Mennonite Encyclopedia*, 1955 ed., s.v. "Keller, Ludwig."

75. Ludwig Keller to Anna Brons, 15 September 1897, as cited by Sprunger, 14.

76. Ludwig Keller to Anna Brons, 28 November 1886, as cited by Sprunger, 14.

various branches could join with the Quakers, Schwenkfelders, Arminians, Remonstrants, Dunkers, several branches of the General Baptists, the Hutterian Brethren, several wings of the Presbyterians, etc., in brief all the parties that grew out of old Anabaptism, in an "Old-Evangelical Alliance."[77]

On 20 April 1887 in Berlin, he delivered an address entitled "*Zur Geschichte der Altevangelischen Gemeinden*," in which he specified basic ideas of his vision. He said that since the first century there had always been evangelical brotherhoods outside of the state church, aware of each other and continuing in spiritual succession. Their principles were: (1) a church made up of believers with voluntary adult membership and adult baptism; (2) cooperation between the groups functioning homogeneously; (3) no concept of denominational institution but rather the idea of brotherhood; (4) church discipline through the use of the ban; (5) the practice of Christian charity.[78]

Keller employed several means to institute his vision of a revival of the old evangelical brotherhood. In addition to his books, he published articles in the *Mennonitische Blatter* and *Gemeindeblatt*, two Mennonite periodicals.[79] Keller sought close contact with German and Dutch Mennonite preachers in order to win them over to his ideas. He also established contact with Mennonite historians such as John Horsch, Christian Neff, and Anna Brons through a series of letters. The letters to Horsch are particularly interesting, especially after 1887 when Horsch moved to America. Keller hoped that Horsch could help in spreading the old evangelical brotherhood ideas among the Mennonites in America.[80]

Keller's vision of a renewed old evangelical party eventually proved disappointing. The correspondence between Keller and Horsch as well as

---

77. Elizabeth Horsch Bender, ed. "The Letters of Ludwig Keller to John Horsch, 1885-1893," *The Mennonite Quarterly Review* 21 (July 1947): 202.

78. Friedmann, 162.

79. Keller's books include: *Geschichte der Wiedertäufer und ihres Reiches zu Münster* (1880), *Ein Apostel der Wiedertäufer* (1882), *Die Reformation und die älteren Reformparteien* (1885), *Die Waldenser und die deutschen Bibelübersetzungen* (1886), *Johann von Staupitz und die Anfänge der Reformation* (1888). *See The Mennonite Encyclopedia*, "Keller, Ludwig."

80. *The Mennonite Encyclopedia*, 1955 ed., s.v. "Keller, Ludwig, and the Mennonites." In America Horsch joined with Mennonite John Funk and used the *Herold der Wahrheit*, a Mennonite church paper started by Funk in 1864 to propagate the ideas of Keller. *See* Friedmann, 165-66.

other contact with the Mennonites ended abruptly. In 1892, Keller established the Comenius Gesellschaft, which was a church historical society with its focus on the old evangelical brotherhoods.[81] Keller broke suddenly with the Mennonites because he could not accept their system of being a closed community with strict discipline. Being "a staunch individualist with some inclination toward mysticism, [he] had very little appreciation for this type of church life."[82]

Newman and Keller[83]

Newman sought to relate Keller's ideas in America among his Baptist constituents by a series of articles in *The Western Recorder* and *The Canadian Baptist*.[84] In addition, he provided reviews of Keller's publications to the academic community.[85] In spite of his appreciation for Keller's work, Newman was critical at times. First, he observed that because Keller's work covered such a wide period of history, he tended to make use of secondary sources too frequently, although he said, "A few slips in the use of authorities or inadequate knowledge of certain parts of history should not be regarded as sufficient ground for the damning of an author's work as a whole."[86]

---

81. Friedmann, 171. He established this organization in memory of Johann Amos Comenius (1592-1670), the last bishop of the old church of the Moravian and Bohemian Brethren. It had a three-fold purpose: (1) the publication of Comenius' most important works as well as those of his predecessors and those who held similar ideas; (2) research centering on the old evangelical brotherhood; (3) the collection of books, manuscripts and other documents which had historical importance. *See The Mennonite Encyclopedia*, 1955 ed., s.v. "Comeniusgesellschaft." Newman was an honorary member of the society.

82. *The Mennonite Encyclopedia*, "Keller, Ludwig and the Mennonites."

83. Fountain, 55-60, provides a good comparison between Newman and Keller.

84. *See* Albert Henry Newman, "A German Vindication of Baptist Principles," *The Canadian Baptist*, 30 July 1885, 1 and 6 August 1885, 1. *Also see* Albert Henry Newman, "Dr. Ludwig Keller on the Relation of the Anabaptists to Earlier Evangelical Parties," *The Western Recorder*, 27 May 1897-13 January 1898, 1. (This was a seventeen-part series of articles in which Newman provided a translation of Keller's monograph entitled "The Beginnings of the Reformation and the Heretical Conventicles: Investigations on the History of the Waldenses at the Beginning of the Reformation." Newman made comments throughout the series concerning his appraisal of Keller's work).

85. Albert Henry Newman, "Recent Research Concerning Medieval Sects," *Papers of the American Society of Church History*, First Series, 4 (1891): 170-75.

86. Albert Henry Newman, "Recent Researches Concerning Medieval Sects," 173.

Second, Newman charged that Keller indulged in conjecture and ignored many facts that might modify some of his conclusions.

> While Keller is usually careful to characterize his conjectures as such, or to indicate that the conjectural statement is only probably correct, he often proceeds to build up an elaborate scheme on the basis of the conjecture, and he uses the conjecture in such a way as would lead one to suppose that he has come to regard it as well authenticated fact.[87]

Even though Newman was critical of Keller's work in certain places, his respect is obvious. "[H]e is a writer to whom Baptists should feel deeply grateful, and of whose works they cannot afford to be ignorant."[88] Furthermore, Newman found it hard to accept that Keller was a member of a denomination that practiced infant baptism, especially in light of the conclusions Keller reached concerning the Anabaptists. "So pronounced was his friendship for the 'heretics,' and so sharp his polemics against Luther and Zwingli, that I felt sure that he was a Baptist at heart."[89]

How much influence did Keller's concept of the old evangelical brotherhood have on Newman? Newman admitted that he did not accept all of Keller's historical conclusions.[90] However, his writings frequently mention the ideas of the old evangelical party and their continuation into the period of the Reformation as well as their extension back to apostolic times. Generally, he conceded that his "position is identical with that of Keller as regards the close historical connection of the old evangelical life of the

---

87. *Ibid.*, 174.

88. Albert Henry Newman, "Dr. Ludwig Keller on the Relation of the Anabaptists to Earlier Evangelical Parties," 27 May 1897, 1.

89. Albert Henry Newman, "Dr. Ludwig Keller on the Relation of the Anabaptists to Earlier Evangelical Parties," 27 May 1897, 1. On another occasion Newman said practically the same thing: "If it should be found that Dr. Keller has descended from some persecuted Baptist family of the sixteenth century, and so from the old evangelical part of the medieval time, the result would be quite of a piece with some of the assured results of his own investigations." *See* Albert Henry Newman, "A German Vindication of Baptist Principles," 30 July 1885, 1.

90. For example, Newman said: "I would not go quite so far as Ludwig Keller in laying claim to all the evangelical leaders and parties and all the advocates of civil and religious liberty during the medieval time as members of the one old-evangelical party." Albert Henry Newman, "The Significance of the Anabaptist Movement in the History of the Christian Church," 16.

middle ages with the anti-Pedobaptist movement of the sixteenth century."[91] Moreover, Newman specified that he had "long held" conclusions similar to Keller, "without being able to adduce complete proof of their correctness."[92]

Where did Newman and Keller differ? The difference centered in their appraisal of the medieval trade guilds and secret societies. Keller believed that these organizations were thoroughly imbued with the principles of old evangelical influence and were bearers of such ideas.[93] Newman, while accepting this as a possibility, could not find facts to warrant such a conclusion.[94] Furthermore, he indicated that Keller's sympathy was more with the old evangelical parties before the Reformation, than with the Anabaptists who sought to restore completely the apostolic principle.

> This attitude of Keller toward the evangelical parties of the Reformation time is a partial explanation of his own failure to take his stand in the ranks of the Baptists, where, so far as his convictions are concerned, he seems rightly to belong....[B]ut, like many of the old evangelicals of the medieval time, he is content to hold in abeyance the matter of the right administration of the ordinances, and from inside of one of the new evangelical parties of the state church type to seek to bring about the acceptance of old evangelical teaching and a proper appreciation of the character and importance of the old evangelical movement.[95]

Harold S. Bender

Newman was at the height of his career and had been teaching church history for twenty years in 1897, the year of Harold S. Bender's birth. Bender's career began in the mid-1920s, just a few years before Newman's retirement in 1929.

From the 1920s until his death in 1962, there can be no doubt that Bender was instrumental in causing the field of Anabaptist studies to

---

91. Albert Henry Newman, "Dr. Ludwig Keller on the Relation of the Anabaptists to Earlier Evangelical Parties," 27 May 1897, 1.

92. Albert Henry Newman, "A German Vindication of Baptist Principles," 30 July 1885, 1.

93. Fountain, 59-60.

94. Albert Henry Newman, "Dr. Ludwig Keller on the Relation of the Anabaptists to Earlier Evangelical Parties," 4 November 1897, 1.

95. Albert Henry Newman, "Dr. Ludwig Keller on the Relation of the Anabaptists to Earlier Evangelical Parties," 2 December 1897, 1.

blossom. He was responsible for organizing the Mennonite Historical Library, the Mennonite Historical Society, and for providing numerous publications concerning the Anabaptists.[96]

As Bender embarked on his career in Anabaptist historiography, it is not unusual that he should have corresponded with those whom he considered to be the prominent scholars in the field. One such scholar was Newman. The letters exchanged between Newman and Bender show that Bender greatly appreciated Newman's work in Anabaptist studies.

As president of the Mennonite Historical Society in 1925, Bender helped to organize a celebration of the quadricentennial anniversary of the first adult baptism in Zürich, which occurred in January 1525. Goshen College sponsored the celebration during the second week of June.[97] Bender invited Newman to be the keynote speaker for the program and paid compliment to his career as a church historian:

> you have put us all greatly in your debt through your splendid researches...to say nothing of your brilliant and solid work in the field of Church History at large....It is out of sincere appreciation and recognition of your services to the "Anabaptist" world, that I suggest that we would be highly honored.[98]

Newman accepted the invitation and delivered two addresses: "The Significance of the Anabaptist Movement in the History of the Christian Church," and "Balthazar Hubmaier and the Moravian Anabaptists."[99]

One of the points of discussion in the correspondence between Newman and Bender concerned Bender's desire to build a large collection of Anabaptistica at Goshen College. He consulted Newman at various times regarding Anabaptist documents and where they might be found.[100] In

---

96. *See The Mennonite Quarterly Review* 38 (April 1964). The entire issue is devoted to Bender as a memorial.

97. Harold S. Bender to A.H. Newman, TL, 21 February 1925, A.H. Newman file, Baylor University, 1.

98. *Ibid.*, 1-2.

99. A.H. Newman to Harold S. Bender, LS, 26 February 1925, Harold S. Bender Papers, Archives of the Mennonite Church, Goshen, Indiana, 1.

100. *See* for example, Harold S. Bender to A.H. Newman, TL, 10 March 1925, 2; 8 April 1925, 2; 23 June 1925, 2, A.H. Newman file, Baylor University.

addition, he asked Newman more than once if he knew of someone wealthy among the Baptists who was interested enough in history to finance some of the projects the Mennonites were desiring to undertake.[101] Bender lamented the fact that the Mennonites did not have a greater appreciation of their history which would bring funds to finance some of the historical projects. "We Mennonites have not yet learned to develop the appreciation for the historic as we hope to some day."[102] Newman seemed impressed with the young Bender and his colleague Ernst Correll.

> Goshen College is very fortunate in having on its faculty two such brilliant young scholars as yourself and Correll. I wish we had at Mercer...some historical scholars with the linguistic equipment and the enthusiasm for original research that I see in you two.[103]

So impressed was Newman with Bender's work that he recommended the young scholar's name for membership in the American Society of Church History.[104] Bender returned the favor by securing election for Newman into the Mennonite Historical Society out of respect for Newman's "outstanding contributions and first position in the field of American Anabaptist Historiography."[105]

Newman and Modern Anabaptist Historiography

How useful is Newman's work to modern Anabaptist scholars? There is hardly a reference to Newman in most of the leading works on the Anabaptists today although a few modern scholars refer to Newman's work

---

101. *See* Harold S. Bender to A.H. Newman, TL, 8 April 1925, 2 and 3 January 1929, 2, A.H. Newman file, Baylor University.

102. Harold S. Bender to A.H. Newman, TL, 26 April 1925, 1, A.H. Newman file, Baylor University. *Also see* Bender to Newman 8 April 1925, 2.

103. A.H. Newman to Harold S. Bender, LS, 20 February 1926, Mennonite Historical Archives, Goshen, Indiana, 1-2.

104. A.H. Newman to Harold S. Bender, LS, 3 July 1925, 2 and 3 August 1925, 2, Mennonite Historical Archives, Goshen, Indiana.

105. Harold S. Bender to A.H. Newman, 10 December 1926, Mennonite Historical Archives, Goshen, Indiana.

118

in their bibliographies.[106] But, for the most part, they do not use any of his work extensively. What reasons could account for this?

One explanation is that Newman's work is simply obsolete. The field of Anabaptist historiograpy has grown considerably since Newman's death. Franklin Littell alluded to this in *The Origins of Sectarian Protestantism* (1964). He noted that the "major primary materials have only lately become generally accessible" and that a "structural analysis of Anabaptism...must begin with the romance of source exhumation and rediscovery."[107] Even though Newman used primary sources in *A History of Anti-Pedobaptism*, they were just beginning to become available in his day and many more have been discovered since his death. The field of Anabaptist historiography has also changed significantly since Littell's work. Leonard Gross noted that with the death of Harold S. Bender in 1962, the "Vietnam Era" (1963-78) produced a new emphasis in Anabaptist studies. This period caused scholars to reappraise the "cause and effects of earlier revolutionary eras, including the significance (for Anabaptism) of Thomas Muntzer...and the Kingdom of Münster."[108] Continuing, Gross said:

> If Bender's era was that of establishing a thesis, as it indeed turned out to be, the Vietnam-era approach to Anabaptist studies can now be seen as a needed anti-thesis. Everything and anything within Anabaptist history was open to critique,

---

106. For example: George Huntston Williams, in *The Radical Reformation* (Philadelphia: The Westminster Press, 1962), 491, only cites one article by Newman. He does not mention *A History of Anti-Pedobaptism*. Peter James Klassen, *The Economics of Anabaptism* (London: Mouton and Company, 1964), 143, cites three of Newman's works in his bibliography. John Christian Wenger, *Even Unto Death* (Richmond: John Knox Press, 1961, 126, cites *A History of Anti-Pedobaptism* in his bibliography. George Huntston Williams and Angel M. Mergal, eds. *Spiritual and Anabaptist Writers* (Philadelphia: The Westminster Press, 1957), Vol. 25, *The Library of Christian Classics*, ed. by John Baillie, John T. McNeill, and Henry P. Van Dusen, cites only *A History of Anti-Pedobaptism*. Franklin Hamlin Littell, *The Anabaptist View of the Church* (Boston: Star King Press, 1958), 217, cites *A History of Anti-Pedobaptism*.

107. Franklin Hamlin Littell, *The Origins of Sectarian Protestantism* (New York: The Macmillan Company, 1964), 142-43.

108. Leonard Gross, foreword to *Becoming Anabaptist*, by J. Denny Weaver (Scottdale, PA: Herald Press, 1987), 10. *Also see* James M. Stayer, "The Anabaptists," in *Reformation Europe: A Guide to Research*, ed. Steven Ozment (St. Louis: Center For Reformation Research, 1982), 135-59.

with a number of scholars pushing hard to unseat, consciously, the work of earlier generations.[109]

From 1978 until present, Gross notes that a type of synthesis has prevailed in Anabaptist studies, seeking to combine the work of previous Anabaptist historiography with that of the revisionists in the Vietnam era.[110] It can be surmised, therefore, that at least four eras can be located in modern Anabaptist historiography: the early period beginning with the late nineteenth century work by Keller, Horsch, and others; the Bender era; the Vietnam era; and the current period. Primary materials for Anabaptist studies have been discovered in each of these eras. Newman's work is located in the early period (although he did participate Bender era) and many new revelations concerning the nature of the Anabaptists have since been recorded.

Evidence exists that Newman's work was becoming outdated as early as 1914. A. J. Rowland, Secretary of the American Baptist Publication Society wrote to Newman in 1914 regarding the sales of *A History of Anti-Pedobaptism*. He said:

> I find we still have a couple of hundred copies of your "History of Anti-Pedobaptism," and this will be enough to last us for some time to come, as the demand for the book in recent years has not been great. Perhaps if you wish to make additions or corrections you might go over the volume and send the material to us so that if necessary we can change the plates or make new plates in view of the possibility of our issuing another edition.[111]

Another reason modern scholars in Anabaptist studies generally do not use Newman's work relates to his assumptions about the movement which have become outdated. One of Newman's basic ideas was that the Anabaptists maintained a spiritual kinship with the Medieval dissent groups,

---

109. Gross, 10-11. Stayer calls the work of the earlier Anabaptist scholars "free church historiography." He said their purpose was to "make the ugly duckling of the Reformation into its most beautiful swan." Concerning the work of revisionists, Stayer said, "the net effect of the new research has been to accomplish a major revision, which can be summarized as ending both the isolation of the Anabaptist field and the idealization of the Anabaptists" (p. 136).

110. Gross, 11.

111. A. J. Rowland to Albert Henry Newman, TL, 9 November 1914, Albert Henry Newman File, Baylor University. Newman never revised the book.

most notably, the Waldensians. But Littell noted that in modern Anabaptist historiography, "the evidence is too slight to sustain the weight of [these]...theses."[112]

Newman's purpose as an Anabaptist scholar is another explanation of why his work is no longer used. He desired to study the Anabaptists for the purpose of understanding Baptist history, which in turn would address the problems the Baptists of his day were encountering. "Much of his writing bore directly upon the problems that were troubling the best minds of the denomination."[113] The majority of his publications are in periodicals or journals whose primary reading audience was Baptist. Therefore he served as an interpreter of the Anabaptists to his Baptist readers, attempting to show that the Anabaptists were the spiritual forefathers of the Baptists. Newman's Anabaptist writings, especially *A History of Anti-Pedobaptism*, are largely interpretive in character. He told the story of the Anabaptists largely through emphasis on the characters within the movement. The strength of his work was in its interpretive quality, not that it revealed new material. He served as a popularizer of the Anabaptist movement rather than a discoverer.

> I have no ambition to be regarded as a discoverer. I am content to examine carefully such historical materials as interest me, and are accessible, and it is my aim to interpret and apply judiciously such materials as I may have occasion to reproduce.[114]

---

112. Littell, *The Origins of Sectarian Protestantism*, 153. Litell mentions specifically the work of Keller and Albert Ritschl although the comment would apply to Newman as well. Keller concentrated on identifying the Anabaptists with the Waldensians while Ritschl attempted to identify them with the Franciscan order.

113. Eby, 123.

114. Albert Henry Newman, "The Whitsitt Controversy," 223.

Conclusion

Newman developed an interest in studying the Anabaptists as a result of two factors in his overall historiography. First, his favorable bias toward his own denomination, the Baptists, caused him to investigate any group prior to the seventeenth century which had similar qualities. He saw in the Anabaptist movement the antecedents of the rise of seventeenth-century Baptists. Similarly, a second reason for Newman's interest in the Anabaptists related to his use of the Spiritual Kinship Theory of Baptist origins. Newman saw a close kinship between Anabaptists and Baptists. Therefore, he sought to investigate the former in order to shed further light on the nature of the latter group.

Newman served as one of the pioneers in modern Anabaptist historiography by assigning to the movement its rightful place in Reformation historiography, helping to destroy the false interpretation that all Anabaptists shared the same traits as the fanatic radicals at Münster. He was among the first scholars to provide different classifications of Anabaptists.

Although Newman is recognized by some modern Anabaptist scholars as a leader in the early days of Anabaptist historiography, his work is seldom used. This is because of the dramatic changes in the field of Anabaptist studies due to the discovery of new primary source materials and the publication of better interpretations. Many of Newman's ideas about the Anabaptist movement are outdated such as the notion that the sixteenth-century Anabaptists were descendents of the medieval Waldensians. Newman was not a discoverer of Anabaptist history. He was a popularizer of the movement, primarily to his own denomination the Baptists, with the hope that his work would stimulate Baptists to investigate their history further.

CHAPTER IV

ALBERT HENRY NEWMAN AND BAPTIST HISTORIOGRAPHY

Introduction

Before the nineteenth century Baptist historians worked largely as compilers and recorders of events. The work of American Baptist compilers such as John Comer, John Callender, Benjamin Griffith, John Stanford, Morgan Edwards, John Asplund, and Isaac Backus served as important source material for later historians. But these men could not be classified as historians because, while the "historian seeks to relate and interpret what has happened as well as to describe it; the chronicler...simply records events and describes activities as they occur."[1]

In England, Thomas Crosby provided a break with the American trend in the eighteenth century. His *A History of the English Baptists* (1738-40) represents the first attempt to write a history of Baptists. He tried "to correct what he considered to be the inaccurate accounts of the Baptists given by other writers."[2] Crosby attempted to defend believer's baptism; dissociate English Baptists from continental Anabaptists, especially those of the

---

1. W. Morgan Patterson, "Baptist Historiography in America in the Eighteenth Century," *Review and Expositor* 52 (October 1955): 483. Patterson surveys the work of each of these eighteenth century Baptist chroniclers.

2. B. R. White, "The Task of the Baptist Historian," *The Baptist Quarterly* 22 (October 1968): 399. White has two articles specifically on Crosby's life and work. *See* "Thomas Crosby, Baptist Historian," *The Baptist Quarterly* 21 (October 1965): 154-68 and (January 1966): 219-34.

Münster type; and provide an overall defense of the Baptist denomination. Furthermore, he desired to see a union between the General and Particular Baptists of England.[3] Crosby was the first Baptist historian to popularize the notion of tracing a continuity of Baptist teachings from New Testament times to the present as he attempted to show "that Baptist principles not only root in the New Testament but also can be traced through various groups since then."[4]

The beginning of the nineteenth century brought several new presentations of Baptist history. Adam Taylor, disturbed by Crosby's attempts to promote union between the General and Particular Baptists, sought to defend the principles of the General Baptists in his *A History of the English General Baptists*, 2 vols. (1818). Joseph Ivimey, in his *A History of the English Baptists*, 4 vols. (1811-30), attempted to prove that English Baptists were the true followers of the Reformation tradition and had pursued that tradition to its logical consequences.[5] Ivimey also perpetuated Crosby's views concerning a spiritual succession of Baptist-like ideas.[6] In America, David Benedict published *A General History of the Baptist Denomination in America and Other Parts of the World* (1813), and was the first significant advocate of spiritual kinship in America.[7]

---

3.   White, "The Task of the Baptist Historian," 399-400.

4.   McBeth, 57. Patterson, *Baptist Successionism*, 24, shows that Crosby's work was among those cited by the lineal successionists of the nineteenth century. Though Crosby did not espouse lineal succession, he failed to make critical distinctions at times. Patterson notes the difference between Crosby and the lineal successionists: "individuals and groups which had previously been characterized by Crosby and others as possessing one or two features in common with Baptists became Baptists in everything but name....Thus, a casual observation of similarity by Crosby was eventually adjudged proof of the Baptist nature of a sect by later uncritical historians."

5.   McBeth, 57.

6.   *Ibid.*

7.   *Ibid.* McBeth identifies four categories concerning Baptist origins: "The Outgrowth of English Separatism," "Anabaptist Influence," "Continuation of Biblical Teachings," and "Succession of Baptist Churches" (*see* 49-60). There is a slight difference between Torbet's typology and McBeth's. Torbet lists only three categories: "The Successionist Theory," "Anabaptist Spiritual Kinship Theory," and "English Separatist Descent Theory" (Torbet, 18-21). McBeth divides Torbet's spiritual kinship category into "Anabaptist Influence" and "Continuation of Biblical Teachings," and implies that the "Anabaptist Influence" category is a

The writing of Baptist history blossomed during the last quarter of the nineteenth century, especially in America. This chapter is divided into two major sections. The first section will discuss the most significant Baptist historians who were contemporary with Newman and their ideas concerning the issue of Baptist origins. The second section of the chapter will concentrate on the Whitsitt Controversy at the Southern Baptist Theological Seminary. This dispute, involving Newman, concerned one of the major denominational conflicts of the era; it was based on differing understandings of Baptist history.

Baptist Historiography and the Issue of Baptist Origins

Chapter two showed how the general field of church history grew into a professional discipline during Newman's career. Baptist historiography essentially followed the same course of development. During this "golden age" of Baptist historical writing, Baptists were concerned with several issues. These may be gathered into three categories: conflict concerning Baptist origins; theological problems related to the Fundamentalist/Modernist struggle; and controversy surrounding the Social Gospel movement.[8] Because Newman devoted most of his work to the first category and little written attention to the latter two, this section will be confined to issues related to different interpretations of Baptist origins.

Thomas Armitage

Thomas Armitage migrated from England, where he was born in 1819, to America in 1838. He converted from Methodism to the Baptist denomination after grappling with the issue of baptism. Although Armitage spent his career as a pastor rather than a professional historian, he wrote one of the most important Baptist histories of his era, *A History of the Baptists:*

---

more modern offshoot of the spiritual kinship theory. While he does not use the same terminology as Torbet's "Spiritual Kinship Theory," the categories do correspond.

8. *See* Robert T. Handy, "Themes for Research in Baptist History Since 1865," *The Chronicle* 16 (July 1953): 134-39; Winthrop S. Hudson, "Themes for Research in Baptist History," *The Chronicle* 17 (January 1954): 3-23; Edwin S. Gaustad, "Themes for Research in American Baptist History," *Foundations* 6 (April 1963): 146-73; and Dwight A. Honeycutt, "A Study of the Life and Thought of Henry Clay Vedder," (Th.D. diss., New Orleans Baptist Theological Seminary, 1984), 3.

Traced By Their Vital Principles and Practices, From the Time of Our Lord and Saviour Jesus Christ to the Year 1886.[9]

Armitage holds a distinct place in Baptist historiography. He was the first to see clearly the implausibility of lineal succession. He reached four conclusions concerning successionist claims:

> 1. That Christ never established a law of Christian primogeniture by which he endowed local churches with the exclusive power of moral regeneration, making it necessary for one church to be the mother of another, in regular succession, and without which they could not be legitimate churches.
>
> 2. Our Lord never promised an organic visibility to his Church in perpetuity, amongst any people or in any age.
>
> 3. Christ never promised to his churches their absolute preservation from error.
>
> 4. The world is vastly more indebted to a line of individual men who have contended for the truth, each by himself, than to any organic churches, which can be traced by visible succession from the Apostles, under any name whatever.[10]

Armitage claimed that the attempt to provide an unbroken succession of churches "is in itself an attempt to erect a bulwark of error."[11] Furthermore, a contradiction exists when Protestants, who argue convincingly against papal succession, invent their own type of lineal descent. Such an argument was "necessary only to such Churches as regulate their faith and practice by tradition, and for their use it was invented."[12]

Yet, in keeping with Crosby, Ivimey, and Benedict, Armitage held to spiritual succession. He argued that "true lineage from the Apostolic Churches...rest[s] in present conformity to the apostolic pattern."[13] Armitage admitted that the thesis of his *A History of the Baptists* was "to follow certain

---

9. Thomas Armitage, *A History of the Baptists: Traced By Their Vital Principles and Practices, From the Time of Our Lord and Saviour Jesus Christ to the Year 1886* (New York: Bryan, Taylor and Company, 1887).

10. *Ibid.*, 3-6.

11. *Ibid.*, 2.

12. *Ibid.*

13. *Ibid.*, 1.

truths through the ages...down to their chief conservators of this time, the Baptists."[14]

Clearly, Newman did not originate the Spiritual Kinship Theory of Baptist origins. He was already well into his academic career when Armitage's *A History of the Baptists* was published, and his ideas of spiritual kinship could not have come solely from Armitage. Instead, it seems that he refined a theory that was already prevalent among writers of Baptist history, extending as far back as Crosby, Ivimey, and Benedict. Newman carried the concept further than any of the previous historians by his extensive research in the dissenting sects (especially the Anabaptists) throughout the history of the church.

Henry Clay Vedder

Born just six months after Newman, Henry Clay Vedder was probably the most prolific Baptist historian during Newman's career. Both men were students at the Rochester Theological Seminary, with Newman graduating in 1875, and Vedder the following year.

In 1894, Vedder accepted the chair of church history at Crozer Theological Seminary thereby ending a career as a journalist on the editorial staff of *The Examiner*, a post he had held since his graduation from Rochester Theological Seminary. During his years at Crozer, Vedder underwent a significant change in his theological outlook.[15] Along with Shailer Matthews and Walter Rauschenbusch, Vedder became a significant spokesperson among Baptists for the Social Gospel Movement.[16] Vedder's change in thinking occurred gradually between 1908 and 1911, just before the publication of his *Socialism and the Ethics of Jesus* (1912). Hanley points to three influences which brought about this shift in Vedder's thought: the acceptance of the theory of evolution; a Marxist economic interpretation of

---

14. *Ibid.*, 11.

15. This change has been documented well in Honeycutt's dissertation. Also *see* Robert B. Hanley, "Henry Clay Vedder: Conservative Evangelical to Evangelical Liberal," *Foundations* 5 (April 1962): 135-57 and G. Keith Parker, "Henry Clay Vedder, Church Historian," *The Quarterly Review* 31 (October 1970): 65-85.

16. Honeycutt, 82.

128

history; and a philosophy of pragmatism.[17]   Although Vedder encountered
attacks from fellow Baptists for his theological change of opinion, he was
never forced to resign his position at Crozer.[18]

Much of Vedder's work as a historian of the Baptists came during his
"orthodox" period.[19]   Concerning Baptist origins, Vedder clearly did not
advocate lineal succession. "Our theory of the church as deduced from the
Scriptures requires no outward and visible succession from the apostles."[20]
Vedder seemed to adhere to a type of spiritual kinship theory, though not as
pronounced as Newman's.[21] There were three editions of his *A Short History
of the Baptists* and each edition vigorously rejected lineal succession while
maintaining that Baptist-like principles did exist throughout the history of the
church.

> The attempt has been made, at one time or another, to identify
> as Baptists nearly every sect that separated from the Roman
> Church. It will not suffice to prove that most of these sects
> held certain doctrines from which the great body of Christians
> had departed—doctrines that Baptists now hold, and that are
> believed by them to be clearly taught in the New
> Testament—or that the so-called heretics were often more
> pure in doctrine and practice than the body that assumed to be

17. Hanley, 137-144.

18. Honeycutt points out that neither Crozer nor its board of trustees was related officially to
the Baptist convention in the North because the convention was not formally established until
1907, after the founding of the school. The school was formally incorporated by the state of
New York in 1910. Because the school was autonomous, it was more open to different ideas
and Vedder was relatively safe from censure. Honeycutt further admits that this environment
of freedom served to stimulate the development of Vedder's theological thought. *See*
Honeycutt, 44-45.

19. Parker, 72. This does not imply that Vedder ceased his historical work after his
theological change. However, most of his work on Baptist history dates from the early period,
with the exception of *A Short History of Baptist Missions* (1927).

20. Henry Clay Vedder, *A Short History of the Baptists*, 2d rev. ed., (Philadelphia: American
Baptist Publication Society, 1907), 7.

21. Some of Newman's writings reveal that he was more sympathetic with the successionists.
"For myself, I am anxious to find as many Baptists as possible in every land and in every age.
What I object to is the determination to prove an unbroken succession by hook or by crook,
and the seeming implication that such succession is essential to present day baptism." (*See*
Albert Henry Newman to T. T. Eaton, cited in Albert Henry Newman, "The Whitsitt
Controversy," 150). Vedder showed no evidence of identification with lineal successionist
claims.

the only orthodox and Catholic Church. This is quite different from proving the substantial identity of these sects with modern Baptists....It is one thing to prove that the various heretical sects bore testimony...[to] truth held by a modern denomination; and quite another thing to identify...these sects with any one modern body.[22]

McBeth places Vedder in the same category with Newman in reference to Baptist origins although he qualifies his statement by saying, "[t]hough Vedder sought to trace Baptist principles through the centuries, he recognized that Baptist history reached 'solid ground' only in the early seventeenth century."[23]

Although not mentioned in Vedder's first edition of *A Short History of the Baptists*, the two revised editions highlight the fact that the Mennonites influenced John Smyth and the rise of the General Baptists. He related that while in Holland, Smyth became acquainted with Arminian theology, and "here it is also reasonable to suppose, he learned the Mennonite theory of the nature of the church."[24] Although Vedder recognized the Anabaptist influence on the rise of the Baptists, he did not discuss the issue as comprehensively as did Newman.[25]

Newman and Vedder had some similarities in their approaches to Baptist history. Yet, the two men differed in their careers. Vedder used his craft as a historian to advocate the Social Gospel, and as a result, experienced a radical shift in theology. Newman's career and theology underwent no such change. Vedder's literary output was greater than that of Newman. This is due, at least in part, to the move that Newman made to Baylor University in 1901. Had he remained at his position at McMaster, he would have been in closer contact with the "cutting edge" of his field and probably would have generated more research. Vedder and Newman were

---

22. Vedder, *A Short History of the Baptists* (1891), 45-46; (1897), 46-47; (1907), 8.

23. McBeth, 58. He is citing a statement by Vedder, found in *A Short History of the Baptists*, rev. ed., (1897), 135; (1907), 201. Torbet identifies Vedder within the "English Separatist Descent" camp while McBeth placed him in the "Continuation of Biblical Teachings" category. McBeth's classification seems to be more accurate.

24. Vedder, *A Short History of the Baptists*, rev. ed., (1897), 136; (1907), 203.

25. *See* Albert Henry Newman, *A History of AntiPedobaptism: From the Rise of Pedobaptism to A.D. 1609*, 339-93.

separated by the differences between the intellectual climates of the Northeast and Texas.

William Thomas Whitley

Many Baptist historians in the late nineteenth century emphasized the theory that the Anabaptists influenced the rise of the seventeenth-century Baptists. Gradually, however, during the early years of the twentieth century, some Baptist historians began to move away from this idea, thereby rejecting notions of spiritual succession.[26] "This amounts to a revolution not just in Baptist historiography but in their whole attitude to their past."[27]

William Thomas Whitley, a major force in English Baptist historiography during this era, serves as an example of this change among Baptist historians. Whitley was a prolific historian. He wrote numerous journal articles and several books concerning Baptist history, including *A History of the British Baptists* (1923), and *The Baptists of London* (1928). He also edited early Baptist source materials which included *Minutes of the General Assembly of the General Baptist Churches in England*, and *The Works of John Smyth*.[28]

Whitley, early in his career, accepted the idea of Anabaptist influence on the rise of the Baptists. In 1909 he wrote, "The General Baptists are an English outgrowth of the Continental Anabaptists," and made reference to "the constant interaction of the Dutch Anabaptists and the English, for at least half a century."[29] Some fourteen years later, however, Whitley changed

---

26. In addition to Newman, Walter Rauschenbusch held to spiritual succession and emphasized Anabaptist influence on the rise of the English Baptists, while many other Baptist historians were moving away from the concept. Sellers mistakenly comments: "At the very time therefore that mainstream American Baptist scholars were repudiating the Anabaptist heritage...an advanced liberal was rediscovering it....Almost single-handed, Rauschenbusch had guaranteed that for a generation only Baptists of the theological and political left would care to appropriate the Anabaptists as their spiritual forebears." Sellers disregards Newman, who certainly was not on the theological or political left. *See* Ian Sellers, "Edwardians, Anabaptists and the Problem of Baptist Origins," *The Baptist Quarterly* 29 (July 1981):, 101.

27. Sellers, 99.

28. McBeth, 50.

29. William Thomas Whitley, ed., *Minutes of the General Assembly of the General Baptist Churches in England*, Vol. 1, (London: Kingsgate Press, 1909), ix, xi, as cited by *Ibid.*

his mind and rejected Anabaptist influence. In *A History of the British Baptists*, he included a section entitled, "Origin Independent of the Anabaptists." Whitley began the section by saying, "Baptists are to be sharply distinguished from the Anabaptists of the Continent, some of whom took refuge in England as early as 1530."[30] Moreover, he concluded that "[i]t is unexcusable today to confound the continental Anabaptists of the sixteenth century with the English Baptists of the seventeenth."[31] Whitley attributed the rise of the Baptists to the publication of the Scriptures in the vernacular and "to the consequent emergence of questions about the Church."[32]

Henry Sweetser Burrage

Another Baptist historian contemporary with Newman, Henry Sweetser Burrage, became one of the first scholars to espouse totally the concept that Baptists find their roots only within English Separatism, thereby discounting Anabaptist influence.[33] Burrage, having spent a year at the University of Halle in Germany (1868-69), came back to the United States and worked primarily in the area of local Baptist history within the New England context. He edited the periodical *Zion's Advocate* from 1873-1905. Beginning in 1907, Burrage served as the state historian in Maine. He also wrote several important Baptist works including *A History of the Baptists in New England* (1894).[34]

Burrage's son, Champlin, shared his father's convictions concerning Baptist beginnings. Champlin Burrage spent most of his career in the study of Cretan archeology. But his thesis for the B. Litt. degree from Oxford was published as *The Early English Dissenters in Light of Recent Research*, 2 Vol. (1912). In this work the younger Burrage expounded upon the issues stirred up during the Whitsitt Controversy, and agreed basically with Whitsitt's conclusions. He also discounted any influence upon the rise of English

---

30. W. T. Whitley, *A History of the British Baptists* (London: Charles Griffin and Company, 1923), 17.

31. *Ibid.*, 18.

32. *Ibid.*

33. Sellers, 100.

34. *Who Was Who in America*, 1943 ed., s.v. "Burrage, Henry Sweetser."

Baptists by the Anabaptists. "The name 'Baptist' or 'Baptists' appears never to have been applied before 1641 to those English people who espoused the cause of Anabaptism."[35] He also concluded that "the word Anabaptist even in these early times was evidently employed as a generic term to designate separatists, or indeed any persons of irregular or fanatical religious opinions."[36]

Baptist Historiography After Newman's Era

During the early years of the twentieth century, the English Separatist Descent concept of Baptist origins became the most widely accepted theory.[37] In 1953, Winthrop Hudson's article, "Baptists Were Not Anabaptists," brought the discussion of Baptist origins into the modern era. Hudson began the article with a forceful statement:

> The single most confusing element in the attempt to understand the Baptist heritage and to clarify the theological convictions which led Baptists to adopt their distinctive witness has been the identification of the Baptists with the Continental Anabaptists.[38]

He then summarized his thesis in five points. First, the early Baptists were adamant in their repudiation of the name Anabaptist, believing it to be an unjust term placed upon them. Second, early Baptists clearly rejected certain distinctive features of Anabaptism such as opposition to civil magistracy, Christians holding public office, military service, oaths, going to court, the doctrine of soul sleep, the belief that Christ received his flesh apart from Mary, and rejection of original sin. Third, the early Baptists had all been Separatists before they adopted Baptist views. Fourth, to account for the rejection of infant baptism does not necessitate a hypothesis of Anabaptist influence. Fifth, when Smyth opted to follow the Anabaptists, the remainder

---

35. Champlin Burrage, *The Early English Dissenters in the Light of Recent Research*, Vol. 1, *History and Criticism* (Cambridge: The University Press, 1912), 26.

36. *Ibid.*, 41.

37. Sellers, 99.

38. Winthrop S. Hudson, "Baptists Were Not Anabaptists," *The Chronicle* 16 (October 1953): 171. *Also see* Winthrop S. Hudson, "Who Were the Baptists?" *The Baptist Quarterly* 16 (July 1956): 303-312; and 17 (April 1957): 53-55.

of his church which returned to England dissociated themselves from him, thereby rejecting any Anabaptist influence.[39]

Another position, developed in modern Baptist historiography and contrary to Hudson's article, could be considered a modern outgrowth of the spiritual kinship theory. This viewpoint recognizes Anabaptist influence, yet it does not espouse spiritual succession of Baptist principles, the belief of early advocates of Anabaptist influence. There are several modern Baptist scholars who support this viewpoint.[40]

Most of those who promote this position emphasize a narrow point of contact: "*some* English Baptists (the General Baptists) may have been influenced by *some* of the Anabaptists (the Dutch Mennonites) at a *specific time* (the early seventeenth century).[41] They point to various similarities between the General Baptists and the Mennonites such as believers' baptism, religious liberty, separation of church and state, and Arminian views concerning salvation.[42]

Scholars accepting this position include Alfred Clair Underwood, who in *A History of the English Baptists*, said "It is impossible to believe that John Smyth's contacts with the Mennonites did not inoculate him with some of their ideas."[43] Furthermore, he concluded that even though most of the English General Baptists rejected Smyth upon their return to England, his influence continued in the area of oaths and magistrates. Underwood noted that with the Restoration of 1660, certain General Baptists opted for prison rather than recite an oath of allegiance. Nevertheless, Underwood concluded that there are many probabilities and warned against being too dogmatic.[44]

---

39. Hudson, "Baptists Were Not Anabaptists," 171-76. Other scholars who reject Anabaptist influence are H. Leon McBeth, William G. McLoughlin, and Robert Torbet.

40. It should be noted that Ernest A. Payne, an English Baptist historian wrote a direct rebuttal of Hudson's article for *The Baptist Quarterly Review*. *See* Ernest A. Payne, "Who Were the Baptists?" *The Baptist Quarterly Review* 16 (October 1956): 339-42.

41. McBeth, 53. The emphasis is McBeth's.

42. *Ibid.*

43. A. C. Underwood, *A History of the English Baptists* (London: Kingsgate Press, 1947), 52.

44. *Ibid.*, 54-55. Underwood recognized that there could have been other factors contributing to the General Baptist rejection of oaths and magistrates such as a "prevailing biblicism" or influence from the Quakers. Therefore, it is difficult to make a dogmatic

William R. Estep, also an advocate of the Anabaptist influence position, concentrated on Thomas Helwys, who led the remainder of Smyth's congregation back to England. He concluded:

> There is no doubt that Helwys did not reproduce the Waterlander faith and practice in every detail. There were significant differences. But the determinative features of his theology...are Anabaptist remolded in the midst of controversy and in the light of his own understanding of the Bible. This is not to deny the role of the Scriptures in the formulation of Helwys' Baptist faith but it is to recognize the molding influence that enabled him to recognize in the New Testament the essential features of that faith we readily recognize as Baptist.[45]

Furthermore, Estep concluded that the Particular Baptists, influenced by Anabaptism, arose out of English Separatism, by way of the General Baptists, although the influence was "mediated more by books and tracts than by personal contact."[46]

The discussion concerning Baptist beginnings has experienced a transformation during the twentieth century. At the beginning of the century, the English Separatist descent ideas were in vogue among many Baptist scholars. Ideas concerning succession, both lineal and spiritual were being discounted (with the exception of Newman and Rauschenbusch). By mid-century the most vocal champion of the English Separatist theory was Winthrop S. Hudson. The evidence suggests that Newman maintained his belief in spiritual kinship throughout his career even though the theory lost support among Baptist historians in the early years of the twentieth century. In recent years, however, some Baptist scholars have given more attention to

---

statement in support of direct Mennonite influence upon the General Baptists. Nevertheless, the Christological similarities between Mennonites and General Baptists as well as refusals to allow marriages outside of their communion may be used to support the influence theory.

45. W. R. Estep, "Anabaptists and the Rise of English Baptists," *The Quarterly Review* 29 (January 1969): 57. The first half of this article appeared in *The Quarterly Review* 28 (October 1968): 43-53. Another article by Estep representing this position is, unfortunately, unpublished. It is entitled "On the Origin of English Baptists," (1980).

46. W. R. Estep, "Anabaptists and the Rise of English Baptists," Part 2, 62. Other modern scholars holding to the Anabaptist influence theory are Ernest A. Payne, James D. Mosteller and Mennonite scholars Irvin B. Horst and Harold S. Bender. *See* McBeth, 53.

the idea of Anabaptist influence, yet without advocating any type of spiritual succession.

The Whitsitt Controversy

During the last decade of the nineteenth century, the issue of Baptist beginnings became a factor that almost split the Southern Baptist Convention. The incident, which brought forth serious doubts concerning the perpetuity of Baptist churches from apostolic times, centered around William Heth Whitsitt, president of the Southern Baptist Theological Seminary in Louisville, Kentucky. Newman, at the time living in Toronto, Canada, assumed the role of mediator in the controversy.

The Beginning of the Controversy

The Whitsitt Controversy was the symptom of a much greater problem in the Southern Baptist Convention, namely, conflict concerning Landmarkism's claims of lineal succession.[47] As history grew into a professional discipline, Baptist historians began to discount the claim of a lineal succession of Baptist churches. At the heart of the Whitsitt Controversy was a confrontation between Landmarkists, desiring to retain their lineal successionist claims, and the practical application of scientific history to the issue, which discounted this view regarding Baptist beginnings.

Born in 1841, Whitsitt graduated from Union University in Jackson, Tennessee in 1861. After serving as a scout for the Confederate Army during the Civil War, Whitsitt attended the University of Virginia briefly and the Southern Baptist Theological Seminary (1866-68). He then spent two years in Germany studying at the universities of Leipzig and Berlin. In 1872, Whitsitt accepted the chair of Ecclesiastical History at the Southern Baptist Theological Seminary. Upon the death of John Albert Broadus in 1895, Whitsitt assumed the presidency of the seminary.[48]

The controversy surrounding Whitsitt began with his publication of an article entitled "Baptists" for *Johnson's Universal Cyclopedia.* The article,

47. Beck, 73.

48. Norman Wade Cox and Judson Boyce Allen, eds., *Encyclopedia of Southern Baptists* (Nashville: Broadman Press, 1958), s.v. "Whitsitt, William Heth," by Gaines S. Dobbins.

consisting of five pages, sought to depict Baptist history and doctrine. While describing the origin of the name "Baptist" Whitsitt wrote:

> Some have fancied that the new title was claimed and maintained because of the change in the form of administering baptism, which is alleged to have occurred about the year 1641, when immersion was substituted in the place of sprinkling and pouring.[49]

Whitsitt stated that before 1641, Baptists did not practice immersion regularly as a form of baptism and also that the mode of Roger Williams' baptism in 1639 was probably sprinkling. "These seemingly innocuous pronouncements set off an unparalleled furor across the South and ignited a tension-filled situation among Southern Baptists."[50]

These conclusions were not new to Whitsitt. They were the result of three months study in England thirteen years earlier, where he encountered various sources related to early Baptist history, including the famous "Kiffin Manuscript," a part of the "Jessey Church Records." Analysis of these documents provided the evidence that led Whitsitt to his conclusions. The "Kiffin Manuscript" provides the explanation for the recovery of immersion as the regular form of baptism among the Particular Baptists.

> 1640, 3d Mo: The Church became two by mutuall consent just half being wth Mr P. Barebone, & ye other halfe with Mr H. Iessey Mr Richard Blunt wth him being convinced of baptism yt also it ought to be by diping ye Body into ye Water, resembling Burial & riseing again. 2 Col: 2. 12, Rom: 6. 4 had sober conferance about in ye Church, & then wth some of the forenamed who also ware so convinced: And after Prayer & conferance about their so enjoying it, none haveing then so so [sic] practised in England to professed Believers, & hearing that some in ye Nether Lands had so practised they agreed & sent over Mr Rich. Blunt (who understood Dutch) wth Letters of Comendation, who was kindly accepted there, & returned wth Letters from them Io: Batte a Teacher there, & from that Church to such as sent him.
>
> 1641: They proceed on therein, viz, Those Persons yt ware persuaded Baptism should be by dipping ye Body had mett in

49. Charles Kendall Adams, ed., *Johnson's Universal Cyclopedia* (New York: D. Appleton and Company, 1893), s.v. "Baptists," by William H. Whitsitt, as cited by Beck, 87.

50. Beck, 88.

tow Companies, & did intend so to meet after this, all these agreed to proceed alike togeather.[51]

Upon discovery of this document in 1880, Whitsitt published his findings anonymously in two editorials in *The Independent*, a nondenominational periodical. These two editorials related Whitsitt's ideas in a written debate over the question of baptism with Dr. Henry Dexter of the *Congregationalist*. The language of the *Independent* editorials was stronger than that of the later encyclopedia article. For instance, concerning Roger Williams in the *Independent*, Whitsitt said:

> Roger Williams never was a Baptist in the modern sense – that is, never was immersed; and the ceremony referred to was anabaptism, rebaptism by sprinkling, and not "catabaptism" or baptism by immersion....The burden of proof rests entirely upon those who assert that Williams was immersed.[52]

Because the editorials were anonymous, there was no response from Whitsitt's Baptist constituents until he acknowledged authorship of them subsequent to the publication of the encyclopedia article thirteen years later. He then proceeded to write additional articles and a book, *A Question in Baptist History* (1896), in order to explain and defend his position.[53] In the introduction Whitsitt posed two questions which identified the purpose of the book.

> Whether the immersion of adult believers was practiced in England by the Anabaptists before the year 1641? Whether these English people first adopted immersion for baptism and thus became Baptists in or about the year 1641?[54]

After publication of *A Question in Baptist History*, reactions from opposing sides came forth, both in denominational papers and in state conventions and associations.[55] The most severe reaction came from *The*

51. Champlin Burrage, *The Early English Dissenters In Light of Recent Research*, Vol. 2, (Cambridge: The University Press, 1912), 302-3.

52. *Independent* 31 (2 September 1880): 17.

53. Beck, 88.

54. William H. Whitsitt, *A Question in Baptist History*, (Louisville: Charles T. Dearing, 1896), p. 5.

55. James Thomas Meigs, "The Whitsitt Controversy," *The Quarterly Review* 31 (January 1971): p. 48.

Western Recorder, the Baptist state paper for Kentucky. Whitsitt's critics basically used two strategies. First they attempted to discredit the authenticity of the Kiffin Manuscript by arguing that it was a forgery. Second, they contended that Whitsitt's views were too uncertain and narrow to present a credible case. The two most vocal antagonists toward Whitsitt were Thomas Treadwell Eaton, editor of *The Western Recorder* and John T. Christian, who wrote a counter-argument to Whitsitt's position in *Did They Dip?*.[56]

Beck argued that Whitsitt's major error was that he first published his findings in non-Baptist literature. The decade of the 1890s found Southern Baptists exerting their denominational pride. Many Baptists felt betrayed that Whitsitt would choose first to release his findings outside of the denomination. "This facet of the issue was clear and little confusion clouded the minds of Baptists....No unanimity existed on the historical question, but everyone agreed on the problem of publication."[57]

In defense of Whitsitt, E. B. Pollard argued that his reasons for publishing the articles anonymously outside of Southern Baptist periodicals were due to his knowledge that they would elicit criticism, not only upon himself, but also upon the seminary. This he wanted to avoid. Also, he wanted the ideas to be judged on their own merits and related them "in the form of a challenge, as from an outsider, in order to incite Baptists to a profounder interest in the study of their own history."[58] The resulting

---

56. *Ibid.* Eaton was a trustee at the seminary and also pastor of the Walnut Street Baptist Church in Louisville, Kentucky. It was Christian who challenged the authenticity of the Kiffin Manuscript and the Jessey Church Records. Beck details both the criticism and support for Whitsitt. *See* pp. 90-109.

57. Beck, 93. Beck reasons that the intense denominational rivalry during the late nineteenth century made Whitsitt's publication of his findings in nondenominational literature such a crucial mistake. For instance, she cited W. A. Jarrel of Dallas who said "Does not Dr. Whitsitt's method of getting his absurdities before the people clearly indicate an intention to furnish the enemy with a permanent club and to set himself up as infallible." *See* W. A. Jarrel, "Dr. Kerfoot's Apology for Dr. Whitsitt," *Baptist Standard*, 4 June 1896, 3, as cited by Beck, 94.

58. E. B. Pollard, "The Life and Work of William Heth Whitsitt," *The Review and Expositor* 9 (April 1912): 173. Concerning the editorials for *The Independent*, Whitsitt said: "What I wrote was from a Pedobaptist standpoint with a view to stimulating historical inquiry, with no thought that it would injure the Baptists and with no intention to disparage Baptist doctrines or practices." William Heth Whitsitt to the Board of Trustees, LS, no date, William Heth

controversy became so intense that Whitsitt resigned from his post in May 1898. From there he retired to Virginia where he died in 1911.

Newman and the Whitsitt Controversy

Interestingly, when the controversy surrounding Whitsitt began, both sides appealed to Newman for support. Eaton, leading opponent of the pro-Whitsitt forces, traveled with his family for a summer to Newman's retreat in Canada and "visited Dr. Newman often to discuss the matter."[59] On the opposing side, two Whitsitt supporters wrote letters to Newman. Archibald Thomas Robertson, professor of New Testament at the seminary wrote:

> The elements that have rallied around Dr. Eaton have nearly all been opposed to the Seminary in reality and will be satisfied with nothing short of the humiliation of Dr. Whitsitt. That we are determined shall not happen because of its manifest injustice and because it would throttle the rest of the faculty and put us under the power of the Western Recorder. This paper is the chief exponent of backwardism and mossbackism among us.[60]

In addition, an unidentified trustee from St. Louis wrote to Newman and declared that he was "in no humor to accept peace on any terms." Appealing to his expertise as a historian, he asked for Newman's impressions and suggestions as to what course of action to take. "Being an educator, historian, and a Southern Baptist I feel that you may be really helpful in this way. You understand the situation."[61]

Why did both sides elicit Newman's support? Two reasons are apparent. The most prominent reason involves the Spiritual Kinship Theory. This was a type of successionist view which gave Newman a measure of

Whitsitt Personal Papers and Correspondence, 1858-1909, Southern Baptist Theological Seminary, Louisville, Kentucky. Microform Copy.

59. Breazeale, 90-91. Breazeale quoted this from a personal interview with Mrs. Frederick Eby, Newman's daughter.

60. A. T. Robertson to A. H. Newman, LS, 18 February 1897, Albert Henry Newman Papers, 2.

61. Letter from a trustee of the Southern Baptist Theological Seminary to A. H. Newman, L, 23 August 1897, Albert Henry Newman Papers, 1,3.

identity with the lineal successionists.[62] The pro-Whitsitt forces were attracted to Newman because they knew that he attempted to derive his conclusions on the basis of fact and not tradition. Therefore, both sides in the controversy had a point of contact with Newman and desired his support.[63]

A second reason for Newman's appeal to both sides was his conciliatory personality. Though Newman had been involved in controversies in the past (Rochester Theological Seminary and Southwestern Baptist Theological Seminary), he had a reputation for fairness and a personality that eschewed controversy. "Contentiousness had no place in his make-up; he never would engage in controversy."[64] Therefore, his personality induced both sides to see him as a "safe" referee.

Newman chose to enter the controversy by writing a comprehensive analysis. This took the form of a series of articles for *The Christian Index* which were edited and published by George A. Lofton in a volume called *A Review of the Question* (1897). Newman's conciliatory nature is evident at the beginning of his appraisal of the controversy. He recognized that the controversy had two sides with good people supporting each and that his "convictions...that the piety, the honesty, and the learning of the denomination are not all on one side, will tend to make [him] obnoxious to both parties."[65] However, he recognized that truth and peace were more important than popularity and that while he might not be able to influence the extremes on either side, he hoped to be able to reach the large majority in the middle.[66] He then sought to justify his position as mediator by referring to three qualifications which made him a competent judge: (1) he was a Southern Baptist who took an interest in the welfare of the

---

62. *See* William W. Barnes, *The Southern Baptist Convention: 1845-1903* (Nashville, Broadman Press, 1954), 100-103.

63. This idea is in keeping with Fountain's contention in his thesis. It is apparent in the title, "A. H. Newman's Appropriation of the Spiritual Kinship Theory of Baptist Origins as a Historiographical *Via Media*."

64. Eby, *Newman the Church Historian*, 140.

65. Albert Henry Newman, "The Whitsitt Controversy," 146.

66. *Ibid.*, 146-47.

Convention; (2) his years of residence outside of the realm of the Southern Baptist Convention made him free of partisan assumptions; and (3) his career as a church historian gave him a measure of expertise in the examination of the causes of historical controversies.[67] Throughout his analysis Newman declared his non-partisanship with statements such as "I am no partisan of Dr. Whitsitt's,"[68] and "this controversy is none of mine."[69]

After setting forth his introductory remarks, Newman turned to a critique of Whitsitt. First, he concluded that Whitsitt's article in *Johnson's Universal Cyclopedia* (1893) was fair with no pejorative overtones. "He [Whitsitt] evidently had due consideration for the sensibilities of his brethren who lay stress on apostolic succession."[70] Concerning the 1880 editorials in *The Independent*, Newman's comments were more severe. He criticized the editorials for being negative toward Baptists.

> Were it not that he claims the authorship of the article, one would be inclined to suspect that he had simply furnished the materials and that the editor had wrought them over in such a way as to make them as stinging as possible to the Baptists. It is exceedingly unfortunate that having committed such an indiscretion Dr. Whitsitt should have proclaimed himself the author of a performance so little to his credit as a denominational leader.[71]

Further criticism of Whitsitt centered on the proposition that he was too polemical against the successsionists in his conclusions. According to Newman, Whitsitt resented the successionist view to the extent that he de-emphasized any Baptist qualities in the evangelical sects throughout history and stressed their non-Baptist characteristics. Newman believed that Whitsitt desired "to score a point against the successionists at the expense of the Christian heroes of the past centuries."[72]

---

67. *Ibid.*, 147.

68. *Ibid.*, 224.

69. *Ibid.*, 230.

70. *Ibid.*, 158.

71. *Ibid.*, 159.

72. *Ibid.*, 161-62.

A final critique by Newman presumed that Whitsitt desired to claim personal prestige for his historical conclusions. Newman agreed with Whitsitt's findings concerning the introduction of immersion in 1641. "I do not think that your opponents have brought forward as yet anything decisive in favor of an earlier date than 1641 for the introduction of immersion among English Antipedobaptists."[73] However, it is interesting to note a particular statement by Newman concerning Whitsitt's conclusions. Newman claimed that he had reached the same conclusion "years ago" independently of the source that Whitsitt initially based his conclusions upon in 1880.[74] In another article published in 1899, Newman claimed to have made the discovery "about twenty years ago."[75] That would place his discovery around 1879, a year before Whitsitt published his findings in *The Independent*. W. O. Carver suggested that Whitsitt was anxious to publish his findings in *The Independent* because H. C. Vedder, Henry Dexter, and Newman were "already pressing hard on his heels with their studies in the same field."[76]

This raises two interesting questions. First, was Newman's harsh criticism of Whitsitt's claims to originality the result of professional jealousy? This is a difficult question to answer. Eby's treatment of Newman's personality suggested that this kind of feeling would have been unlikely.[77] Yet there may have been some feeling of pride on Newman's part which persuaded him to contend that Whitsitt was not the originator of the historical conclusion. The second obvious question concerns speculation as to why Newman did not publish the findings in 1879 if he discovered them

---

73. Albert Henry Newman to W. H. Whitsitt, LS, 23 November 1896, William Heth Whitsitt Personal Papers and Correspondence, 1.

74. *Ibid.*, 185. Newman claimed that his discovery came from the quotations from George Gould's book *Open Communion and the Baptists of Norwich*, published in 1860. Newman said the book contained quotations from the same records that Whitsitt based his conclusions on, yet Whitsitt did not refer to the book. Essentially, Newman argued here that Whitsitt was not the originator of the discovery concerning the recovery of immersion in 1641.

75. Albert Henry Newman, "A Review of Dr. Christian's Articles," *The Western Recorder*, 25 May 1899, 3.

76. W. O. Carver, "William Heth Whitsitt: The Seminary's Martyr," *The Review and Expositor* 51 (October 1954): 457.

77. Eby, *Newman the Church Historian*, 112-53.

before Whitsitt. This question is more difficult to answer. Because Newman was at Rochester at that time, and since lineal successionist claims were not as prevalent in the North, he would not have received the same degree of criticism as Whitsitt. Perhaps Newman did not consider the information important enough to publish. Unfortunately, no evidence in Newman's writings or personal files suggests a clear answer to this question.

Newman's critique of the anti-Whitsitt forces centered on their historical method. In a review of John Tyler Christian's book *Did They Dip?*, he disagreed with Christian's assertion that the normal mode of baptism among the Anabaptists was immersion.[78] He attacked Christian's use of sources saying that he quoted extensively from modern writers and did so without any discretion or "regard to their qualifications to speak authoritatively on the matters involved in the discussion."[79] Newman also supported the authenticity of the Kiffin Manuscript against Christian's charges of forgery,[80] and in private correspondence with Whitsitt, expressed his opinion of Christian's book with more candor.

> I have just looked over J. T. C.'s book. It fairly bristles [?] with blunders....I am not at all sure that it is worth your while to expose its multitudinous errors.[81]

Newman finished his analysis of the controversy by summarizing his critique in six conclusions. First, he said that Whitsitt never should have written the editorials for *The Independent* because of their ambivalent tone toward Baptists. Second, Whitsitt wrote the editorial out of his own ambitious desires to be seen as an original discoverer. Third, Whitsitt was

---

78. Albert Henry Newman, "The Whitsitt Controversy," 218.

79. *Ibid.*, 220. Newman's tone throughout this review was scathing, yet he remained within the field of historical research and did not resort to personal attacks. He concluded that Christian's findings in the book were completely untenable based upon the historical evidence.

80. Albert Henry Newman, "A Review of Dr. Christian's Articles," *The Western Recorder*, 25 May 1899, 3 and 1 June 1899, 3. In this two part article Newman traced the path of the Kiffin Manuscript and the Jessey Church Records through their various owners. *See also:* Albert Henry Newman, "Can An Alibi Be Established," *The Western Recorder*, 7 July 1898, 2 and "The Early Custodians of the 'Jessey Church Records' and the Kiffin Manuscript," *The Western Recorder*, 7 April 1898, 2.

81. Albert Henry Newman to W. H. Whitsitt, LS, 29 December 1896, William Heth Whitsitt Personal Papers and Correspondence.

misled at times because of his over-reliance on other historians, especially Henry Dexter, a Congregationalist historian, who was at times hostile toward Baptists. Fourth, Whitsitt should not be dismissed from his position because his conclusions had long been accepted by historians who specialized in Baptist history.[82] Fifth, Whitsitt's opponents should continue to maintain their lineal succession views, but with a tolerant attitude toward differing ideas. Sixth, Newman called for peace and reconciliation between the two groups.[83]

At the end of his examination of the controversy, Newman said, "I do not wish to be regarded as a champion of the theory of the late introduction of proper baptism among English anti-Pedobaptists."[84] Evidently, many people took this as a statement that Newman was moving away from Whitsitt's conclusions in favor of successionist claims. In a letter to Whitsitt in early 1899, Newman declared that this supposed change of his views was erroneous. Although this letter is not included in the collection of the Whitsitt Papers at the Southern Baptist Theological Seminary, the contents of Newman's letter can be surmised from Whitsitt's response.

> Your letter of the 4th instant [sic] brings me sincere joy. Certainly it was an agreeable sensation to be assured in your own hand that you have not renounced your views regarding the reintroduction of immersion in the year 1641....Yet the impression that you have renounced your views has been so often conveyed...that multitudes of people on both sides of the issue have quietly settled down to the conclusion that it must be a correct impression....You have been greatly misunderstood. Only plain speech will put you right.[85]

---

82. This raises a question as to why other historians had not received the same criticism if Whitsitt's conclusions had long been accepted. It can probably be answered in two points. First, with Whitsitt's findings, Southern Baptist successionists had their first serious challenge from one of their own. Second, although Newman was from the South, until 1901 all of his historical work was in northern Baptist schools. Since lineal succession was not as prevalent there, northern Baptist historians such as Burrage, Vedder, and Newman would not have received as much criticism for teaching and holding to the conclusions that cost Whitsitt his position.

83. Albert Henry Newman, "The Whitsitt Controversy," 211-15.

84. *Ibid.*, 230.

85. William H. Whitsitt to Albert Henry Newman, LS, 6 February 1899, Albert Henry Newman Papers.

Newman's Appraisal in Retrospect

Charles William DeWeese discussed Newman's involvement in the Whitsitt Controversy within the broader context of a discussion of his contributions to Baptist historiography. He concluded that Newman misunderstood both the seriousness and the significance of the controversy for Southern Baptists. As evidence of this conclusion DeWeese cited the following statement by Newman:

> if Dr. Whitsitt's opponents should seek to secure his condemnation by the Southern Baptist Convention, I have not the slightest doubt but that he would be enthusiastically sustained by an overwhelming majority.[86]

DeWeese pointed out that regardless of Newman's misplaced confidence, Whitsitt was forced eventually to resign his post at the seminary. He suggested that Newman's sixteen years in Canada prior to the controversy caused him to misjudge the mood of Southern Baptist life.[87] This quote from Newman, however, does not necessarily show that Newman misunderstood the situation. It is not uncommon during controversies for both sides to claim the majority of "grass root" support. Both sides may have evidence to support their claim. Many Southern Baptists sustained Whitsitt in spite of the criticism against him and the eventual outcome of the controversy.

There is evidence, however, that at its beginning, Newman may have underestimated the seriousness of the attacks on Whitsitt. In correspondence with Whitsitt, Newman quipped, "You are doubtless enjoying your fame."[88] Six days later Newman wrote another letter to Whitsitt which began with the statement,

> Of course I did not suppose that you were really enjoying the attacks that are being _____ in your teachings, but I suppose that in view of the continued prosperity of the seminary and the larger measure of denominational confidence you still

---

86. Albert Henry Newman, "The Whitsitt Controversy," 213, as cited by Charles William DeWeese, "The Contributions of A. H. Newman to Baptist Historiography," *Baptist History and Heritage* 7 (January 1972): 11.

87. DeWeese, 11.

88. Albert Henry Newman to William Heth Whitsitt, LS, 7 November 1896, William Heth Whitsitt Personal Papers and Correspondence.

enjoy, you were able to accept the situation with a degree of equanimity.[89]

Although there is no surviving letter, Whitsitt probably responded to Newman during the six days between the two letters and informed him as to the seriousness of the attacks.

Regardless of Newman's estimate of the seriousness of the controversy in the early days, by 1897 he became fully aware of its explosive nature. The letters Newman received from A. T. Robertson (18 February 1897) and from the anonymous trustee from St. Louis (23 August 1897) would have been sufficient evidence to convince him of the seriousness of the matter. Also, Newman was cognizant of events occurring in the Southern Baptist Convention through interaction with the Baptist state newspapers.[90]

DeWeese further argued that Newman did not understand the importance of the controversy when he wrote that the controversy "is occupying the attention of the Southern Baptists to an extent wholly disproportionate to its importance."[91] However, in "The Whitsitt Controversy," Newman said, "That the subject-matter of the controversy is a matter of apparently slight importance, detracts nothing from the seriousness of the actual situation."[92] In light of this statement it is clear that Newman only regarded the "subject–matter" of the controversy (i.e. the recovery of immersion among English Baptists) as insignificant. But he knew the controversy itself was a serious threat to the Southern Baptist Convention. It is understandable how Newman could believe that the subject matter of the controversy was insignificant. It has already been stated that Newman arrived at similar conclusions many years before the controversy began.

---

89. Albert Henry Newman to William Heth Whitsitt, LS, 23 November 1896, William Heth Whitsitt Personal Papers and Correspondence, 1.

90. During the years of the Whitsitt Controversy, Newman contributed thirty-nine articles to *The Western Recorder* and the series of twenty-six articles to *The Christian Index*, which were published together in *A Review of the Question*. Many of the articles for *The Western Recorder* were editorial responses to other writers which give evidence to the fact that he kept informed of the activities in the Convention. The topics for these articles varied as not all concentrated on the Whitsitt Controversy. However, since Newman had such frequent contact with these periodicals in the South, he would have been informed of the Controversy.

91. Albert Henry Newman, "A Review of Dr. Christian's Articles," 25 May 1899, 3.

92. Albert Henry Newman, "The Whitsitt Controversy," 145.

Also, he knew that the majority of Baptist historians accepted the conclusion that immersion was not the regular mode of Baptism among Baptists until 1641. From a scholarly perspective, the subject matter was insignificant because the issue had been settled years before. But on the popular level within the Southern Baptist Convention, the issue was more volatile than in the North or in Canada where the majority of other Baptist historians operated.

Finally, DeWeese argued that Newman misunderstood the seriousness of the controversy on the basis of a statement made in "A Review of Cr. Christian's Articles." Newman said, "the present controversy...has been of incidental benefit in stimulating an interest in Baptist history."[93] DeWeese then surmised that on the contrary, the controversy produced an intense interest in Baptist history. In defense of Newman, DeWeese made his statement seventy-three years after the fact. Newman's comment came at the immediate conclusion of the controversy. He was not able to see the final results of the conflict as DeWeese later could. The context of the quote cited by DeWeese shows that Newman was not just lamenting a lack of interest in Baptist history. Rather, he desired to see an interest in the objective study of history as a discipline.

> Baptists have done far less than their share of historical research. The present controversy, that has been productive of so much harm, has been of incidental benefit in stimulating an interest in Baptist history. But interest stimulated by partisan considerations is not the kind of interest that leads to trustworthy results. The true historian must rise superior, as far as possible, to partisan, or even to denominational interests.[94]

From Newman's perspective there would not have been much interest in the field of Baptist history except from a partisan standpoint.

Newman attempted to serve as peacemaker in the Whitsitt Controversy. Unfortunately, he was not successful. Whitsitt resigned his position as president of the seminary in 1898. The Southern Baptist

93. Albert Henry Newman, "A Review of Dr. Christian's Articles," 1 June 1899, 3, as cited by DeWeese, 12.

94. Albert Henry Newman, "A Review of Dr. Christian's Articles," 1 June 1899, 3.

Convention remained divided on the issue, even though the tension eased with Whitsitt's resignation. Newman's desire for an increase of interest in Baptist history from a non-partisan perspective seems to have been accomplished. Though the advocates of lineal succession won the battle with his resignation, Whitsitt's conclusions became the norm after the beginning of the twentieth century.

Conclusion

Newman's career corresponded with the era when Baptist historiography was developing into a professional discipline. During his career, although issues such as the Social Gospel and Fundamentalism were of interest to historians, Newman's main focus concerned Baptist beginnings. The Anabaptist spiritual kinship theory superseded the claims of those who advocated a lineal succession of Baptist churches that could be traced to the first century. By the early years of the twentieth century, the spiritual kinship theory was replaced by the English Separatist descent theory, which sought to identify Baptist origins within English Separatism and reject any connection with the Anabaptists. Newman did not follow the trend of Baptist historiography into the twentieth century. He remained committed to spiritual kinship. By the middle of the twentieth century, many Baptist historians advocated a connection between the Anabaptists and the rise of the Baptists, though discounting any claims of spiritual kinship. Newman's use of the spiritual kinship theory helped lay the groundwork for further investigations into Anabaptist influence by later historians.

CHAPTER V

CONCLUSION

Albert Henry Newman's life and career were a part of a period of American history which saw rapid changes in many facets of society. During the late nineteenth and early twentieth centuries, America changed from an agrarian nation to one of the industrial leaders of the world. The nation participated in a bloody "war to end all wars" in Europe. Movements such as the Social Gospel and Fundamentalism caused a stir in the religious community. Progress in the sciences, due largely to Darwin's theory of evolution, spawned the rise of disciplines such as psychology and sociology.

Newman grew up during the Reconstruction era in the South. He attended Mercer University and then moved to Rochester, New York for seminary training at the Rochester Theological Seminary. From there, his intentions were to continue his studies in Germany, but he decided instead to spend a year in study at the Southern Baptist Theological Seminary, located at that time in Greenville, South Carolina. This decision marks the first major watershed in Newman's life. His career would doubtless have been much different if he had been schooled in Germany. His intentions were to study Old Testament and Semitic languages. He would, most likely, have never become a church historian if he had continued with his original plans. Even if he had become a historian after he returned to the United States, Newman's approach to history would have been significantly changed by German methodology.

Newman began his teaching career in 1877 by returning to Rochester to fill the vacancy created by the death of R. J. W. Buckland, professor of church history. This position permanently changed Newman's career from Old Testament scholar to church historian. But in 1881, he lost his position after being involved in a controversy at the seminary over homiletics professor W. C. Wilkinson. Newman's support of Wilkinson conflicted with president A. H. Strong. After he made critical comments about Strong during a chapel service, Newman was forced to resign. Surprisingly, Strong harbored no bitter feelings against Newman and was instrumental in helping Newman secure his next teaching position at Toronto Baptist College (later to become McMaster University) in Toronto, Canada. Newman remained in this position for twenty years.

In 1901, after twenty-five years in the North, Newman accepted a teaching position at Baylor University in Waco, Texas. Almost immediately he regretted accepting the position. Upon returning to Canada after visiting at Baylor and agreeing to accept the position, he tried to reverse his decision, but B. H. Carroll, chairman of the school's board of trustees, refused to let Newman break the contract. The Baylor Theological Department officially became the Baylor Theological Seminary in 1905. Renamed Southwestern Baptist Theological Seminary in 1908, it relocated to Fort Worth, Texas in 1910. Newman remained with the seminary until 1913 when acting as dean, he attempted to change the curriculum. This conflicted with seminary president B. H. Carroll's wishes as and resulted in Newman's dismissal.

The move to Texas is another turning point of Newman's career. After 1901 his literary output decreased. This was due in part to the fact that Texas was still considered somewhat of a frontier state at the beginning of the twentieth century. Newman did not have as much access to the new developments in his field as he did when he was a part of the academic community in the north. Furthermore, most of his writing was done at his summer home during the summer break while in Canada. In Texas he did not have this luxury or the time for such activity.

From Southwestern Newman returned to Baylor where he taught until 1920. He then accepted a position with Mercer University in Macon, Georgia where he taught until 1928. He finished his teaching career in 1929 after one year as visiting professor at McMaster University. Upon retirement, Newman moved to Austin, Texas to live with his daughter and son-in-law. He died in 1933 after being struck by an automobile.

A study of Newman's work as a historian reveals that he did not make the same transition in his methodology that the discipline of church history made at the beginning of the twentieth century. Church history grew into a professional discipline during the late nineteenth century. During that period three types of historiographical expressions can be identified. Sectarian historians worked largely as denominational apologists intent on proving an unbroken organic connection between their confessional stance and the apostolic church. J. M. Carroll, author of *The Trail of Blood*, which attempted to connect Baptists organically through the dissenting sects in church history, serves as an example of this methodology. At the other extreme were the scientific historians. These historians attempted to remove all *a priori* conclusions (including speculations about God) and biases from their work and base their conclusions only on what the sources revealed. Ephraim Emerton, professor of Ecclesiastical History at Harvard University, serves as a good example of this methodology. The third school of historiography was the theological historians. These scholars, of whom Philip Schaff serves as an example, based their conclusions on primary sources, but they differed from the scientific historians over the starting point for historical work. The theological church historians generally started with the assumption that the history of the church was the study of the movement and activity of God interacting with the church. The scientific church historians viewed the church as an institution composed of humans and therefore they were not interested in speculation about God or his activity.

Newman cannot be identified completely as a disciple of any one of these three schools of historiographical thought. His use of the Spiritual Kinship theory of Baptist origins was a type of successionism but he did not advocate any type of organic connection between Baptists and the dissenting sects. Therefore, he did not fit squarely into the sectarian camp. He had very little in common with the scientific approach except for their use of sources, and therefore was not a part of that school of thought either. Newman may have been more comfortable among the theological historians, but he had differences with them as seen by his incongruence with Philip Schaff over both ecumenism and approach to church history.

Scientific Historiography became the dominant methodology among church historians by the beginning of the twentieth century. The combination of the American Society of Church History with the American Historical Association in 1897 signals the triumph of scientific church history. Newman did not make the shift in his historiography to the scientific methodology. Evidence of this is found in the decreasing popularity of his work, *A Manual of Church History* as the twentieth century progressed, in spite of the revision completed in 1933. Whereas Newman's work decreased in its popularity, *A History of the Christian Church* (1918), by scientific church historian Williston Walker increased in popularity and remains a popular church history text.

One of Newman's research interests was the Anabaptists. During the late nineteenth century in Baptist circles, ideas of lineal succession were common. This prevailing atmosphere coupled with a strong Baptist bias and his use of the Spiritual Kinship Theory generated Newman's interest in the Anabaptists. Newman had the notion that modern Baptists are the inheritors of apostolic Christianity, a Baptist bias. He believed that the Baptist denomination, more closely than any other, exemplified all the characteristics of the first-century church. Therefore, he was interested in any group which resembled the Baptists. He found many similarities with the Anabaptists and sought to know all that he could about that sixteenth-century movement and its connection with the rise of the seventeenth-century Baptists in England. Though he was no champion of lineal succession, Newman did accept the idea that there was a "spiritual" succession of apostolic characteristics which can be identified in the dissenting sects. This theory caused him to study the dissenting sects and discover their apostolic traits, which gave them a "kinship" with the Baptists. According to Newman, the Anabaptists represented the most complete renewal of apostolic Christianity before the rise of the Baptists. The Spiritual Kinship Theory and his favorable Baptist bias are the two guiding principles in all of Newman's historiography.

Newman was a pioneer in the field of Anabaptist studies, one of the first to break from traditional pejorative interpretations which viewed all Anabaptists as fanatics in light of the Munster fiasco. He was one of the first historians to suggest different categories within the movement and delineate the distinctive characteristics of each group. Though he recognized kinship, Newman was able to distinguish between the Anabaptists and the Baptists, unlike many other Baptist writers of his day.

Very little reference is made to Newman by modern Anabaptist scholars. His *A History of Anti-Pedobaptism: From the Rise of Pedobaptism to 1609*, is sometimes cited in bibliographies, and occasionally, one or two of his articles are included. But, for the most part, Newman's work is overlooked by modern Anabaptist scholars. This is due to several factors. First, Newman's work is simply obsolete. Many new sources and discoveries have been made in the field of Anabaptist studies since Newman's time primarily through the work of the Mennonites. Second, some of Newman's conclusions about the Anabaptists are discounted by modern writers as a result of innovations in the field. Third, Newman's purpose for studying the Anabaptists was not to be a discoverer, but to serve as an interpreter of that movement to his Baptist audience. He wanted to bring his Baptist constituency to an appreciation of their heritage by showing that they had many similarities with the Anabaptists. Consequently, most of Newman's Anabaptist studies are for Baptist periodicals.

Another important research topic for Newman was Baptist history, more specifically, investigations into Baptist origins. The field of Baptist historiography developed in a manner parallel to the field of general history. Consequently, Baptist history grew into a professional discipline in the late nineteenth century as well. The predominant ideas about lineal succession were gradually replaced by those historians, similar to Newman, who advocated spiritual kinship. By the beginning of the twentieth century, a new theory of Baptist origins became the dominant view. This theory sought to trace Baptist beginnings to the English Separatist movement in England and gave less emphasis to Anabaptist influence.

By the middle of the twentieth century the English Separatist Descent theory was the prevailing interpretation of Baptist origins among historians.

But gradually, Baptist scholars have turned back to investigating the contributions that Anabaptists provided to the founding of the Baptist movement. Another interpretation, the Anabaptist Influence theory has developed as the major alternative to the English Separatist Descent theory. This view is similar to the Spiritual Kinship theory in that it emphasizes the similarities between Baptists and Anabaptists, but discounts any type of spiritual kinship with dissenting groups throughout church history.

Newman was a brilliant scholar. He was a linguist who mastered several foreign and ancient languages. This served as a useful tool for his research, especially his work on the dissenting sects. But Newman's methodology failed to keep pace with the rest of the field of church history. As a general historian, he did not make the transition to scientific historiography which became the predominant methodology at the beginning of the twentieth century. As an Anabaptist scholar, Newman's work was supplanted by the studies of the Mennonites, primarily led by Harold S. Bender. As a Baptist historian, Newman's use of the Spiritual Kinship theory was no longer the major interpretation motif after the beginning of the twentieth century. This failure to make the transition in methodology and outlook can perhaps be attributed to one major change in his career. The move from McMaster University to Baylor University in 1901 caused him to lose contact with the current developments in the field of church history. Though he had access to the major periodicals and even contributed articles, he lost contact with the most stimulating academic community by being so far away from the northern institutions of learning. Also, the infancy status of the theological department at Baylor and later that of Southwestern Baptist Theological Seminary proved a hindrance to Newman's ability to remain current in his research.

This study of Newman's life and work as a historian leads naturally to some further questions and areas of potential research. First, the sectarian historiography of the nineteenth century needs further examination. How much affect did Romanticism within the area of American historiography have on the sectarian approach? Was the sectarian methodology, which assumed organic connection with the apostolic church, prevalent in all the major Protestant denominations or just several? What similarities or differences existed between the Protestant sectarian historians and Catholic historians? How much did the mood of anti-Catholicism, fueled by the large numbers of Catholic immigrants to America in the middle of the nineteenth century, affect the rise of sectarian historiography?

A second topic which needs further investigation is the development of Baptist historiography since the beginning of the denomination in the seventeenth century. W. Morgan Patterson's study of Baptist historiography in the eighteenth century needs to be expanded further to include the seventeenth, nineteenth, and twentieth centuries. For example, what can be determined about the methodology of early Baptist historians such as Thomas Crosby? Also, there are certain questions which need to be answered concerning Baptist historiography. How much did nineteenth century Baptist historians contribute to the rise of Anabaptist historiography among the Mennonites? What affect has revivalism in America had on Baptist historians and their conclusions? How did the Social Gospel movement, led by Baptist historian Walter Rauschenbusch, affect other Baptist historians? How much has Fundamentalism contributed to the work of Baptist historians? Do Fundamentalist Baptist historians differ from non-Fundamentalists in their methodology?

BIBLIOGRAPHY

Primary Sources

Books

Newman, Albert Henry., ed. *A Century of Baptist Achievement*. Philadelphia: The American Baptist Publication Society, 1901.

_____. *A History of Anti-Pedobaptism; From the Rise of Pedobaptism to A.D. 1609*. Philadelphia: The American Baptist Publication Society, 1897.

_____. *A History of Baptist Churches in the United States*. The American Church History Series, Vol. 2. New York: The Christian Literature Co., 1894; reprint, Philadelphia; The American Baptist Publication Society, 1898.

_____. *Liberty of Conscience: A Fundamental Baptist Principle*. Toronto: Standard Publishing Company, 1883.

_____. ed. *Memoir of Daniel Arthur McGregor*. Toronto: Dudley and Burns, Printers, 1891.

_____. *A Manual of Church History*. Vol. 1, *Ancient and Mediaeval Church History (To A.D. 1517)*. Philadelphia: The American Baptist Publication Society, 1899; reprint, Valley Forge: The Judson Press, 1933.

_____. *A Manual of Church History*. Vol. 2, *Modern Church History (A.D. 1517-1932)*. Philadelphia: The American Baptist Publication Society, 1902; reprint, Valley Forge: The Judson Press, 1931.

Translated Works

_____. Trans. of Augustine's: "Acts or Disputations Against Fortunatus the Manichaean." In *A Select Library of the Nicene and Post-Nicene Fathers*, Edited by Philip Schaff, 113-24. Buffalo: The Christian Literature Company, 1887.

_____. Trans. of Augustine's: "Concerning the Nature of Good, Against the Manichaeans." In *A Select Library of the Nicene and Post-Nicene Fathers*, Edited by Philip Schaff, 351-65. Buffalo: The Christian Literature Company, 1887.

_____. "Early Christian Biblicism." Trans. of H. Achelis'"Das Christentum in den ersten drei Jahrhunderten." *The Mennonite Quarterly Review* 4 (January 1930): 51-59.

_____. Trans. *Hermeneutics of the New Testament*, by Albert Immer, 1877.

_____. Trans. of Augustine's: "On Two Souls, Against the Manichaeans." In *A Select Library of the Nicene and Post-Nicene Fathers*, Edited by Philip Schaff, 95-107. Buffalo: The Christian Literature Company, 1887.

Scholarly Articles

_____. "Adam Pastor, Anti-Trinitarian AntipaedoBaptist." *Papers of the American Society of Church History*, Second Series, 5 (1917): 75-99.

_____. "The Antipedobaptist Holy Catholic Apostolic Church." *The Crozer Quarterly* 1 (October 1924): 379-95.

_____. "The Authority of Christian Consciousness." *The Southwestern Theological Review* 1 (1903): 106-15.

_____. "Balthazar Hubmaier and the Moravian Anabaptists." *The Goshen College Record*, Review Supplement 27 No. 10 (1926): 4-22.

_____. "Baptist Churches Apostolical." In *Baptist Doctrines: Being in Exposition, in a Series of Essays by Representative Baptist Ministers, of the Distinctive Points of Baptist Faith and Practice*, Edited by Charles A. Jenkens, 236-82. St. Louis: C.R. Barns, 1892.

_____. "Baptist Ministerial Education Seventy-Five Years Ago." *The Rochester Theological Seminary Bulletin* 76 (July 1925): 345-61.

_____. "Baptist Pioneers in Liberty of Conscience." *The Review and Expositor* 6 (April 1909): 239-55.

_____. "Biblical Theology – Its Nature, Presuppositions, Methods and Perils." *The Baptist Quarterly Review* 6 (April 1884): 240-56.

_____. "A Biographical and Bibliographical Account of Dr. H. A. W. Meyer." *The Baptist Quarterly (Philadelphia)* 8 (October 1874): 438-57.

_____. "The Calvinism of Calvin." *The Review and Expositor* 6 (October 1909): 562-76.

_____. "The Credibility of Christ's Discourses as Reported by John." *The Baptist Quarterly (Philadelphia)* 8 (July 1874): 307-20.

_____. "Dr. Goodspeed's New Book." *The McMaster University Monthly* 10 (November 1900): 84.

_____. "The Early Waldenses." *The Baptist Quarterly Review* 7 (July 1885): 300-22.

_____. "Fifty Years of Progress in Church History." *The Review and Expositor* 7 (January 1910): 65-79.

_____. "Four Hundred Years of Lutheranism." *The Review and Expositor* 15 (January 1918): 3-23.

_____. "George Burman Foster." *The McMaster University Monthly* 5 (December 1895): 97-99.

_____. "Heimgegangen – Philip Schaff." *The McMaster University Monthly* 2 (November 1893): 83.

_____. "A Higher Critic of our own Time: W. C. Wilkinson as Theologian and Critic." *The Review and Expositor* 20 (April 1923): 138-55.

_____. "History of Baptist Organization." *The Review and Expositor* 8 (July 1911): 363-77.

_____. "Introductory Essay on the Manichaean Heresy." In *A Select Library of the Nicene and Post-Nicene Fathers*, Vol. IV. Edited by Philip Schaff, Buffalo: The Christian Literature Company, 1887.

_____. "Liberty and Creed." *The Southwestern Theological Review* 1 (1903): 140-60.

_____. "The Moravian Baptists." *The Baptist Quarterly Review* 9 (January 1887): 41-62.

_____. "Opportunities for Baptists in Present Religious Progress." *Proceedings of the Baptist Congress* 16 (1898): 47-56.

_____. "An Orthodox Heretic of the Fourth Century." *The Crozer Quarterly* 3 (July 1926) 307-24, supplemental note, 351-52.

_____. "The Peasants War." *The Baptist Quarterly Review* 11 (January 1889): 48-65.

_____. "Proposed Series of Denominational Histories." *Papers of the American Society of Church History*, First Series, 3 (1890): 209-13.

162

_____. "Recent Changes in the Theology of Baptists." *The American Journal of Theology* 10 (October 1906): 587-609.

_____. "Recent Research Concerning Medieval Sects." *Papers of the American Society of Church History*, First Series, 4 (1891): 167-221.

_____. "The Reformation from a Baptist Point of View." *The Baptist Quarterly Review* 6 (January 1884): 47-67.

_____. "Roger Williams." *The Magazine of Christian Literature* 5 (1891-92): 271-82.

_____. "Sabbath Observance." *Proceedings of the Baptist Congress* 8 (1890): 163-65.

_____. "The Significance of the Anabaptist Movement in the History of the Christian Church." *The Goshen College Record*, Review Supplement 27 (January 1926): 15-22.

_____. "Some Aspects of Early Protestant Theology." *The Baptist Quarterly Review* 5 (October 1883): 417-39.

_____. "Some Recent Literature on the Anabaptist Movement." *The Southwestern Theological Review* 1 (1903): 2-16.

_____. "The Sources of Luke's Gospel." *The Baptist Quarterly (Philadelphia)* 9 (July 1875): 306-21.

_____. "Strong's Systematic Theology." *The Review and Expositor* 2 (January 1905): 41-66.

_____. "The Thirty Years' War," Part I. *The McMaster University Monthly* 1 (June 1891): 12-26."The Thirty Years' War," Part II. *The McMaster University Monthly* 1 (June 1891): 104-17.

_____. "Truth-Speaking." *The McMaster University Monthly* 9 (October 1899): 1-5.

_____. "The Whitsitt Controversy." In *A Review of the Question*. Edited by George A. Lofton. Nashville: University Press Company, 1897.

_____. "Wiclif and the Mendicant Friars." *The McMaster University Monthly* 5 (November 1895): 59-66.

Reviews

_____. Review of *Das apostolische Symbol im Mittlealter: Eine Skizze*, by Von D. Friedrich Wiegand. *The American Journal of Theology* 9 (October 1905): 777.

_____. Review of *The Athanasian Creed and its Early Commentaries*, by A. E. Burn. *The American Journal of Theology* 1 (January 1897): 216-218.

_____. Review of *Athanasiana: Literar-und dogmengeschichtliche Untersuchungen*, by Von Alfred Stulcken. *The American Journal of Theology* 4 (October 1900): 624-25.

_____. Review of *Die Bekehrung Johannes Calvins*, by Von Lic. A. Lang. *The American Journal of Theology* 2 (April 1898): 432-33.

_____. Review of *Canada Under British Rule*, by John G. Bourinot. *The McMaster University Monthly* 10 (April 1901): 325.

_____. Review of *Cardinal Albrecht von Brandenburg und das neue Stift zu Halle, 1520-1541*, by Von Paul Redlich. *The American Journal of Theology* 6 (January 1902): 163-65.

_____. Review of *The Censorship of the Church of Rome and Its Influence Upon the Production and Distribution of Literature*, by George Haven Putnam. *The American Journal of Theology* 12 (April 1908): 295-99.

_____. Review of *Die Christliche Liebesthätigkeit im Mittlelalter*, by G. Uhlhorn. *The Baptist Quarterly Review* 7 (October 1885): 524-25.

_____. Review of *Cyprian von Karthago und die Verfassung der Kirche*, by Otto Ritschl. *The Baptist Quarterly Review* 8 (January 1886): 129-31.

_____. Review of *David Friedrich Strauss: Sein Leben und Seine Schriften unter Heranziehung seiner Briefe dargestellt*, by Von Karl Harraens. *The American Journal of Theology* 7 (January 1903): 205-06.

_____. Review of *Die Deutsche Bibelubersetzung der mittelalterlichen Waldenser*, by Hermann Haupt. *The Baptist Quarterly Review* 7 (October 1885): 526.

_____. Review of *The Early Christian Conception of Christ: Its Significance and Value in the History of Religion*, by Otto Pfleiderer. *The American Journal of Theology* 9 (October 1905): 773-75.

164

_____. Review of *The English Reformation and Puritanism With Other Lectures and Addresses*, by Eri B. Hulbert. *The American Journal of Theology* 12 (April 1908): 317-19.

_____. Review of *Fürstbischof Martin Brenner: Ein Characterbild aus der steirischen Reformations-Geschichte*, by Von Leopold Schuster. *The American Journal of Theology* 3 (October 1899): 804-08.

_____. Review of *Geschichte Der Evangelischen Kirche in Deutschland*, by Von R. Rocholl. *The American Journal of Theology* 1 (October 1897): 1071-74.

_____. Review of *Die Geschichte der Florilegien vom V.-VIII. Jahrhundert*, by Von Theodor Schermann. *The American Journal of Theology* 9 (October 1905): 777.

_____. Review of *Die Geschichtsquellen Des Bisthums Münster*, by von. H. Detmer. *The American Journal of Theology* 6 (July 1902): 595.

_____. Review of *Die Gottes- und Logos-Lehre Tertullians*, by Von Johannes Stier. *The American Journal of Theology*, 4 (October 1900): 625-27.

_____. Review of *Die Gottesbeweise Bei Thomas Von Aquin Und Aristoteles*, by Von Eugen Rolfes. *The American Journal of Theology* 3 (October 1899): 749-50.

_____. Review of *Die Gratia Christi et de Libero Arbitrio*, by K. Krough-Tönning. *The American Journal of Theology* 3 (October 1899): 819-20.

_____. Review of *The Hibbert Lectures, 1887*, by A. H. Sayce. *The Baptist Quarterly Review* 10 (April 1888): 251-54.

_____. Review of *Historische Arbeiten, vornehmlich zur Reformationszeit*, by Von C. A. Cornelius. *The American Journal of Theology* 5 (January 1901): 168-70.

_____. Review of *History of the Christian Church*, Vol. 1-4, by Philip Schaff. *The Baptist Quarterly Review* 7 (July 1885): 378-80.

_____. Review of *History of the Christian Church*, Vol. 5, Part II: *The Middle Ages, From Boniface VIII, 1294 to the Protestant Reformation, 1517*, by Philip Schaff. *The American Journal of Theology* 15 (January 1911): 123-25.

_____. Review of *History of the Christian Church Since the Reformation*, by S. Cheetham. *The American Journal of Theology* 12 (April 1908): 316-17.

_____. Review of *History of the Church of the United Brethren in Christ*, by Daniel Berger. *The American Journal of Theology* 2 (January 1898): 180-83.

_____. Review of *History of English Commerce and Industry*, by L. L. Price. *The McMaster University Monthly* 10 (April 1901): 325.

_____. Review of *History of the Huguenot Emigration to America*, by Charles W. Baird. *The Baptist Quarterly Review* 7 (July 1885): 380-82.

_____. Review of *History of Methodism*, by Holland N. McTyeire. *The Baptist Quarterly Review* 7 (October 1885): 519-21.

_____. Review of *A History of the Plymouth Brethern*, by William Blair Neatby. *The American Journal of Theology* 7 (January 1903): 166-68.

_____. Review of *The Hulsean Lectures, 1885*, by W. Cunningham. *The Baptist Quarterly Review* 9 (July 1887): 398-99.

_____. Review of *The Inquisition – A Political and Military Study of its Establishment*, by Hoffman Nickerson. *Church History* 1 (September 1932): 180-81.

_____. Review of *Der Katholicismus als Princip des Fortschritts*, by Von Hermann Schell. *The American Journal of Theology* 4 (January 1900): 224-25.

_____. Review of *Die Ketzergeschichte des Urchistenthums, Urkundlich Dargestellt*, by Adolf Hilgenfeld. *The Baptist Quarterly Review* 6 (October 1884): 522-28.

_____. Review of *Kirchengeschichte Deutschlands*, by Von Albert Hauck. *The American Journal of Theology* 4 (January 1900): 190-91.

_____. Review of *Die Kirchenrechtsquellen Des Patriarchats Alexandrien*, by Von Wilhelm Riedel. *The American Journal of Theology* 5 (April 1901): 372-73.

_____. Review of *Lectures on the Origin and Growth of Religion as Illustrated by the Religion of the Ancient Babylonians*, by A. H. Sayce. *The Baptist Quarterly Review* 10 (April 1888): 251-54.

_____. Review of *Lehrbuch der Dogmengeschichte*, by Adolf Harnack. *The Baptist Quarterly Review* 8 (July 1886): 411-14.

_____. Review of *The Life of Father Hecker*, by Walter Elliott. *The American Journal of Theology* 3 (October 1899): 816-19.

_____. Review of *Luther und die Kirchengeschichte nach seinen Schriften, zunächst bis 1521*, by Von W. Kohler. *The American Journal of Teology* 6 (July 1902): 591-92.

_____. Review of *Melanchthon's Lehre von der Bekehrung: Eine Studie zur Entwicklung der Anschauung Melanchthons uber Monergismus und Synergismus unter besonderer Berücksichtigung der psychologischen Grundlage und der prädestinationischen Konsequenzen*, by Von Ernst Friedrich Fischer. *The American Journal of Theology* 9 (October 1905): 778-79.

_____. Review of *Messiah's Second Advent: A Study in Eschatology*, by Calvin Goodspeed. *The McMaster University Monthly* 10 (November 1904): 84.

_____. Review of *Les Moines De Constantinople*, by Victor Lecoffre. *The American Journal of Theology* 3 (January 1899): 177-181.

_____. Review of *Die Neubesetzung Der Deutschen Bistümer unter Papst Innocenz IV, 1243-1254*, by Von P. Aldinger. *The American Journal of Theology* 6 (October 1902): 797-98.

_____. Review of *Die Origenistischen Streitigkeiten im sechsten Jahrhundert und das fünfte allgemeine Concil*, by Von Dr. Franz Diekamp. *The American Journal of Theology* 6 (April 1901): 369-70.

_____. Review of *Paul and the Revolt Against Him*, by William Wilkinson. *Theologische Literaturzeitung*, 39 (October 1914): 648-49.

_____. Review of *Practica Inquisitionis Heretice Pravitatis*, by Bernardo Guidonis. *The Baptist Quarterly Review* 9 (January 1887): 145-47.

_____. Review of *Quellen und Forschungen zur Geschichte der oberdeutschen Taufgesinnten in 16. Jahrhundert: Pilgram Marbecks Antwort auf Kaspar Schwenkfelds Beurteilung des Buches der Bundes-bezeugung von 1542*, edited by J. Loserth. *The Mennonite Quarterly Review* 4 (April 1930): 149-54.

_____. Review of *Realencyklopädie Für Protestantische Theologie und Kirche*, by J. J. Herzog and D. Albert Hauck. *The American Journal of Theology* 5 (January 1901): 127-28.

_____. Review of *Die Reformation und Gegenreformation in den Innerösterreichischen Ländern im XVI Jahrhundert*, by Von Johann Loserth. *The American Journal of Theology* 4 (January 1900): 195-98.

_____. Review of *Der Reformkatholizismus die Religion der Zukunft*, by Von Josef Müller. *The American Journal of Theology* 4 (January 1900): 225-27.

_____. Review of *S. Austin* [Augustine of Canterbury] *and his Place in the History of Christian Thought*, by William Cunningham. *The Baptist Quarterly Review* 9 (July 1887): 398-99.

_____. Review of *Seventeen Lectures on the Study of Medieval and Modern History*, by William Stubbs. *The Baptist Quarterly Review* 9 (July 1887): 396-98.

_____. Review of *A Short History of Monks and Monasteries*, by Alfred Wesley Wishart. *The American Journal of Theology* 5 (January 1901): 179-81.

_____. Review of *Der Sogenannte Praedestinatus: Ein Beitrag zur Geschichte des Pelagianism*, by Von D. Hans von Schubert. *The American Journal of Theology* 9 (October 1905): 775-77.

_____. Review of *Die Universitäten des Mittelalters*, by P. Heinrich Denifle. *The Baptist Quarterly Review* 8 (July 1886): 408-11.

_____. Review of *Usprung,* [sic] *Entwickelung* [sic] *und Schicksale der Taufgesinnten oder Mennoniten*, by A. Brons. *The Baptist Quarterly Review* 8 (April 1886): 273.

_____. Review of *Die Waldenser und ihre einzelnen Gruppen bis zum Anfang des 14, Jahrhunderts*, by D. Karl Müller.*Ueber die Inquisition gegen die Waldenser in Pommern und die Mark Brandenburg*, by W. Wattenbach. *Ueber das Verhältnis der Taboriten zu den Waldesiern des 14, Jahrhunderts*, by W. Preger. *Historie des Vaudois d'Italie depuis leurs Origines jusqu' a nos Jours*, by Em. Comba. *The Baptist Quarterly Review* 10 (January 1888): 128-31.

_____. Review of *Die "Wiedertäufer" im Herzogtum Jülich*, by Von Dr. Karl Rembert. *The American Journal of Theology* 4 (July 1900): 615-18.

_____. Review of *Wyclif and Hus*, by Johann Loserth. *The aptist Quarterly Review* 7 (October 1885): 523-24.

Denominational Writings

_____. "Adoptionism in Early and Mediaeval Times." *The Western Recorder*, 15 December 1910, 1.

168

————. "After Death What?" *The Western Recorder*, 28 December 1906, 2.

————. "The Anabaptists of Switzerland Defended and Befriended by the Dutch." *The Western Recorder*, 25 January 1900, 1.

————. "Augustin on the Goodness of the Creation." *The Western Recorder*, 6 October 1904, 1.

————. "Augustin's Confession." *The Western Recorder*, 7 July 1904, 1.

————. "Baptist Churches Apostolical." *The Canadian Baptist*, 23 November 1882, 2.

————. "Baptist Churches Apostolical." *The Canadian Baptist*, 30 November 1882, 2.

————. "The Baptist Congress." *The Canadian Baptist*, 31 October 1889, 5.

————. "The Baptists." *The Canadian Baptist*, 25 April 1929, 53-56.

————. "Baptists and Higher Education." *The Canadian Baptist*, 11 June 1883, 1.

————. "The Baptists in History." *The Christian Index*, 1 June 1922, 18-22.

————. "The Baptists of Texas and Ministerial Education." *The Western Recorder*, 26 September 1901, 1.

————. "The Bernese Baptists During the Seventeenth Century." *The Western Recorder*, 23 November 1899, 1.

————. "The Bishop of Ely on Baptism." *The Western Recorder*, 11 April 1907, 1.

————. "Can an Alibi be Established." *The Western Recorder*, 7 July 1898, 2.

————. "Canon Bigg on Affusion for Baptism." *The Western Recorder*, 10 February 1910, 1.

————. "The Canon of the Old Testament." *The Western Recorder*, 26 January 1905, 1; 2 Februray 1905, 1.

————. "Causes of the Constant Increase of the Baptist Sect." *The Western Recorder*, 14 December 1899, 1.

————. "Charles Francis Adams on Moses." *The Western Recorder*, 27 December 1900, 1.

_____. "A Christian Philosophy of History." *The Western Recorder*, 31 January 1901, 1.

_____. "Christian Universities and Theological Studies." *The Western Recorder*, 24 April 1902, 1; 22 May 1902, 1.

_____. "Cities vs. Towns." *The Canadian Baptist*, 22 March 1888, 5.

_____. "The College Library." *The Canadian Baptist*, 7 February 1884, 4.

_____. "The Confessions of Augustine." *The Western Recorder*, 5 May 1904, 1.

_____. "Contemporary British Thought." *The Western Recorder*, 20 August 1908, 1.

_____. "Corner-Stone Laying at Baylor University." *The Western Recorder*, 13 March 1902, 1.

_____. "The Decline of Infant Baptism." *The Canadian Baptist*, 11 May 1882, 1.

_____. "The Dedication of the Carroll Building at Baylor University." *The Western Recorder*, 30 April 1903, 16.

_____. "The Deification of Mary, the Mother of Jesus." *The Western Recorder* 12 July 1906, 1; 16 August 1906, 1.

_____. "Delegated Bodies in Connection with Baptist Churches." *The Christian Index*, 14 October 1897 to 14 April 1898. (A series of twenty-six weekly articles).

_____. "The 'Dictionary of Christ and the Gospels' on Baptism and Other Matters." *The Western Recorder*, 7 February 1907, 1.

_____. "The 'Dictionary of Christ and the Gospels' on Baptism and Other Matters." *The Canadian Baptist*, 28 February 1907, 3.

_____. "Dr. Briggs on 'Catholicism.'" *The Western Recorder*, 29 October 1903, 1.

_____. "Dr. Briggs on the Means of Attaining to Catholicity." *The Western Recorder*, 3 December 1903, 1.

_____. "Dr. Carroll's Review of the 'Manual of Church History.'" *The Baptist Standard*, 22 March 1900.

_____. "Dr. Dexter and Early Baptist History." *The National Baptist*, 4 June 1891.

170

_____. "Dr. Lindsay on the Anabaptists." *The Western Recorder*, 1 August 1907, 1.

_____. "Dr. Ludwig Keller on the Relation of the Anabaptists to Earlier Evangelical Parties." *The Western Recorder*, 27 May 1897, 1; 1 July 1897, 2; 15 July 1897, 1; 29 July 1897, 1; 12 August 1897, 1; 26 August 1897, 1; 9 September 1897, 1; 23 September 1897, 1; 7 October 1897, 1; 21 October 1897, 1; 4 November 1897, 1; 18 November 1897, 1; 2 December 1897, 1; 16 December 1897, 1; 30 December 1897, 1; 13 January 1898, 1; 27 January 1898, 1.

_____. "The Doukhobortsi." *The Western Recorder*, 16 February 1899, 1.

_____. "The Dutch Reformed Churches During the Nineteenth Century." *The Western Recorder*, 28 August 1902, 1.

_____. "The Early Custodians of the 'Jessy Church Records; and the Kiffin Manuscripts." *The Western Recorder*, 7 April 1898, 2.

_____. "The English Reformation: Cromwell and his 'Ironsides.'" *The Standard*, 23 April 1910, 5-6.

_____. "Erasmus and the Anabaptists." *The Western Recorder*, 22 February 1900, 1.

_____. "Erasmus on Biblical Study." *The Western Recorder*, 31 May 1900, 1.

_____. "Erasmus on Christ and Christianity." *The Western Recorder*, 26 April 1900, 1.

_____. "F. C. Conybeare on Infant Baptism." *The Western Recorder*, 27 December 1906, 1.

_____. "F. C. Conybeare on Infant Baptism." *The Canadian Baptist*, 10 January 1907, 2-3.

_____. "The Free Church of Scotland and the United Free Church." *The Western Recorder*, 4 December 1902, 1.

_____. "From Dr. Newman." *The Canadian Baptist*, 18 April 1901, 245.

_____. "From an Early Letter of Luther on Infant Baptism." *The Western Recorder*, 7 November 1907, 1.

_____. "From Puritan to Papist." *The Western Recorder*, 2 November 1905, 1.

_____. "Further Extracts from the Minutes of an Old English Baptist Association." *The Western Recorder*, 13 October 1898, 1; 20 October 1898, 1.

_____. "The Genesis of the Theological Seminary." *The Baptist Standard*, 3 June 1909, 6-7.

_____. "A German Vindication of Baptist Principles." *The Canadian Baptist*, 30 July 1885, 1.

_____. "A German Vindication of Baptist Principles." *The Canadian Baptist*, 6 August 1885, 1.

_____. "A Handsome Present." *The Canadian Baptist*, 22 December 1892, 1.

_____. "Harnack on the Formation of Churches and its Importance." *The Western Recorder*, 5 March 1903, 1.

_____. "Harnack on the Missionary Method of the Early Christians." *The Western Recorder*, 2 April 1903, 1.

_____. "Harnack's Latest and Best Book." *The Western Recorder*, 29 January 1903, 1.

_____. "The Hauck Herzog Encyclopaedia on Baptism." *The Western Recorder*, 19 December 1907, 1.

_____. "Henry Jessy's Interpretation of Contemporary Events." *The Western Recorder*, 29 November 1900, 1.

_____. "Home Missions." *The Canadian Baptist*, 3 May 1885, 5.

_____. "An Ill-Considered Challenge." *The Canadian Baptist*, 10 November 1898, 712.

_____. "An Important Work on the Anabaptists and their Predecessors." *The Western Recorder*, 27 September 1900, 1.

_____. "Jewish Proselyte Baptism." *The Western Recorder*, 22 March 1900, 1.

_____. "John Foster." *The Western Recorder*, 10 August 1899, 1.

_____. "John Milton on Christian Baptism." *The Western Recorder*, 5 May 1898, 1; 19 May 1898, 1.

_____. "Kattenbusch on the History of Baptism." *The Western Recorder*, 6 February 1908, 1.

172

_____. "The Key of Truth." *The Western Recorder*, 17 November 1898, 1; 22 December 1898, 1; 19 January 1899, 1.

_____. "Kautsky on Munzer and the Anabaptists." *The Western Recorder*, 25 October 1900, 1.

_____. "The Last Book and the Last Days of John Smyth." *The Western Recorder*, 29 March 1906, 1.

_____. "Liberty of Conscience, A Fundamental Baptist Principle." *The Canadian Baptist*, 20 September 1883, 2.

_____. "Liberty of Conscience in 1649." *The Western Recorder*, 4 July 1901, 1.

_____. "The Loose-From-Rome Movement in Austria." *The Western Recorder*, 5 June 1913, 1.

_____. Luther on Baptism." *The Western Recorder*, 20 July 1905, 1.

_____. "Luther's Baptismal Booklet of 1526." *The Western Recorder*, 18 October 1906, 1.

_____. "The Making of a Professor." *The Canadian Baptist*, 11 August 1904, 5.

_____. "The McGregor Memoir." *The Canadian Baptist*, 25 June 1891, 4.

_____. "The McGregor Memoir." *The Canadian Baptist*, 17 September 1891, 4.

_____. "The McGregor Memorial." *The Canadian Baptist*, 16 April 1891, 4.

_____. "The McGregor Volume and the Orphan Children." *The Canadian Baptist*, 14 April 1892, 1.

_____. "McMaster Library – Missing Books." *The Canadian Baptist*, 21 November 1895, 1.

_____. "McMaster University." *The Canadian Baptist*, 12 July, 1888, 4.

_____. "The McMaster University Monthly." *The Canadian Baptist*, 23 July 1891, 4.

_____. "Medieval Eclipse of Missions." *The Baptist Union*, 16 November 1895, 9; 23 November 1895, 9; 30 November 1895, 9; 7 December 1895, 11; 14 December 1895, 9.

_____. "Meeting of the American Society of Church History." *The Canadian Baptist*, 23 January 1890, 1.

_____. "Melchoir Hoffann, Jan Matthys and the Munster Kingdom." *The Baptist Standard*, 12 September 1901, 3.

_____. "The Mennonites." *The Baptist Standard*, 10 October 1901, 2.

_____. "Michael Servetus." *The Western Recorder*, 5 December 1901, 1.

_____. "Ministerial Education." *The Canadian Baptist*, 27 February 1890, 4.

_____. "Minutes of an English Baptist Association of Olden Time." *The Western Recorder*, 16 June 1898, 1.

_____. "The Moravian Anabaptists." *The Baptist Standard*, 26 September 1901, 5.

_____. "The Moriscos of Spain." *The Western Recorder*, 31 March 1904, 1.

_____. "Mourner's Benches." *The Western Recorder*, 27 January 1898, 2.

_____. "Muller's History of the Anabaptists of Bern." *The Western Recorder*, 26 October 1899, 1.

_____. "The Muratorian Fragment." *The Western Recorder*, 13 April 1905, 1.

_____. "My Oldest Book." *The Western Recorder*, 25 February 1904, 1.

_____. "My Successor." *The Canadian Baptist*, 6 June 1901, 356.

_____. "My Summer Peregrinations." *The Western Recorder*, 5 July 1900, 1.

_____. "The New Catechism." *The Canadian Baptist*, 23 February 1899, 21.

_____. "The New Edition of Kessler's Sabbata." *The Western Recorder*, 16 July 1903, 1.

_____. "The New Testament Canon." *The Western Recorder*, 30 March 1905, 1.

_____. "The New Testament Canon." *The Western Recorder*, 18 March 1909, 1.

174

_____. "A New Theory of the Diaconate." *The Canadian Baptist*, 25 February 1886, 1.

_____. "An Official Roman Catholic Pronouncement on the Exaltation of the Priesthood." *The Baptist Standard*, 24 October 1929, 2.

_____. "An Official Roman Catholic Pronouncement on the Exaltation of the Priesthood." *The Canadian Baptist*, 29 August 1929, 4.

_____. "The Opponents of Infant Baptism and Related Errors in the Reformation Time." *The Baptist Standard*, 8 August 1901, 1.

_____. "Origen, Eusebius and Athanasius." *The Western Recorder*, 4 May 1905, 1.

_____. "A Personal Word." *The Canadian Baptist*, 6 June 1901, 356.

_____. "The Pioneer Fathers." *The Canadian Baptist*, 11 July 1929, 5.

_____. "The Pistis Sophia on Baptism." *The Western Recorder*, 15 September 1898, 1.

_____. "The Pontificate of Leo XIII." *The Western Recorder*, 10 July 1902, 1.

_____. "Presbyterianism in England and Scotland." *The Western Recorder*, 9 October 1902, 1.

_____. "Prof. Rauschenbusch on the Rise of Infant Baptism." *The Western Recorder*, 11 August 1898, 1.

_____. "Professor Franklin Howard Kerfoot, D.D." *The Canadian Baptist*, 3 March 1898, 136-37.

_____. "Professor Newman and the Whitsitt Controversy" *The Canadian Baptist*, 20 August 1896, 541.

_____. "Robert Hall." *The Western Recorder*, 21 September 1899, 1.

_____. "A Review of Dr. Christian's Articles." *The Western Recorder*, 25 May 1899, 3; 1 June 1899, 3.

_____. "The Roman Curia as it is Today." *The Western Recorder*, 6 March 1913, 1.

_____. "Schade's Philosophy of History." *The Western Recorder*, 7 March 1901, 1.

————. "Schade's Views on Church History and Eschatology." *The Western Recorder*, 11 April 1901, 1.

————. "Scottish Presbyterianism from 1733 to 1843." *The Western Recorder*, 6 November 1902, 1.

————. "A Seventeenth Century Presbyterian on Liberty of Conscience." *The Western Recorder*, 22 August 1901, 1.

————. "The Six Principles." *The Western Recorder*, 30 March 1899, 1.

————. "The Society of Jesus." *The Western Recorder*, 13 February 1902, 1.

————. "Some Baptist Appelations." *The Canadian Baptist*, 16 February 1928, 6.

————. "Some Biblical Anabaptists." *The Baptist Standard*, 19 September 1901, 5.

————. "Some Criteria for Early Antipedobaptist Documents." *The Western Recorder*, 3 September 1903, 2.

————. "Some Early English Baptist Church Books." *The Western Recorder*, 1 August 1912, 1.

————. "Some Mediaeval Antinomians." *The Western Recorder*, 11 August 1904, 1.

————. "Some Millenarian Anabaptists." *The Baptist Standard*, 22 August 1901, 3.

————. "A Specimen of Seventeenth Century Polemics." *The Western Recorder*, 21 January 1904, 1.

————. "Staupitz and Luther." *The Western Recorder*, 9 August 1900, 1; 30 August 1900, 1.

————. "Toleration and Liberty of Conscience." *The Western Recorder*, 31 October 1901, 1.

————. "Traces of Baptist Teaching and Practice During the First Sixteen Christian Centuries." *The Baptist Standard*, 17 October 1901, 1; 24 October 1901, 5; 31 October 1901, 5; 7 November 1901, 5; 21 November 1901, 5-6; 5 December 1901, 2-3.

————. "A Valuable Household Book." *The Canadian=Baptist*, 6 December 1900, 773.

————. "Was Milton a Baptist?" *The Western Recorder*, 4 February 1909, 1.

176

_____. "What Drs. Bright and Strong Think." *The Canadian Baptist*, 21 March 1888, 2.

_____. "Why Milton was not a Baptist." *The Western Recorder*, 22 April 1909, 1.

Unsigned Articles

_____. "The Amenities of Anglicanism." *The Canadian Baptist*, 4 January 1883, 4.

_____. "Anabaptism in the Presbyterian Church." *The Canadian Baptist*, 26 March 1885, 4.

_____. "The Baptist Encyclopedia." *The Canadian Baptist*, 26 April 1883, 4.

_____. "Baptist Progress and Prospects." *The Canadian Baptist*, 8 February 1883, 4.

_____. "The Baptist Theological Colleges of Great Britain." *The Canadian Baptist*, 19 October 1882, 4.

_____. "The Christian Mirror." *The Canadian Baptist*, 22 March 1883, 4.

_____. "College News." *The McMaster University Monthly* 1 (June 1891): 40-41.

_____. "Discarding Old Friends." *The Canadian Baptist*, 8 March 1883, 4.

_____. "Early Dated Baptists." *The Canadian Baptist*, 12 June 1890, 2.

_____. "Editorial Notes." *The Canadian Baptist*, 10 January 1889, 4.

_____. "Editorial Notes." *The Canadian Baptist*, 17 January 1889, 4.

_____. "Editorial Notes." *The Canadian Baptist*, 24 January 1889, 4.

_____. "Editorial Notes." *The Canadian Baptist*, 31 January 1889, 4.

_____. "Editorial Notes." *The Canadian Baptist*, 7 February 1889, 4-5.

_____. "Editorial Notes." *The Canadian Baptist*, 14 February 1889, 4.

_____. "Editorial Notes." *The Canadian Baptist*, 21 February 1889, 4-5.

_____. "Editorial Notes." *The Canadian Baptist*, 28 February 1889, 4.

_____. "Editorial Notes." *The Canadian Baptist*, 7 March 1889, 4.

_____. "Editorial Notes." *The Canadian Baptist*, 14 March 1889, 4.

_____. "Editorial Notes." *The Canadian Baptist*, 21 March 1889, 4-5.

_____. "Editorial Notes." *The Canadian Baptist*, 28 March 1889, 4.

_____. "Editorial Notes." *The McMaster University Monthly* 1 (January 1892): 179-83.

_____. "Editorial Notes." *The McMaster University Monthly* 2 (April 1893): 340-41.

_____. "Examinations." *The Canadian Baptist*, 4 January 1883, 4.

_____. "The 'Examiner' and John Milton." *The Canadian Baptist*, 8 January 1885, 4.

_____. "How it Works." *The Canadian Baptist*, 4 January 1883, 4.

_____. "Leaving Secular Business." *The Canadian Baptist*, 22 March 1883, 4.

_____. "Methodist Union." *The Canadian Baptist*, 1 February 1883, 4.

_____. "More Ministers Wanted." *The Canadian Baptist*, 25 January 1883, 4.

_____. "A New Scheme of Christian Union." *The Canadian Baptist*, 18 January 1883, 4.

_____. "Pastors' Salaries." *The Canadian Baptist*, 22 February 1883, 4.

_____. "The Radicalism of the Swiss Protestants." *The Canadian Baptist*, 14 September 1882, 4.

_____. "Rev. John Harvard Castle, D.D." *The Canadian Baptist*, 26 June 1890, 4-5.

_____. "Salutatory." *The Canadian Baptist*, 3 January 1889, 4.

_____. "The Saratoga Bible Convention." *The Canadian Baptist*, 29 March 1883, 4.

_____. "Some Recent Bequests." *The Canadian Baptist*, 1 March 1883, 4.

_____. "The Strong Point." *The Canadian Baptist*, 17 May 1883, 4.

178

_____. "A Work for Churches and Parents." *The Canadian Baptist*, 1 February 1883, 4.

_____. "Up With the Times." *The Canadian Baptist*, 19 April 1883, 4.

Encyclopedia Articles

Bender, Harold S., ed. *The Mennonite Encyclopedia*. Scottdale, PA: The Mennonite Publishing House, 1957. S.V. "Helwys, Thomas," by Albert Henry Newman.

Cathcart, William., ed. *The Baptist Encyclopedia*. Philadelphia: Louis H. Everts, 1881. S.V. "Anabaptists," by Albert Henry Newman.

Encyclopedia Britannica. 11th ed. 1910. S.V. "American Baptists," by Albert Henry Newman.

Hastings, James, ed. *Dictionary of Christ and the Gospels*. New York: Charles Scribner's Sons, 1908. S.V. "Abgar," " Supper," "Christ in the Middle Ages," by Albert Henry Newman.

_____., ed. *Encyclopedia of Religion and Ethics*. New York: Charles Scribner's Sons, 1911. S.V. "Aeons," by Albert Henry Newman.

Hauck, Albert, ed.
Realencyklopädie für protestantische Theologie und Kirche, 3rd ed. Leipzig: J. C. Hinrichs, 1896. S.v.*"Englische Theologie des 19. Jahrhundert,"* "Manning, James," "Williams, Roger," "Hackett, Horatio Balch," "Hall, Robert," "Fuller, Andrew," "Fuller, Richard," "Foster, John," "Clarke, John," by Albert Henry Newman.

Jackson, Samuel Macaulay, ed.
The New Schaff-Herzog Encyclopedia of Religious Knowledge. Grand Rapids: Baker Book House, 1949. S.V. "Agenda," "Ambrosiaster," "Antinomianism and Antinomian Controversies," "Apollinaris of Laodicea," "Baptists," "Blaurer, Margaretha," "Bunyan, John," "Charlemagne," "Charles V," "Christmas," Clarke, John," "Communism," "Dogma," "Dogmatics," Foster, John," "Fuller, Andrew," "Fuller, Richard," "Hacket, Horatio Balch," "Hall, Robert," "Holy Roman Empire," "Huguenots," "Ignatius of Loyola," "Jesuits," "Laity," "Leland, John," "Liberty, Religious," "Manning, James," "Marbeck, Pilgram," "Nerses," "Nestorius," "Paulicians," "Peter of Bruys," "Philipi," "Philip IV," "Reublin, Wilhelm," "Rice, Luther," "Rogers, John," "Saravis, Adrian," "Theoligical Seminaries," "Twin (Dwin, Dvin, Devin)," "Ubbonites," "Williams, Roger," by Albert Henry Newman.

Der Protestantismus am Ende des XIX Jahrhunderts in Wort und Bild. S.V. *"Der Protestantismus in Nord-America*, by Albert Henry Newman.

Singer, Isidore, ed. *The Jewish Encyclopedia*. New York: Funk and Wagnall's, 1901. S.V. "Abelard, Peter,"Abelites," by Albert Henry Newman.

Unpublished Newman Materials

Albert Henry Newman Papers. Microfilm. Nashville: The Historical Commission of the Southern Baptist Convention.

Albert Henry Newman File. Waco, Texas: The Texas Collection, Baylor University.

Albert Henry Newman File. Fort Worth, Texas: A. Webb Roberts Library, Southwestern Baptist Theological Seminary.

Albert Henry Newman File. Hamilton, Ontario: Canadian Baptist Archives, McMaster Divinity College.

Unpublished Primary Materials

Alumni Files, Rochester, New York. Samuel Colgate Historical Library, Crozer Rochester Divinity School.

Benajah Harvey Carroll Papers. Fort Worth, Texas. A. Webb Roberts Library, Southwestern Baptist Theological Seminary.

Emmons, Martha. Personal interview, 8 March 1989.

Faculty Minutes. Fort Worth, Texas. A. Webb Roberts Library, Southwestern Baptist Theological Seminary.

Secondary Sources

Books

Adams, Herbert Baxter. "On Methods of Teaching History." In *Methods of Teaching History*, ed. G. Stanley Hall, 176. Boston: Ginn, Heath and Company, 1885.

Ahlstrom, Sydney E. *A Religious History of the American People*. New Haven: Yale University Press, 1972.

_____., ed. *Theology in America*. Indianapolis: Bobbs-Merrill Company, 1967.

Aland, Kurt. *A History of Christianity*, 2 Vols. Translated by James L. Schaaf. Philadelphia: Fortress Press, 1985.

Armitage, Thomas. *A History of the Baptists: Traced by Their Vital Principles and Practices, From the Time of Our Lord and Saviour Jesus Christ to the Year 1889*. New York: Byran Taylor and Company, 1889.

Arnold, Gottfried. *Unparteyische kirchen-und Ketzer-Historie*. Frankfurt, 1699.

Ausubel, Herman. *Historians and Their Craft*. New York: Columbia University Press, 1950.

Bainton, Roland. *Christendom: A Short History of Christianity and Its Impact on Western Civilization*. New York: Harper and Row, 1964.

Baker, Robert A. *Tell the Generations Following: A History of Southwestern Baptist Theological Seminary 1908-1983*. Nashville: Broadman Press, 1983.

Barnes, William W. *The Southern Baptist Convention: 1845-1953*. Nashville: Broadman Press, 1954.

Bassett, John S. *The Middle Group of American Historians*. New York: MacMillan Company, 1917.

Bellot, H. Hale. *American History and American Historians*. London: Athlone Press, 1952.

Bender, Harold S. *The Anabaptists and Religious Liberty in the Sixteenth Century*. Philadelphia: Fortress Press, 1970.

Bloch, Marc. *The Historian's Craft*. Translated by Peter Putnam. New York: Vintage Press, 1953.

Bowden, Henry Warner. ed. *A Century of Church History: The Legacy of Philip Schaff*. Carbondale, IL: Southern Illinois University Press, 1988.

_____. *Church History in the Age of Science*. Chapel Hill: University of North Carolina Press, 1971.

Burrage, Champlin. *The Early English Dissenters in Light of Recent Research*. 2 Vols. Cambridge: The University Press, 1912.

Carr, Edward Hallett. *What is History?* London: McMillan and Company Ltd., 1961.

Carroll, James Milton. *The Trail of Blood*. Lexington, KY: Ashland Avenue Baptist Church, 1931.

Clasen, Claus Peter. *Anabaptism: A Social History 1525-1618*. Ithaca: Cornell University Press, 1972.

Commager, Henry Steele. *The American Mind: An Interpretation of American Thought and Character Since the 1880s*. New Haven: Yale University Press, 1950.

_____. *The Era of Reform: 1830-1860*. Malabar, FL: Robert E. Krieger Publishing Company, 1860.

Douglas, Crerar, ed. *Autobiography of Augustus Hopkins Strong*. Valley Forge: Judson Press, 1981.

Dowell, Spright. *A History of Mercer University 1833-1953*. Macon, GA: Mercer University Press, 1958.

Dryer, George Herbert. *History of the Christian Church*, 5 Vols. Cincinnati: Jennings and Pye, 1896-1903.

Eby, Frederick. *Newman the Church Historian*. Nashville: Broadman Press, 1946.

Estep, William R. *The Anabaptist Story*. Grand Rapids: William B. Eerdmans Publishing Company, 1975.

Fisher, George Park. *History of the Christian Church*. New York: Charles Scribner's Sons, 1887.

Gonzalez, Justo L. *The Story of Christianity*, 2 Vols. San Francisco: Harper and Row, 1983-84.

Gooch, G. P. *History and Historians in the Nineteenth Century*. New York: Longmans, Green and Company, 1913.

Gould, George. *Open Communion and the Baptists of Norwich*. Norwich: J. Fletcher, 1860.

Graves, J. R. *Old Landmarkism: What is It?* 2d ed. Memphis: Baptist Book House, 1881.

Gross, Leonard. Foreword to *Becoming Anabaptist*, by J. Denny Weaver. Scottdale, PA: Herald Press, 1987.

Guilland, Antoine. *Modern Germany and Her Historians*. estport, CT: Greenwood Press, 1970.

Hall, G. Stanley, ed. *Methods of Teaching History*. Boston: Ginn, Heath and Company, 1885.

Harnack, Adolf von. *History of Dogma*, 7 Vols. Translated from the 3rd German Ed. by Neil Buchanan. New York: Russell and Russell, 1958.

Herbst, Jurgen. *The German Historical School in American Scholarship*. Ithaca: Cornell University Press, 1965.

Higham, John, Leonard Krieger, and Felix Gilbert, eds. *History*. Englewood Cliffs, NJ: Prentice-Hall, 1965.

Hofstadter, Richard. *Social Darwinism in American Thought*. Philadelphia: University of Pennsylvania Press, 1955.

Holt, W. Stull. *Historical Scholarship in the United States*. Seattle: University of Washington Press, 1967.

Hudson, Winthrop S. *American Protestantism*. Chicago: University of Chicago Press, 1961.

_____. *Baptist Concepts of the Church*. Chicago: Judson Press, 1959.

_____. *Baptist Confessions*. Valley Forge: Judson Press, 1963.

_____. *Baptists in Transition: Individual and Christian Responsibility*. Valley Forge: Judson Press, 1979.

_____. *The Great Tradition of the American Churches*. New York: Harper, 1953.

_____. *Religion in America: An Historical Account of the Development of American Religious Life*. New York: The MacMillan Company, 1987.

Hurst, John Fletcher. *History of the Christian Church*, 2 Vols. New York: Eaton and Mains: 1897-1900.

Hutchison, William R. *The Modernist Impulse in American Protestantism*. Oxford: Oxford University Press, 1976.

Hutchinson, William T., ed. *The Marcus W. Jernegan Essays in American Historiography*. Chicago: University of Chicago Press, 1937.

Iggers, Georg G. *The German Conception of History*. Middletown, CT: Wesleyan University Press, 1968.

Johnston, Charles M. *McMaster University: The Toronto Years*. Vol. 1. Toronto: University of Toronto Press, 1976.

Jones, Howard Mumford. *The Life of Moses Coit Tyler*. Ann Arbor: The University of Michigan Press, 1933.

Kautsky, Karl. *Communism in Central Europe in the Time of the Reformation.* Translated by J. L. and E. G. Mulliken. London: T. Fisher Unwin, 1897.

Klassen, Peter James. *The Economics of Anabaptism.* London: Mouton and Company, 1964.

Klassen, Walter. *Anabaptism: Neither Catholic Nor Protestant.* Ontario: Conrad Press, 1973.

Kraus, Michael. *A History of American History.* New York: Farrar and Rinehart, 1937.

_____. *The Writing of American History.* Norman: The University of Oklahoma Press, 1953.

Kummel, Werner George. *The New Testament: The History of the Investigation of Its Problems.* Translated by S. McLean Gilmour and Howard C. Kee. Nashville: Abingdon Press, 1972.

Latourette, Kenneth Scott. *A History of Christianity.* New York: Harper and Brothers, 1953.

Levin, David. *History as Romantic Art.* Stanford: Stanford University Press, 1959.

Littell, Franklin Hamlin. *The Anabaptist View of the Church,* 2d ed. Boston: Starr King Press, 1958.

_____. *The Origins of Sectarian Protestantism.* New York: The MacMillan Company, 1963.

Lotz, David W., ed. *Altered Landscapes: Christianity in America: 1935-1985.* Grand Rapids: William B. Eerdmans Publishing Company, 1989.

Marsden, George M. *Fundamentalism and American Culture.* Oxford: Oxford University Press, 1980.

McBeth, H. Leon. *The Baptist Heritage.* Nashville: Broadman Press, 1987.

_____. *A Sourcebook For Baptist History.* Nashville: Broadman Press, 1990.

McGlothlin, William J. *Baptist Beginnings in Education: A History of Furman University.* Nashville: The Sunday School Board, 1926.

McIntire, C. T., ed. *God, History and Historians.* New York: Oxford University Press, 1977.

McLoughlin, William G. *Modern Revivalism: Charles Grandison Finney to Billy Graham*. New York: The Ronald Press Company, 1959.

Mueller, William A. *A History of Southern Baptist Theological Seminary*. Nashville: Broadman Press, 1959.

Neill, Stephen and N. T. Wright. *The Interpretation of the New Testament: 1861-1986*. London: Oxford University Press, 1988.

Nichols, James H. *Romanticism in American Theology: Nevin and Schaff at Mercersburg*. Chicago: University of Chicago Press, 1961.

Patterson, Morgan W. *Baptist Successionism: A Critical View*. Valley Forge: Judson Press, 1969.

Payne, Ernest Alexander. *The Anabaptists of the Sixteenth Century and Their Influence in the Modern World*. London: C. Kingsgate Press, 1949.

Price, J. M., ed. *Southwestern Men and Their Messages*. Kansas City: Central Seminary Press, 1948.

Ragsdale, Bartow Davis. *Story of Georgia Baptists*. Vol. 1, *Mercer University: Penfield Period and Related Interests*. Atlanta: Foote and Davies Co., 1932.

Ray, Jeff D. *B. H. Carroll*. Nashville: Sunday School Board of the Southern Baptist Convention, 1927.

_____. *The Round-Up*. Baylor University, 1902-20. carborough, L. R. *A Modern School of the Prophets*. Nashville: Broadman Press, 1939.

Schaff, David S. *The Life of Philip Schaff*. New York: Charles Scribner's Sons, 1897.

Schaff, Philip. *Amerika*. 2nd ed. Berlin: Wiegandt and Grieben, 1858.

_____. *History of the Apostolic Church With a General Introduction to Church History*. Translated by Edward D. Yeomans. New York: Charles Scribner, 1853.

_____. *History of the Christian Church*, 7 Vols. Grand Rapids: Wm. B. Eerdmans Publishing Company, 1867.

_____. *What is Church History? A Vindication of the Idea of Historical Development*. Philadelphia: J. B. Lippincott and Company, 1846.

Seth, James. *A Study of Ethical Principles*. 12th ed. New York: Charles Scribner's Sons, 1911.

Sheldon, Henry Clay. *History of the Christian Church*, 5 Vols. New York: Thomas Y. Crowell and Co., 1894.

Shriver, George H. *Philip Schaff: Christian Scholar and Ecumenical Prophet.* Macon GA: Mercer University Press, 1987.

Smithson, Robert Jamieson. *The Anabaptists: Their Contribution to Our Protestant Heritage.* London: J. Clarke and Company, 1935.

Stayer, James M. "The Anabaptists." In *Reformation Europe: A Guide to Research*, ed. Steven Ozment, 135-59. St. Louis: Center For Reformation Research, 1982.

Strong, Augustus Hopkins. *Philosophy and Religion.* New York: A. C. Armstrong and Son, 1888.

Torbet, Robert G. *A History of the Baptists.* Valley Forge: Judson Press, 1950.

Tripathi, Amales. *Evolutions of Historiography in America, 1870-1910.* Calcutta: World Press Private, 1956.

Troeltsch, Ernst. *The Social Teaching of the Christian Church*, 2 Vols. Translated by Olive Wyon. New York: The MacMillan Company, 1931.

Tull, James E. *Shapers of Baptist Thought.* Valley Forge: Judson Press, 1972.

Underwood, A. C. *A History of the English Baptists.* London: Kingsgate Press, 1947.

Vedder, Henry Clay. *A Short History of the Baptists.* Philadelphia: American Baptist Publication Society, 1891.

_____. *A Short History of the Baptists*, 2d ed. Philadelphia: American Baptist Publication Society, 1897.

_____. *A Short History of the Baptists*, 2d rev. ed. Philadelphia: American Baptist Publication Society, 1907.

_____. *A Short History of Baptist Missions.* Philadelphia: Judson Press, 1927.

Walker, Williston. *A History of the Christian Church.* New York: Charles Scribner's Sons, 1918.

Wenger, John Christian. *Even Unto Death.* Richmond: John Knox Press, 1961.

Whitley, William Thomas. *A History of the Britist Baptists.* London: Charles Griffin and Company, 1923.

186

_____. ed. *Minutes of the General Assembly of the General Baptist Churches in England*, Vol. 1. London: Kingsgate Press, 1909.

Whitsitt, William Heth. *A Question in Baptist History*. Louisville: Charles T. Dearing, 1896.

Williams, George Huntston. "Church History: From Historical Theology to the Theology of History." In *Protestant Thought in the Twentieth Century*, ed. Arnold S. Nash, 147-78. New York: The MacMillan Company, 1951.

_____. *The Radical Reformation*. Philadelphia: The Westminster Press, 1962.

Williams, George Hunston and Angel M. Mergal, eds. *Spiritual and Anabaptist Writers*. Vol. 25 of the *Library of Christian Classics*. London: SCM Press LTD, 1957.

Articles

Adams, Herbert Baxter. "New Methods of Study in History." *Journal of Social Science* 18 (May 1884): 213-65.

_____. "Seminary Libraries and University Extension." *Johns Hopkins University Studies in Historical and Political Science* 5 (1887): 443-69.

_____. "Special Methods of Historical Study." *Johns Hopkins University Studies in Historical and Political Science*, Second Series 1-2 (January-February 1884): 5-23.

Ahlstrom, Sydney E. "The Problem of the History of Religion in America." *Church History* 39 (June 1970): 224-35.

Anderson, Galusha. Review of *A History of Anti-Pedobaptism From the Rise of Pedobaptism to A. D. 1609*, by Albert Henry Newman. *The American Journal of Theology* 2 (January 1898): 184-86. Andrews, Charles M. "These Forty Years." *American Historical Review* 30 (January 1925): 225-50.

Bender, Elizabeth Horsch. "The Letters of Ludwig Keller to John Horsch." *The Mennonite Quarterly Review* 21 (July 1947): 175-204.

Bender, Harold. "The Historiography of the Anabaptists." *The Mennonite Quarterly Review* 31 (April 1957): 88-104.

Bowden, Henry Warner. "Science and the Idea of Church History, An American Debate." *Church History* 36 (September 1967): 308-26.

Brown, W. J. T. "The Munster Anabaptists." *The Baptist Quarterly*, n.s. 14 (July 1951): 133-36.

Burrage, Henry S. "Thomas Munzer." *The Baptist Quarterly* 11 (April 1877): 129-47.

Carver, W. O. "William Heth Whitsitt: The Seminary's Martyr." *The Review and Expositor* 51 (October 1954): 449-69.

Dawson, J. M. "Obituary of A. H. Newman." *The Christian Century* 50 (12 July 1933): 914.

Deweese, Charles William. "The Contributions of Albert Henry Newman to Baptist Historiography." *Baptist History and Heritage* 7 (January 1972): 2-14.

Durnbaugh, D. F. "Theories of Free Church Origin." *The Mennonite Quarterly Review* 42 (April 1968): 83-95.

Dyck, Cornelius J. "The Place of Tradition in Dutch Anabaptism." *Church History* 43 (January 1974): 34-49.

Emerton, Ephraim. "The Study of Church History." *Unitarian Review and Historical Magazine* 19 (January 1883): 1-18.

Estep, W. R. "A. H. Newman and Southwestern's First Faculty." *The Southwestern Journal of Theology* 21 (Fall 1978): 83-98.

_____. "Anabaptists and the Rise of English Baptists," Part 1. *The Quarterly Review* 28 (October 1968) 43-53.

_____. "Anabaptists and the Rise of English Baptists," Part 2. *The Quarterly Review* 29 (January 1969): 50-62.

_____. "Newman of McMaster and Southwestern." *Theodolite* 8 (Issue Number 2, 1987): 22-33. Everts, W. W. "Baptist Succession." *The Baptist Quarterly* 11 (October 1877): 409-15.

Farrar, A. J. D. "Continental Anabaptists and Early English Baptists." *The Baptist Quarterly*, n.s. 2 (January 1924): 30-36.

Friedmann, Robert. "John Horsch and Ludwig Keller." *The Mennonite Quarterly Review* 21 (July 1947): 160-74.

_____. "Old Evangelical Brotherhoods: Theory and Fact." *The Mennonite Quarterly Review* 36 (October 1962): 349-54.

Friesen, Abraham. "The Marxist Interpretation of the Reformation." *Archiv fur Reformationsgeschichte* 64 (January 1973): 34-55.

Garrison, W. E. Review of *A History of Christianity*, by Kenneth Scott Latourette. In *The Christian Century* 70 (19 August 1953): 941.

Gausted, Edwin S. "Themes for Research in American Baptist History." *Foundations* 6 (April 1963): 146-73.

Gerrish, B. A. Review of *History of the Christian Church*, rev. ed. by Williston Walker. In *The Journal of Religion* 40 (January 1960): 55.

Gilmour, J. L. "Albert Henry Newman." *The McMaster University Monthly* 10 (November 1901): 49-55.

Handy, Robert T. "Themes for Research in Baptist History Since 1865." *The Chronicle* 16 (July 1953): 134-39.

Hanley, Robert B. "Henry Clay Vedder: Conservative Evangelical to Evangelical Liberal." *Foundations* 5 (April 1962): 135-57.

Harnack, Adolf. "The Relation Between Ecclesiastical and General History." *The Contemporary Review* 86 (December 1904): 846-59.

Heath, Richard. "Early Anabaptism: What it Meant and What We Owe to It." *The Contemporary Review* 67 (April 1895): 578-91.

Hill, Christopher. "History and Denominational History." *The Baptist Quarterly* 22 (April 1967): 65-71.

Hillerbrand, Hans J. "The Origin of Sixteenth-Century Anabaptism: Another Look." *Archiv fur Reformationsgeschichte* 53 (April 1962): 152-80.

Holt, W. Stull. "Historical Scholarship in the United States, 1876-1901: As Revealed in the Correspondence of Herbert Baxter Adams." *Johns Hopkins University Studies in Historical and Political Science* 56 (1938): 7-300.

Hudson, Winthrop S. "Baptists Were Not Anabaptists." *The Chronicle* 16 (October 1953): 171-79.

_____. "Shifting Trends in Church History." *Journal of Bible and Religion* 28 (April 1960): 235-38.

_____. "Themes for Research in Baptist History." *The Chronicle* 17 (January 1954): 3-23.

_____. "Who Were the Baptists?" *The Baptist Quarterly* 16 (October 1956): 303-12.

_____. "Who Were the Baptists?" *The Baptist Quarterly* 17 (April 1957): 53-55.

Iggers, Georg G. "The Image of Ranke in American and German Historical Thought." *History and Theory, Studies in the Philosophy of History* 2 (1962): 17-40.

Jameson, John F. "The American Historical Review." 15 (October 1909): 1-20.

_____. "Early Days of the American Historical Association, 1884-1895." *American Historical Review* 40 (October 1934): 1-19.

Jarrel, W. A. "Dr. Derfoot's Apology for Dr. Whitsitt." *Baptist Standard* 4 June 1896, 3.

Keller, Amalie. "Ludwig Keller: Scholar With a Mission." *Mennonite Life* 8 (October 1953): 159-60, 192.

Keller, Ludwig. "An Apostle of the Anabaptists." Translated by Henry S. Burrage. *Baptist Quarterly Review* 7 (January 1885): 28-47.

Klassen, Walter. "Modern Anabaptist Research." *The Baptist Quarterly* 18 (January 1959): 12-25.

Krahn, Cornelius. "Ludwig Keller: a Prophet and a Scholar." *Mennonite Life* 21 (April 1966): 81-84.   Lipscomb, David. "The Baptists." *Gospel Advocate* 8 (12 June, 1866): 369-74.

_____. "Church of Christ in the Dark Ages. "*Gospel Advocate* 8 (21 August 1866): 533-36.

Littell, Franklin H. "The Importance of Anabaptist Studies." *Archiv fur Reformationsgeschichte* 58 (January 1967): 15-28.

Lyon, David Gordon. "Crawford H. Toy." *Harvard Theological Review* 13 (January 1920): 2-22.

Meigs, James Thomas. "The Whitsitt Controversy." *The Quarterly Review* 31 (January 1971): 41-61.

Moncrief, J. W. Review of *A Manual of Church History* Vol. I, by A. H. Newman. *The American Journal of Theology* 4 (October 1900): 851-52.

Parker, G. Keith. "Henry Clay Vedder, Church Historian." *The Quarterly Review* 31 (October 1970): 65-85.

Patterson, W. Morgan. "Baptist Historiography in America in the Eighteenth Century." *Review and Expositor* 52 (October 1955): 483-93.

Payne, Ernest Alexander. "History: Too Much or Too Little?" *The Baptist Quarterly* 22 (October 1968): 387-97.

190

_____. "John Horsch: Mennonite Historian." *The Baptist Quarterly*, n.s. 13 (January 1949): 29-33.

_____. "Who Were the Baptists?" *The Baptist Quarterly* 16 (October 1956): 339-42.

Penzel, Klaus. "The Reformation Goes West: The Notion of Historical Development in the Thought of Philip Schaff." *Journal of Religion* 62 (July 1982): 219-41.

Platner, J. Winthrop. Review of *A Manual of Church History*, Vol. I, by A. H. Newman. *American Historical Review* 6 (October 1900): 120-21.

Pollard, E. B. "The Life and Work of William Heth Whitsitt." *The Review and Expositor* 9 (April 1912): 169-84.

Robertson A. T. Review of *A Manual of Church History*, Vol. I and II, by A. H. Newman. In *The Baptist Review and Expositor* 1 (April 1904): 118.

Schaff, Philip. "The Anabaptists in Switzerland." *The Baptist Quarterly Review* 11 (July 1889): 263-76.

Sellers, Ian. "Edwardians, Anabaptists and the Problem of Baptist Origins." *The Baptist Quarterly* 29 (July 1981): 97-112.

Smucker, Donovan E. "Anabaptist Historiography in the Scholarship of Today." *The Mennonite Quarterly Review* 22 (April 1948): 116-27.

Sprunger, Mary. "Anna Brons and Ludwig Keller." *Mennonite Life* 40 (June 1985): 10-16.

Swing, Albert T. Review of *A Manual of Church History*, by A. H. Newman. In *The Bibliotheca Sacra* 60 (April 1903): 388-90.

Wallace, O. C. S. "Toronto Letter." *The Watchman* 7 March 1895, 27.

Wamble, Hugh. "Landmarkism: Doctrinaire Ecclesiology Among Baptists." *Church History* 33 (December 1964): 429-47.

Westin, Gunnar. "Who Were the Baptists?" *The Baptist Quarterly* 17 (April 1957): 55-60.

White, B. R. "The Task of a Baptist Historian." *The Baptist Quarterly* 22 (October 1968): 398-408, 428.

_____. "Thomas Crosby, Baptist Historian," Part 1. *The Baptist Quarterly* 21 (October 1965): 154-68.

_____. "Thomas Crosby, Baptist Historian," Part 2. *The Baptist Quarterly* 21 (January 1966): 219-34.

Windsor, Justin. "Perils of Historical Narrative." *The Atlantic Monthly* 66 (September 1890): 289-97.

_____. "Secretary's Report of the Organization and Proceedings." *Papers of the American Historical Association* 1 (1885): 5-19.

Willet, Hugh M. "The Meeting of the Mercer Trustees." *The Christian Index*, 1 March 1928, 23.

Zenos, A. C. Review of *A History of Baptist Churches in the United States*, by A. H. Newman. In *The Presbyterian Reformed Revuew* 6 (July 1895): 553.

Encyclopedias

Adams, Charles Kendall, ed. *Johnson's Universal Cyclopedia*. New York: D. Appleton and Company, 1893.

Bender, Harold S., ed. *The Mennonite Encyclopedia*. Scottdale, [PA: The Mennonite Publishing House, 1957. S.V. "Historiography," by Quintus Leatherman; "Keller, Ludwig," by Christian Neff; "Keller, Ludwig, and the Mennonites," by Robert Friedmann; "Newman, Albert Henry," by Harold S. Bender.

Cox, Norman Wade and Judson Boyce Allen, eds. *Encyclopedia of Southern Baptists*. Nashville: Broadman Press, 1958. S.V. "Southern Baptist Theological Seminary," by Leo T. Crimson; "Toy, Crawford Howell," by Gaines S. Dobbins.

Dictionary of Canadian Biography, 1982 ed. S.V. "McMaster, William."

Lippy, Charles H. and Peter W Williams, eds. *Encyclopedia of the American Religious Experience*. New York: Charles Scribner's Sons, 1988. S.V. "The Historiography of American Religion," by Henry Warner Bowden.

The New Schaff-Herzog Encyclopedia of Religious Knowledge. S.V. "Conant, Thomas Jefferson;" "Neander, Johann August Wilhelm;" "Newman, Albert Henry."

Who Was Who in America, 1943 ed., S.V. "Burrage, Henry Sweetser."

Unpublished Works

Beck, Rosalie. "The Whitsitt Controversy: A Denomination in Crisis." Ph.D. diss., Baylor University, 1984.

Breazeale, Jerry. "Albert Henry Newman, Historian and Theologian." Th.D. diss., New Orleans Baptist Theological Seminary, 1960.

Bryan, Philip R. "A Critique of the English Separatist Descent Theory in Baptist Historiography." M.A. thesis, Baylor University, 1966.

Fountain, Mark Steven. "A. H. Newman's Appropriation of the Spiritual Kinship Theory of Baptist Origins as a Historiographical *Via Media*." Th.M. thesis, Southern Baptist Theological Seminary, 1986.

Honeycutt, Dwight A. "A Study of the Life and Thought of Henry Clay Vedder." Th.D. diss., New Orleans Baptist Theological Seminary, 1984.

Jones, Archie H. "American Protestantism and the Science of History." Ph.D. diss., University of Chicago, 1954.

Lindsay, Jonathan A. "A Critical Evaluation of William Warren Sweet as a Writer of American Church History." Ph.D. diss., Southern Baptist Theological Seminary, 1967.

Moore, Leroy. "The Rise of American Religious Liberalism at Rochester Theological Seminary." Ph.D. diss., Claremont Graduate School, 1966.

Phillips, Myer. "A Historical Study of the Attitude of the Churches of Christ Toward Other Denominations." Ph.D. diss., Baylor University, 1983.

Riley, William F. "The Influence of Turner's Frontier Thesis upon American Religious Historiography." M.A. thesis, Western Kentucky University, 1974.

Tull, James E. "A Study of Southern Baptist Landmarkism in Light of Historical Baptist Ecclesiology." Ph.D. diss., Columbia University, 1960.

DDS